DIGITAL DISINFORMATION IN AFRICA

The Digital Africa series explores how digital technologies have opened new spaces for the exercise of democratic rights and freedoms in Africa, as well as how repressive regimes have used digital technologies to diminish or remove those rights. The series foregrounds vital new research from across the continent that combines empirical rigor with theoretical sophistication in order to offer new, more nuanced perspectives on the interactions between digital technology and social life on the continent. The books in the this series provide an important corrective to existing studies that have overwhelmingly focused on the Global North by providing a platform for African scholars to present their own in-depth analysis of the relations between digital technologies and social and political power on the continent.

Each volume is co-edited by the series editor in collaboration with an established scholar in the field, and each features rich case studies authored by emerging and established African scholars involved in the African Digital Rights Network. Thanks to contributors' diverse disciplinary and professional backgrounds, each chapter offers uniquely practical suggestions for policy, practice and further research.

Titles include:

Digital Citizenship in Africa: Technologies of Agency and Repression
Digital Disinformation in Africa: Hashtag Politics, Power and Propaganda
Digital Surveillance in Africa: Power, Agency and Rights

Digital Disinformation in Africa

Hashtag Politics, Power and Propaganda

Edited by

Tony Roberts and George Hamandishe Karekwaivanane

LONDON • NEW YORK • OXFORD • NEW DELHI • SYDNEY

Zed

Bloomsbury Publishing Plc

50 Bedford Square, London, WC1B 3DP, UK

1385 Broadway, New York, NY 10018, USA

29 Earlsfort Terrace, Dublin 2, Ireland

First published in Great Britain 2024

Series design by Toby Way

A catalogue record for this book is available from the British Library.

A catalog record for this book is available from the Library of Congress.

ISBN: HB: 978-1-3503-1921-9
PB: 978-1-3503-1920-2
ePDF: 978-1-3503-1923-3
eBook: 978-1-3503-1922-6

Series: Digital Africa

Typeset by Deanta Global Publishing Services, Chennai, India
Printed and bound in Great Britain

To find out more about our authors and books visit www.bloomsbury.com
and sign up for our newsletters.

To Sonia Sinanan for giving me reason and direction
To Tapiwa, my joy and my hope

Contents

Figures and tables

Figures

Tables

Contributors

Nkem Agunwa is an experienced communicator and digital campaigner focusing on human rights activism, including freedom of expression, police brutality, democracy and good governance. She has a decade's experience in national and international organizations, and her expertise in digital mass mobilization has led to impactful campaigns. As the Africa Program Manager at WITNESS, Nkem supports activists and legal experts across Africa to defend human rights through video and technology while countering manipulated media. She also contributes thought leadership on mis/disinformation in Africa and the importance of prioritizing community-focused solutions.

Edmilson Angelo is a doctoral researcher at the Institute of Development Studies (University of Sussex), where his study focuses on online/offline spaces of citizenship in Angola. He holds a bachelor's degree in politics and international relations from Westminster University and a master's in African studies from the University of Oxford as well as an executive certification from the Harvard Kennedy School in Policy Design. Edmilson is a visiting lecturer at St. Mary's University and Royal Holloway, University of London. He has a decade of practitioner experience as founder of leading Angola non-profit Change 1's Life, and he acts as a consultant for a range of national and international public and private bodies. Edmilson is also a columnist and analyst on African politics for the *BBC*, *SIC Portugal* and other international channels and newspapers including *Ver Angola*, *RTP*, *DW* and *RTC Cape Verde*.

Atnafu Brhane Ayalew is a digital rights activist based in Ethiopia. In 2012, he cofounded the blogging collective Zone9 Bloggers and conducted extensive social media campaigns on the rule of law, constitutionalism and freedom of expression. In 2016, the collective accepted awards from Reporters Without Borders, Human Rights Watch, Martin Ennals and Committee to Protect Journalists. In 2014, Atnafu was arrested and charged with Ethiopia's antiterrorism proclamation and was imprisoned for eighteen months. From 2018 to 2019, Atnafu was Digital Integrity Fellow at Open Technology Fund and worked with human rights defenders and human rights organizations in Ethiopia to create awareness of digital literacy, privacy and security. He co-founded the Network for Digital Rights in Ethiopia and is Programme Director and cofounder of the Center for Advancement of Rights and Democracy. He co-authored the 'Ethiopia Digital Rights Landscape Report' for the African Digital Rights Network.

Yohannes Eneyew Ayalew is a PhD candidate and teaching associate at the Faculty of Law, Monash University, Australia. His project looks at how to balance freedom of expression and privacy on the internet under the African human rights system. In 2022, he was a visiting scholar at the Law and Technology Research Group, Faculty of Law, Ghent University. Prior to this, he was a lecturer in Law at the School of Law, Bahir Dar University in Ethiopia, where he was teaching and researching on Media Law and Human Rights. He holds a Master of Laws (LL.M) in International Human Rights Law (University of Groningen), LL.M in Public International Law (Addis Ababa University) and a Bachelor of Laws (LL.B) from Wollo University. His research interest spans the areas of internet freedom, intermediary liability, African human rights law, international human right law and third world approaches to international law (TWAIL).

Rutendo Chabikwa is an interdisciplinary PhD candidate at the University of Oxford, Oxford Internet Institute (OII). Her doctoral research focuses on how Zimbabwean women and queer people experience their citizenship when they engage/encounter state actors on social media. Outside her doctoral work, she researches AI-related policies in Africa and investigates the role that feminist interventions can play in mitigating gender inequality. She is the author of the article 'Women, Peace and Security in Zimbabwe – The Case of Conflict in Non-War Zones' (2021). Her non-academic work has been published in *New Daughters of Africa* (2019) and *When Three Sevens Clash* (2023).

Seyoung Jeon is an independent researcher working at the intersection of tech and politics. Along with her experience in the public sector and in the tech industry, a significant part of her research has been dedicated to tracking online disinformation campaigns targeting elections in African countries. Seyoung holds a Master of Philosophy degree in Politics and International Studies from the University of Cambridge, where she conducted her work on election disinformation aided by a research partnership with Twitter's Election Integrity Program. Her other research interests include the digital dimension of hybrid warfare and the privatization of security in conflict zones.

George Hamandishe Karekwaivanane is a senior lecturer in the Centre of African Studies at the University of Edinburgh. He has two main areas of research. The first focuses on the social, political and economic impacts of digital media in Africa. A recent publication in this area is the edited book *Publics in Africa in a Digital Age*. The second research area focuses on the social and political history of law. This work examines the mutually constitutive relationship between law, society and politics in African history. Some of his publications in this area include the monograph *The Struggle over State Power in Zimbabwe: Law and Politics Since 1950* and the edited book *Pursuing Justice in Africa: Competing Imaginaries and Contested Practices*. He is currently working on a monograph on the history of activist lawyers in Zimbabwe. He serves on the editorial boards of the *Journal of Southern African Studies*, *Black Histories* and the *South African Historical Journal*.

Juliet Nanfuka is a researcher who has worked on various initiatives aimed at helping individuals and organizations advocate for an internet that is free, fair and open in Africa. She is a contributing writer for the Africa Digital Rights Network (ADRN) and has also written for the Institute for New Economic Thinking (INET), the Center for International Media Assistance (CIMA) and various publications. She is a member of the UNESCO Information for All Programme (IFAP) Working Group on Information for Development. Juliet works with the ICT policy think tank Collaboration on International ICT Policy for East and Southern Africa (CIPESA).

Tony Roberts is a research fellow at the Institute for Development Studies (UK). After a period as a lecturer in innovation studies at the University of East London, Tony founded and led two international development agencies working in Central America and Southern Africa. When he stood down as Chief Executive of Computer Aid International, he completed his PhD in the use of digital technologies in international development (Royal Holloway, University of London). After a postdoc at the United Nations University, in China, Tony joined the digital research team at IDS where his research focuses on digital inequalities, digital citizenship and digital rights. He co-founded the African Digital Rights Network for whom he has edited the reports *Digital Rights in Closing Civic Space* and *Surveillance Law in Africa*, as well as the Zed Books collected edition *Digital Citizenship in Africa*. His publications are available from his website www.appropr iatingtechnology.org.

Simone Toussi is a member of the Research Group on Political Communication (*Groupe de recherche en communication politique GRCP*) of Laval University, and the Center for the Study of Democratic Citizenship (CECD). She has previously contributed to research on government policies against disinformation and their impact on democracy in Africa, as well as on policies protecting children's rights on the internet, at the Centre for Human Rights (CHR) of the University of Pretoria. She has also contributed to research on data protection policies in Africa with the Directorate-General for Justice and Consumers (DG JUST) of the European Commission. She works at the intersection of information and communication technology (ICT) policy, democracy, and human rights in Africa, with the Collaboration on International ICT Policy for East and Southern Africa (CIPESA).

Dércio Tsandzana is a Mozambican researcher and political scientist with a PhD from Sciences Po, France. He is currently professor of political science at Eduardo Mondlane University. Since 2013, Tsandzana has been working on youth, social media and political participation in Mozambique, including on-line activism for Global Voices International. Tsandzana also undertook research work focusing on digital rights and data privacy with Internews/USAID, Collaboration on International ICT Policy for East and Southern Africa (CIPESA), Paradigm Initiative (PIN), Association for Progressive Communications (APC) and African

Declaration on Internet Rights and Freedoms. Between 2020 and 2023, Tsandzana collaborated as a permanent ICT and human rights researcher at ALT Advisory (Johannesburg). His most recent publication is entitled *Reporting on Everyday Life: Practices and Experiences of Citizen Journalism in Mozambique*. Personal website: www.tsandzana.com.

Wambui Wamunyu, PhD, is a Kenya-based media studies senior lecturer and researcher with experience in teaching, university administration, curriculum development and research publication. A researcher with experience in qualitative and mixed methods studies, she has presented papers at the African Studies Association (ASA), East African Communication Association (EACA) and International Communication Association (ICA) conferences. Wamunyu has been published in the *African Journalism Studies, The International Encyclopedia of Gender, Media, and Communication* and *The Conversation* among other publications. She also curated a cluster of articles published in Visualizing the Virus, a multidisciplinary digital project focused on Covid-19. Her areas of research interest include disinformation, gender and media and the news media's use of digital technologies.

Acknowledgements

This book is a product of the African Digital Rights Network, a group of more than forty activists, analysts and academics from fifteen African countries. It could not have been produced without the inspiration and fortitude of activists and scholars across the continent who have actively harnessed the positive potential of digital technologies for furthering rights and freedoms and those who have resisted and spoken out against its use to stifle dissent, repress agency and reduce the space for digital citizenship. Special thanks go to those external analysts who lent us their expertise by presenting their work at our meetings: Phillip Howard, Nahema Marchal, Wasim Ahmed, Erin Gallagher, Marc Owen Jones and Andres Moreno. Thanks to colleagues at the Institute of Development Studies Amy Cowlard, Sophie Robinson and digital and technology researchers Becky Faith, Kevin Hernandez, Pedro Prieto Martin and Karishma Banga. We are indebted to Nick Wolterman and Olivia Dellow at Zed Books for steering the project and to unnamed reviewers who provided invaluable feedback on the initial book proposal and on manuscript drafts.

Chapter 1

Digital disinformation in Africa

A critical approach

Tony Roberts and George Hamandishe Karekwaivanane

Digital disinformation is a direct threat to democracy and to fundamental human rights in Africa. Disinformation is playing an increasing role in distorting elections, inflaming conflict and disrupting crucial policy debates across the continent on issues including vaccinations, immigration, gender and reproductive rights. The ability of citizens to access trustworthy information, engage in reasoned debate and participate in decision-making about issues that affect their lives is a fundamental human right and a central tenet of democratic citizenship. Disinformation – understood in this book as the intentional deployment of lies to manipulate people's beliefs and behaviour in order to further political interests – runs counter to democratic ideals and violates fundamental human rights. This book analyses examples of disinformation in ten African countries: Nigeria, Cameroon, Angola, Mozambique, Egypt, Ethiopia, Zimbabwe, Kenya, Uganda and the Democratic Republic of Congo.

Powerful groups often use digital disinformation campaigns to close civic space online by attacking individuals or groups to negate their influence on key social issues. The examples in this book show how states often coordinate digital disinformation campaigns to deter opposition voices from participating in public deliberation. This is often achieved by polarizing debate, exacerbating existing social divisions and has the effect of diminishing faith in traditional media and political institutions and closing the civic space available for democratic participation, especially by marginalized groups.

In a session dedicated to the threat of disinformation, the United Nations Human Rights Council (UNHRC 2022) emphasized that disinformation is designed to mislead in ways that violate human rights, including privacy and the freedom of individuals to seek, receive and impart information. The resolution made particular note of the use of disinformation to spread hatred and racism; to incite violence, discrimination and hostility; and to deter women from participating in the public sphere by attacking female journalists, politicians and human rights defenders (ibid). Such coordinated disinformation campaigns represent a direct threat to democracy and political legitimacy.

Disinformation can take the form of a partisan campaign of character assassination during an election or a misogynistic attack on a prominent female politician. It can be used to attack specific individuals, organizations or election candidates or to otherwise manipulate beliefs and behaviours around policy issues such as immigration, vaccinations or climate change. Disinformation has been identified as a key tactic used by powerful actors to shrink the civic space for dissent and political opposition in Africa as documented in our first study (Roberts and Mohamed Ali 2021). This book includes case studies of disinformation campaigns run by foreign powers to influence countries in Africa, but it is primarily about the growing power of African governments themselves to make repressive use of disinformation to further their own power interests.

The case studies in this book include the deployment of state disinformation to neutralize political opposition, enflame ethnic divisions, perpetrate gender-based violence and the use of disinformation as a weapon of war. In every case, the chapter focuses on an episode in which actors intentionally set out to deploy false information to manipulate public beliefs and behaviour in order to secure an intended objective that serves their power interests. It is important to note that these campaigns will often also involve the deployment of misinformation and malinformation. However, in order to ensure focus of analysis across the book we make disinformation, as defined earlier, the central concern of every chapter.

This book is the first collected edition of case studies to document and analyse the deployment of digital disinformation across Africa. This collected edition is the work of the African Digital Rights Network and forms part of their Digital Africa book series. The African Digital Rights Network brings together more than fifty activists, academics and analysts studying digital rights across all regions of Africa. To date, most scholarly attention has focused on investigating disinformation in the global North (see however Wasserman and Madrid-Morales 2022). This book shifts the focus of attention to digital disinformation across Africa, by bringing together, for the first time in a single volume, case studies of digital disinformation campaigns from across the continent. Authors are primarily nationals of the countries they are writing about, and the book is a conscious effort to bring activists and practitioners together with experienced and emerging scholars from a range of disciplines. Academics do not have a monopoly of knowledge about disinformation, and we believe that taking a holistic approach to disinformation requires its grounding in a rich appreciation of local history, politics and culture. We, therefore, see the authors' diverse backgrounds, their different perspectives and the many registers they employ as important assets in this volume.

As the title implies, the overarching research questions include documenting and analysing episodes of digital disinformation in Africa through the lens of power, politics and propaganda. In addition, we examine what is distinctively African about this disinformation and what is distinctively digital about it. The book provides a series of case studies that identify four areas in which we argue digital disinformation in Africa is distinctive: with regards to its drivers, dynamics, dimensions and directions (defined as follows).

There is a danger in focusing on one of the elements of the dark side of digital technology that its positive potential is underestimated. That is not our intention. Our focus on digital disinformation should not be interpreted as implying that this is the only, predominant or most important phenomenon within digital communication ecosystems in African countries. This book is part of a book series that includes titles dedicated to illuminating the positive potential of digital technology for opening civic space and facilitating democratic discourse, including our first book *Digital Citizenship in Africa* (ed. Roberts and Bosch 2023). This volume contributes to this wider body of emerging literature that examines the positive and negative social, political and economic impacts of digital technologies in African countries.

Background

The Cambridge Analytica affair dramatically amplified global awareness about digital disinformation. The central focus of analysis of Cambridge Analytica has often been on the company's role in using Facebook user data to profile individuals and micro-target them with falsehoods about the 2016 Brexit referendum and the election of Trump. What is less known is that prior to 2016 Cambridge Analytica also operated in African countries. For example, it was employed in the 2013 Kenyan election, during which it 'manipulated voters with apocalyptic attack ads and smeared opposition candidate Raila Odinga as violent, corrupt and dangerous' (Madowo 2018). During the 2015 election in Nigeria 'Cambridge Analytica also leveraged violent video against opposition candidate Muhammadu Buhari. Anti-Buhari disinformation suggested that Buhari would support Boko Haram, a well-known and feared terrorist group, and would end women's rights' (Jemison 2022). The political objectives of disinformation were to manipulate people's beliefs and voting behaviour in favour of the incumbent President. Since 2016, powerful groups around the world have deployed coordinated campaigns of digital disinformation to further their political and economic objectives, not only in elections but also on key policy issues, including Covid-19 vaccinations, immigration, reproductive rights and ethnic conflicts worldwide.

Since 2016 we have seen a veritable explosion of research on disinformation as scholars and policymakers applied themselves with great urgency to the tasks of understanding the challenges posed by digital disinformation and devising responses to it. A key inflection point in the pace of research was political events in 2016 and 2017 in the United States, the United Kingdom and France and the allegations of Russian interference. A substantial amount of this research has focused on Western countries, spurred on by the concerns about the impact of Russian disinformation in Europe and America. These studies are rooted mainly in Western histories and politics. By contrast, academic research on digital disinformation in Africa has been much more limited in breadth and depth. This is despite the fact that across the continent, digital disinformation is increasingly being used by state and non-state actors, including foreign ones. Examples of such activities abound – from the Guptabots in South Africa, the Varakashi in Zimbabwe and the coordinated activities of the pro-Museveni accounts during the 2021 Ugandan election, to the rival French and Russian disinformation campaigns in the Central African Republic (Meta 2020) and indeed the Nigerian paid Twitter influencers who promoted the cause of the Colombian businessman Alex Saab wanted for money laundering, to name just a few (Silverman 2021).

This recent explosion in digital disinformation on social media has given rise to the technologically deterministic notion that social media is the *cause* of disinformation. However, the truth is that disinformation is as old as politics itself and that it predates the existence of modern African states by decades, if not centuries. Digital technologies do have features that can be used to amplify the deployment of disinformation, but social media is simply the latest medium over which disinformation is deployed to secure political objectives. The next section briefly reviews the long history of disinformation in Africa and global politics.

Historical context of disinformation

Given the dazzling novelties of digital innovation, there always exists a danger that we draw technologically deterministic conclusions about the relationship between social media, disinformation and social outcomes. This book avoids such technologically deterministic analysis by, among other things, examining each episode of disinformation studied in its specific historical and political context.

Disinformation is as old as politics in Africa. Distinct historical eras are replete with examples of disinformation using the information and communication technologies of that era (Posetti and Matthews 2018). We know, for example, that disinformation was deployed to influence public opinion about international politics in ancient Egypt. The Roman General Octavia launched a disinformation campaign to manipulate beliefs and behaviour regarding Mark Anthony while he was in Alexandria as a guest of Queen Cleopatra. Octavia had coins produced and distributed that attacked Mark Anthony's propriety and sobriety by inserting 'short, sharp slogans written upon coins in the style of archaic Tweets' (Kaminska 2017).

The Greek playwright Aeschylus (525–426 BC) wrote that 'truth is the first casualty of war' and, as we see in this book, disinformation remains a key weapon of war 2,000 years later. Although the practice of disinformation is ancient, the word itself is relatively modern. The term disinformation has its origins in the Cold War, a loan word from the Russian 'dezinformatsiya', coined during the battle of ideas waged between the two superpowers the United States and USSR. Although the role of digital disinformation in the Brexit referendum and the Trump election shone a spotlight on Russian disinformation, and although funder priorities have directed a disproportionate amount of research attention on Russian disinformation even a cursory historical approach reveals that powerful groups in all nations deploy disinformation. This is especially the case in times of war and conquest.

The CIA Psychological Operations Manual reminds us that 'Since the dawn of history men have resorted to the same familiar techniques in order to induce in the mind of a rival or opponent an attitude of frame of mind favourable to their own purposes' (CIA 1949). The United States has made perhaps the largest financial investment of any nation in foreign influence, conducting surveillance and projecting soft power through media influence. The foreign intelligence budget of the United States is $85b per year which is approximately the total GDP of Kenya (DNI 2022). As Heidi Tworek observes:

> There is a long, often forgotten history of [American] 'active measures' or disinformation. 'Psychological warfare' was a key concept for the CIA during the Cold War and the Department of Defense during the Vietnam War. After the Vietnam War, the Carter and Reagan administrations both incorporated information into their national security strategies. By 2000, these strategies for active engagement abroad were known in the Department of Defense's Joint Staff Officer's Guide under the acronym of DIME: diplomatic, informational, and economic power. This historical perspective makes recent Russian efforts seem less of an anomaly. (Tworek 2020: 171)

Colonial powers used disinformation extensively to further their economic and political exploitation of Africa and to undermine African national liberation movements (Earle 1997; Rid 2020). Substantial investments were made by colonial powers to establish newspapers and radio media to disseminate disinformation designed to legitimate their interests and undermine the interests of those fighting for freedom (Osbourne 2015). Earlier generations of information and communications technologies, including press and radio media, were used by colonial powers to divide and conquer. Colonial newspapers were established in different parts of the continent to mould the literate African middle class so that it would serve as a buffer against anti-colonial agitation by the working class and the peasantry, who were themselves targeted through radio propaganda (Manqoyi 2018). In Britain, pro-government newspapers used disinformation in their coverage of the South African war (Anglo-Boer war). For example, newspapers like *The Times* claimed that the deaths of tens of thousands of civilian women and children unjustly held in inhumane conditions in British concentration camps resulted from the captives' 'poor hygiene' (Kent 2013). Control of the media enabled colonial powers to manipulate public beliefs and behaviour to support policies that served its imperial interests. These media and methods were part of the colonial legacy passed onto post-colonial African administrations following liberation.

In South Africa, the apartheid state waged a sustained disinformation campaign domestically and internationally to shore up support for structural racial discrimination and demonize its opponents. The state's propaganda operation was coordinated at the Ministerial level and sought to deploy falsehoods to legitimize white supremacy to further the power interests of the white minority against the interests of the vast majority of South Africans (Nixon 2016). In Africa's modern history the use of racialized disinformation deployed through private radio stations was used to manipulate the beliefs and behaviour of the Hutu population towards the Tutsi minority and to coordinate the 1994 Rwandan genocide (Pottier 2002). Radio and mobile phone SMS messages were also used to disseminate untruths to foment ethnic hatred in the 2007 post-election violence in Kenya (Mutahi and Kimari 2017). In recent years the rapid expansion in the ownership of mobile phones and the falling cost of mobile internet has meant that social media including Facebook, Whatsapp and Twitter have become more popular mediums for disseminating disinformation.

This book does not set out to provide a history of disinformation in Africa nor is it primarily a work of political science. However, we maintain that several valuable insights can be derived from examining disinformation in its broader historical and political context. The first is that it ensures that we avoid amplifying the technologically-determinist fallacy that disinformation is *caused* by digital technologies. Instead, it re-directs the focus towards understanding the qualitative differences between disinformation in the digital era when compared to previous forms of disinformation. The second is that the volume of recent research on Russian disinformation distorts the picture about the origins and plurality of powerholders deploying disinformation. This book addresses a gap in the existing literature regarding case studies of disinformation in Africa. While the chapter by Jeon in this collection examines the role of Russian disinformation, we also locate African disinformation in the context of Western colonialism and note the efforts of African governments to expand their domestic capacity to deploy disinformation independently.

Acknowledging that digital technology is not the cause of disinformation has important implications for how we think about solutions. Crucially, there are no technological magic bullets that will solve the problem of disinformation, and narrowly focused technological solutions are always going to be inadequate. We have to think beyond the technologies that enable its spread, identify the power interests that originate disinformation and are served by its deployment, and understand the sociopolitical contexts that make disinformation more likely to be believed.

This introduction is organized as follows. Section 1 explains how we define disinformation in this book and how we distinguish it from related phenomena such as misinformation and fake news. Section 2 focuses on what is distinctively African about digital disinformation in African countries, arguing that African colonial history and distinctive culture and institutions have contributed to distinct patterns of disinformation in African contexts. Section 3 examines the importance of the digital dimension in disinformation, arguing that mobile and internet disinformation is qualitatively distinct from previous forms of state propaganda and disinformation. Section 4 explains the critical approach the book's authors take in studying digital disinformation in Africa and introduces the 4Ds: dimensions, dynamics, drivers and directions of digital disinformation in Africa. Section 5 provides an overview of the case study chapters before Section 6 draws some conclusions from across the ten countries.

Defining disinformation

This book focuses centrally on disinformation. Although the terms disinformation, misinformation, propaganda and fake news have distinct meanings, they are often used interchangeably. To provide some analytical clarity, we begin with some definitions. Wardle and Derakshan (2017) describe a broad 'information disorder' composed of three distinct elements: disinformation, misinformation and mal-information. They define disinformation as false information deliberately created or deployed to harm a person, social group, organization or country. In their information disorder framework, misinformation is information that is false, but which is not created or deployed with the intention of causing harm (this includes the innocent sharing of false information). Mal-information is information that is based on reality, but is used to inflict harm on a person, organization or country (including leaks, harassment and hate speech).

These definitions by Wardle and Derakshan are useful in distinguishing disinformation as *intentional* falsehoods. However, for them, the motivation for such intentional falsehoods is limited to the desire to cause harm. By contrast, Benkler, Faris and Roberts (2018) define disinformation as intentionally manipulating and misleading people in order to achieve distinctly *political* ends. The definition of disinformation offered by Freelon and Wells (2020) specifies a wider range of intentions. They view disinformation as false information that is intentionally spread for profit, to create harm or to advance political or ideological goals. Philip Howard's (2020) definition is more expansive still, defining disinformation as purposefully crafted and strategically placed information that deceives someone – tricks them – into believing a lie or taking action that serves someone else's political interests.

These different definitions help to identify what we see as three key elements of disinformation: deployment of falsehoods, manipulation of beliefs and furthering of interests. Understood in this way, disinformation necessarily involves intentional dissemination of lies to serve political interests. The intended first-order effect of the deployment of disinformation is to manipulate people's beliefs and/or behaviour. The intended second-order effect is that this manipulation should further the political, economic, ideological or power interests of the deployers of disinformation. These three elements are illustrated in Figure 1.1.

Figure 1.1 Three elements of disinformation. *Source*: authors.

These three elements of disinformation are central to our understanding of disinformation and to the analysis of case studies in this book.

(i)   Deploy Lies: relatively powerful actors intentionally deploy falsehoods
(ii) Manipulate Beliefs: to manipulate the beliefs and behaviours of others
(iii) Further Interests: in order to further the power interests of the former.

Not all attempts to influence people's beliefs and behaviour are malevolent. After all, influencing public opinion is the purpose of conventional politics, advertising and propaganda. However, they generally rely on truthful persuasion, are transparent about their funders and are subject to regulation and oversight. It is worth clarifying that disinformation is just one tactic in the broader arena of propaganda. Propaganda can use truthful or untruthful words, disinformation, misinformation or mal-information. Therefore, not all propaganda is disinformation. Instead, disinformation is a subset of propaganda that intentionally deploys false information to (often covertly) manipulate people's beliefs and behaviour. Digital disinformation generally takes place outside any framework of regulation or accountability. The identity of the sponsor or perpetrator of disinformation is often unknown, making accountability extremely difficult even where regulation exists. This is the case globally but the regulatory environment in African countries is underdeveloped and the capacity of civil society is uneven in its ability to hold to account those deploying political lies.

What is African about digital disinformation in Africa?

A book with the title *Digital Disinformation in Africa* must answer the question of whether digital disinformation in Africa is significantly different from digital disinformation anywhere else in the world. The vast majority of disinformation studies to date have focused on examples in the global North. By comparison there has been relatively little attention to the analysis of disinformation across Africa. It would be an epistemic injustice to presuppose that everything we need to know about digital disinformation in Africa has already been learnt by scholars from the global North studying Europe and North America. The framings and findings of scholars from the global North cannot (and should not) simply be cut and pasted across the fifty-five different countries on the African continent.

In order to identify the distinctively African elements of digital disinformation, we approached the subject in the following ways. First, the authors were primarily African scholars with linguistic, social and cultural insight into the countries they were studying. The authors identified disinformation case studies that best illustrated contemporary disinformation in their countries. Second, the authors adopted a historically and politically grounded approach and began each chapter by situating the disinformation episode within its specific historical, sociocultural and political context. This approach revealed continuities between colonial and post-colonial experiences of disinformation that are not a feature of European or North American studies of disinformation. Third, we adopted a case study approach that provided rich empirical detail and in-depth analysis, which revealed ways in which disinformation reflected and reproduced distinctive ethnic and gender stratifications. Fourth, the authors analysed the specific legal, regulatory and institutional environment using their local knowledge of political culture exposing what remedies or mitigation or redress may be viable in specific contexts. The resulting chapters are a testament to both the similarities and distinctive nature of digital disinformation in Africa when compared to other regions.

What is digital about digital disinformation in Africa?

Just as a book with our title must answer the question of what is specifically African about 'Digital Disinformation in Africa', it must also answer the question of what is specifically digital about it. We have seen earlier that disinformation has been a feature of political life in Africa for at least two millennia. Therefore, it is essential to ask what, if anything, has changed now that disinformation is mediated by mobile and internet devices and digital platforms. The 1949 CIA PsyOps manual provides some helpful insights:

> There is nothing fundamentally new about the principles of psychological warfare . . . what is new is the improved techniques of the science of psychology . . . the vastly expanded media for dissemination . . . and the forging of these elements together into *a streamlined precision tool for influencing the thoughts of large masses of people.*

When the CIA spoke of a *'streamlined precision tool for influencing the thoughts of people'* in 1949 they could not yet dream of the level of sophistication that digital technologies would provide for the production and dissemination of disinformation.

To analyse the qualitative differences that digitalization makes, we find the concept of affordances helpful. Affordances are the new action possibilities that a technology enables, invites or facilitates (Gibson 1977; Norman 1988). A door handle has the affordance of openability, inviting the possible action of holding and opening. Affordances are possibilities made available by the design of a technology, but affordances do not determine action, because the same tool can be used in more than one way or not used at all (Hutchby 2001); a cup, for example, has the affordance of conveying liquid to the mouth but it can also be used as a pen holder. Social media platforms afford new action possibilities for disinformation as they enable the sending of text, voice, graphic and video messages to any number of recipients, worldwide, instantly, repeatedly with negligible marginal costs. The concept of affordances helps us to discern the practical difference between deploying disinformation by radio or television and digital social media.

Assessing the digitalization of disinformation Arthur de Liedekerke and Michael Zinkanell (2020) note that:

> What has changed is its ubiquity and its power to shape debates and nudge public opinion at an unprecedented scale. There are many reasons behind this shift, but two intertwined causes deserve particular attention: 'the digital transformation of news from offline to online distribution and the rise of social media platforms as news distribution channels'.

The rapid increase in computing power and the dramatic reduction in the cost of access to mobile and internet technologies has reduced the barriers to deploying disinformation campaigns and created a situation where millions of citizens can be reached immediately, repeatedly and affordably those with the means of propaganda. Digital platforms like Facebook, Google and Twitter provide the big data necessary for machine learning algorithms to psychologically profile and micro-target millions of citizens repeatedly with messages designed to manipulate their beliefs and behaviours and serve the interests of powerholders. These digital affordances of speed, scale and scope are common to digitalization processes across multiple domains, as are the drastically reduced transaction costs. They make digital media more flexible and more powerful means of disinformation than previous mechanisms.

A crucial affordance of digital technologies for disinformation is the ability to micro-target messages for specific communities. Radio and television enable propagandists to reach a mass audience in a single transmission with a single message. By contrast, digital surveillance of the type employed by Cambridge Analytica and Bell-Pottinger allows micro-targeting using thousands of different messages to target specific demographic groups (and even individuals). By analysing data about a person's likes and followers, location and purchasing history, algorithms are used to build psychological profiles of citizens so that messages can be tailored and micro-targeted. These messages are used to manipulate a person's beliefs and behaviours based on what issues they are triggered by online and their identified psychological vulnerabilities (Briant 2020; Nyabola 2018). This process is carried out covertly so that targets do not know they are being manipulated to serve the interests of powerholders.

The move from mass media propaganda to micro-targeted disinformation is a substantial advance in psychological-operations (psy-ops) technology. Being able to reach millions of targets, hundreds of times, with carefully tailored messaging at a relatively low cost, has been a massive boon for repressive governments. It has never been easier or cheaper for governments to repeatedly deploy targeted disinformation to manipulate the beliefs and behaviour of millions of citizens.

However, the affordances of any technology are relational and socially mediated: not everyone has the same capacity or intention to make use of these new action possibilities. Different governments have very different budgets, technical capabilities and political intentions regarding digital disinformation. Technology can only amplify whatever levels of human capacity and intent already exist (Toyama 2011). Furthermore, levels of internet access and social media use vary widely within populations and between countries. There are substantial differences between social media use levels between Africa and other continents. In addition, there are fairly stark differences in social media use levels between African countries. Even within individual countries, there are disparities in social media use which are shaped by factors such as age, gender, income and rural/ urban divides. For this reason, we cannot assume that what holds true about digital disinformation in Tokyo or Toronto holds true for Lusaka or Lubumbashi. From this perspective, the study of digital disinformation is necessarily empirical, contextual and situated. As the case studies in this book illustrate, what we learn about digital disinformation in one continent cannot be assumed to hold true in another. In many locations social media is not widely used at all, so it is also worth pointing out that, because of uneven access to digital media, when we study digital disinformation in Africa, we are often studying a small and often unrepresentative demographic, albeit one disproportionately influential in political life (Tufekci 2014). See for example Angelo's chapter on Angola in this volume.

What is our research approach?

In addition to the concept of affordances, in this volume we also draw on various stage-based approaches to guide empirical investigation as well as elements of the emergent area of critical disinformation studies. These research approaches are explained in this section. In their review of the digital disinformation literature, Freelon and Wells (2020) argue that it is a sub-field that is still in its infancy. They divide the body of existing literature into two main groups. The first group is content studies that draw conclusions about the intended purposes, audiences and the effects that producers of disinformation have. Studies in this first group primarily use qualitative methods. The second group are those studies that focus on the reception of disinformation and seek to determine how exposure to disinformation affects opinions, attitudes, beliefs and behaviours, often by using quantitative surveys or experimental methods. These two approaches cut across the three elements of our definition of disinformation illustrated in Figure 1.1 viz deployment of disinformation, manipulation of beliefs and furthering of specific interests. Exposure studies focus on the middle element: the effect of disinformation on beliefs and behaviours. Content studies work across all three elements. The approach we employ in this book most closely fits the content studies approach identified by Freelon and Wells but takes a specifically situated and critical approach as elaborated in what follows.

Stage-based approaches

To study the deployment of disinformation scholars have used a range of stage-based analytical frameworks to provide clarity about the mechanics of disinformation campaigns. In their study of troll accounts and fake news in the Philippines, Ong and Cabanes (2018) use a marketing science framework to analyse disinformation networks. Their framework has four stages: setting campaign objectives; mapping audiences; establishing the role of each media platform; and translating specific campaign aims into assigned actions. This stage-based analysis has the advantage that it often enables rich descriptive analysis of the mechanisms in play and provides a productive framework for disinformation campaign analysis.

Philip Howard (2020) uses a broader phase-based framework to study 'computational propaganda' in which marketing is the third of three stages. In his book *Lie Machines*, he uses a mechanical metaphor to break down the disinformation process into three stages – production, distribution and marketing. He identifies the different actors and techniques involved in the initial manufacture of political lies, with different personnel involved in disseminating the lies on social media, and a third group responsible for amplifying the message and creating virality. This includes a detailed study of the role of hired trolls, automated software bots and a hybrid of semi-automated troll/bots called cyborgs.

These stage-based approaches align with our research approach both because they overlap with the three stages of our definition of disinformation and because they help to guide and structure empirical analysis to produce rich case study documentation.

Less well-developed in the existing literature is the conceptual analysis of disinformation and focused attention on the power interests that underpin almost all disinformation. We argue that there is a need for research that goes beyond explaining how disinformation campaigns work to apply critical and conceptual lenses to understand who benefits from disinformation and what interests it serves.

Critical disinformation studies

One promising line of analysis is the emerging area of critical disinformation studies. Kuo and Marwick (2021) argue the need for critical disinformation studies to distinguish themselves in four ways:

1. By taking a holistic approach to disinformation that is grounded in history, society, culture and politics.
2. By centring analyses of how social stratification shapes the dynamics of disinformation – including along lines of race and ethnicity, gender, class and sexual identity.
3. By foregrounding questions of power, institutions and economic, social, cultural and technological structures as they shape disinformation.
4. By having clear normative commitments to equality and justice.

Our affinity with this critical approach is evident in a number of ways: each chapter begins with a grounding in the historical and political context of the country which help explain the distinct drivers and dynamics of that episode of disinformation. The way in which gender stratification shapes disinformation is the subject of the first chapter by Agunwa and the chapters by Eyelaw and Behane on Ethiopia and by Chabikwa on Zimbabwe focus centrally on disinformation aimed at fomenting ethnic division. Several chapters focus on the deployment of disinformation during elections, highlighting how powerholders use state institutions to deploy falsehoods to manipulate voters' beliefs and behaviours in order that incumbent rulers can maintain their hold over power (including Karekwaivanane' chapter on Zimbabwe, Nanfuka's chapter in Uganda, Toussi's chapter on Cameroon and Angelo's chapter on Angola).

The final way that Kuo and Marwick (2021) distinguish critical disinformation studies is by having a clear normative commitment to equality and social justice. One way to calibrate a normative commitment to social justice is to use a human rights framework to analyse the dynamics of digital disinformation (Jones 2019). This approach has the advantage of calibrating a clear normative commitment to social justice against a body of internationally agreed human rights law that most governments have committed to. In addition to being signatories of key international human rights conventions, many African governments have also incorporated them into their constitutions and into domestic legislation (Roberts et al. 2021). These commitments include the right to privacy of communication, the right to freedom of political opinion, association and expression; and the right to participate in elections and other decision-making about issues affecting a person's life. As members of the African Digital Rights Network and co-authors of previous landscape studies of digital rights in Africa (Roberts et al. 2021) this normative approach appealed to us.

The four 'D's of disinformation

As editors we did not want to impose a theoretical framework on the authors of this collected edition. We did discuss with them the stage-based approaches to analysing disinformation campaigns, the affordances of social media and critical approaches that foreground power interests. We then left them to choose their own conceptual framings, mindful of the rich diversity of their backgrounds, approaches and perspectives. As we edited various drafts of the chapters it became evident that most chapters engaged with four aspects of disinformation: its dimensions, dynamics, drivers and directions as illustrated in Figure 1.2. We expand on each of these in turn as follows.

Dimensions of disinformation (deployment): Who is involved in devising, deploying and amplifying disinformation? Are the actors military units, militant cadres, intelligence agents or foreign public relations or political marketing companies? What is the scale and significance of disinformation operations? Are these characteristics any different in African countries than elsewhere in the world? Has digitalization made any difference to the dimensions of disinformation and if so how and why?

Dynamics of disinformation (manipulation): What tools, techniques or tactics of disinformation are employed on which digital platforms, over what time periods and in what volumes? Are disinformation campaigns characterized by the use of trolls, bots, cyborgs or celebrity influencers? What is the use of images,

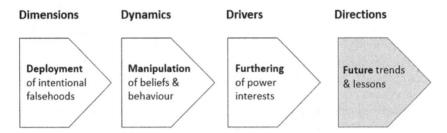

Figure 1.2 The four 'D's of disinformation. *Source*: authors.

memes, sockpuppets, astroturfing or other disinformation techniques? What is the size and demographic of the target audience? Are these dynamics in African disinformation distinct from those used in other parts of the world? To what extent has digitalization changed the dynamics of disinformation compared to pre-existing methods?

Drivers of disinformation (power interests): What motives drive the production and dissemination of disinformation; why does it happen; who benefits and what interests are served? What changes in beliefs or behaviours is the disinformation designed to deliver? Is there any evidence that beliefs or behaviours are changed by disinformation? How are different ethnic, gender, class and sexual identity groups implicated and impacted by digital disinformation? What digital rights are affected by the disinformation and how can they be defended and expanded? Are the drivers of disinformation in Africa any different than in other parts of the world? Are the drivers of disinformation any different in a digital context?

Directions of disinformation (future scenarios): What trends or future directions emerge from the analysis? What lessons and recommendations arise from this analysis of digital disinformation in Africa for future policy, practice and further research? Who needs to do what in order to mitigate or overcome the intentional deployment of lies to manipulate African citizens' beliefs and behaviour to serve other people's interests? (See Figure 1.2.)

Power and disinformation

We argue that all disinformation involves power relationships, so the absence of explicit power analysis is an important conceptual gap in the existing literature. A close analysis of any given disinformation operation soon reveals that it is ultimately tied to power. Disinformation operations are always at some level about the expression, accumulation, reproduction, defence or disruption of social, economic, ideological or political power interests. This book contributes case studies that foreground a range of power relationships that shape digital disinformation in Africa: between countries, between ethnic groups, between genders and between states and citizens and between sides in a conflict. Further research needs to be done to explore how digital disinformation in Africa is both shaped by power and in turn shapes power relationships between corporations, demographic groups and classes of citizens.

Power is an essentially contested concept in the social sciences (Lukes 1974) and so we do not propose to review all of the lengthy debates about it in this chapter. In thinking about how power operates, a useful distinction is between those scholars that see power as an instrument or resource that individuals or institutions wield over others and those who see power as more diffuse, operating everywhere, across networks and social systems (Hayward 1988). From the first perspective the concern is primarily with 'power over' but VeneKlasen and Miller (2002) are among scholars who have elaborated more granular dimensions of power such as 'power within', 'power with' and 'power to' that are helpful in thinking through how to resist and overcome authoritarian 'power over' (McGee 2020). The original source of disinformation narratives is often opaque or anonymous, making concepts of 'hidden power' and 'invisible power' useful for covert agenda setting and the impact of pervasive narratives and their internalization as social norms and values (Gaventa 2006; Baltiwala 2019).

In some cases, digital disinformation is deployed to enable certain actors to maintain power over other individuals or groups. In others, it helps to constitute or reinforce certain gender, ethnic or political power hierarchies. An example illustrated in several chapters in this volume is how disinformation is used to foment anti-immigrant sentiment and reproduce racial hierarchies. In other cases, authoritarian governments use disinformation to protect or consolidate their hold on power. Given the centrality of deceit in disinformation, it is also important to note how disinformation functions to render invisible the hidden operations of power. What is clear from these examples is that a narrowly prescriptive understanding of the relationship between power and disinformation can conceal more than it reveals. In this book, we eclectically draw upon these different approaches to power to tease out how disinformation and power are intertwined. To identify and analyse how power operates in particular disinformation campaigns we ask: what power relations are at play, who benefits and what interests are being served?

The analysis of disinformation is complicated by the fact that different forms of power are often concentrated in the hands of the same groups. Those who possess social power also tend to have economic or political power as well. In addition, they often strive to exclude others from sharing or wresting that power. They also have a vested interest in maintaining a particular social order. Disinformation is one of the tools for prosecuting these social, economic and political power struggles. As such, power provides an important lens through which to think about disinformation. Underlying the examination of the different instances of disinformation in the different chapters of this book is an exploration of how disinformation is implicated in power struggles.

Given the multiple objectives, strategies and tactics of disinformation operations across Africa it was important to us as editors that we were not narrowly prescriptive in imposing specific concepts of power on authors. Furthermore, we do not see the different approaches to power as being mutually exclusive. Instead, the authors have been guided by their empirical data in their selection of a conceptual lens that they employed to analyse the nexus between disinformation and power.

What issues do the chapters address?

The chapters in this book are clustered around three main themes. The first set of papers focuses on digital disinformation's role in creating and maintaining social and political hierarchies. The second set of papers examines the relationship between digital disinformation and conflict. In particular, the chapters explore how disinformation influences how historical and contemporary conflicts are perceived and understood. Finally, the last set of papers analyses the role of digital disinformation in recent elections across the continent. We discuss each cluster of chapters in turn as follows.

The book begins with a set of chapters that attend to the ways that digital disinformation campaigns are used to create and maintain social and political hierarchies. Nkem Agunwa's chapter focuses on gendered disinformation and its impact on women's civic participation in a range of African countries. Gendered disinformation is the intentional spread of deceptive or inaccurate information and images that draw on misogyny and gender stereotypes. This disinformation is typically used to discredit female politicians or silence women's voices in the public sphere. Deploying gendered disinformation in this way has the dual effect of reinforcing gender and political hierarchies. Indeed, Agunwa's study of gendered disinformation reveals that there is considerable overlap between gender and political hierarchies in society. There is a long history of misogynist disinformation; what is new about misogynist disinformation deployed digitally, however, is how the affordances of digital technology enable the financing, coordination and amplification of disinformation at a speed and scale previously impossible. The chapter identifies the mechanisms and dynamics of gendered disinformation and by taking an intersectional approach shows how they particularly affect LGBTQ women. Agunwa concludes that misogynist disinformation tends to involve accusations that women do not conform to oppressive norms of motherhood, heteronormativity and fidelity. The intent of the disinformation is to manipulate public behaviour, silence women's voices and make them retreat from the public realm and from political speech. The chapter analyses online tactics, including doxing, dog-piling and the use of sock-puppets to perpetuate online gender-based violence. On the whole, the chapter argues that gender disinformation contributes to a culture of violence against women that furthers patriarchal interests by diminishing the civic participation of women in Africa.

In his chapter, George Hamandishe Karekwaivanane analyses the disinformation campaign launched to counter the #ZimbabweLivesMatter hashtag that criticized government failings and corruption. After the November 2017 coup that deposed President Robert Mugabe, the incoming president, Emmerson Mnangagwa, began to encourage ruling party supporters to use social media more aggressively to defend the ruling party's political hegemony. The chapter analyses the dynamics of this troll army of 'Varakashi' and their attempts to control and manipulate online political discourse about Zimbabwe. At the heart of the paper is the effort to uncover the anatomy and dimensions of the pro-government network on Twitter that was responsible for deploying disinformation and coordinating attacks on government critics. In terms of methodology, Karekwaivanane combines digital ethnography with the use of social media analytics using NodeXL and other data analytics software tools. By these means seventy-one pro-government accounts were identified and tracked to discern the strategies and tactics of disinformation being deployed. The analysis shows how the Zimbabwean state disinformation machine lacks the large budgets and commercial PR companies that coordinate political campaigns in the global North. Yet what Karekwaivanane characterizes as 'disinformation on a shoestring', succeeds in thrashing opposition figures, disrupting debate and closing civic space. Led unashamedly by senior politicians and amplified by the Varakashi troll-army government disinformation campaigns further vested power interests by intimidating critical voices or *in extremisis* by shutting down the entire internet as it did in 2019.

The second set of chapters focuses on disinformation and conflict. At the heart of military conflict is the struggle for power, be it power over the state or over a specific territory. These power struggles are often accompanied by a contest over the framing of the conflict. The papers in this cluster examine how the dynamics of digital disinformation are used to deploy specific narratives about the conflict. In his chapter Dércio Tsandzana analyses the use of digital disinformation by actors in the military conflict between the Mozambican government and Islamic militants in the north-western province of Cabo Delgado. Mozambique has been experiencing violent conflict in the region since October 2017 following the discovery of large reserves of natural gas. The United States have labelled the main armed group as 'Islamic State in Mozambique' and classified them as a terrorist organization. Huge gas reserves have stimulated a disinformation campaign largely within elite groups to further multi-billion dollar economic interests. He analyses the use of digital disinformation by belligerents on all sides to manipulate domestic and international beliefs about the conflict to advance their military and economic interests. In a country where social media use is less than 10 per cent, Tsandzana notes that disinformation is rarely in local languages; Portuguese disinformation seeks to influence relatively affluent local opinion, and English disinformation is evidence of attempts to influence global decision makers. Tsandzana concludes that this disinformation is driven by political actors exploiting the vacuum of reliable information that is a feature of war. In this case, the insurgents are characterized as the source of disinformation and the government through mainstream media and an army of government-aligned 'digital firefighters' seek to counter disinformation with their own narrative on the war. Independently verifying the claims made by either side is a major challenge in the fog of war. Tsandzana's chapter demonstrates the layered role of disinformation during the conflict. Disinformation was a tool that was actively used by the belligerents to advance specific narratives. However, it was also used by the government as a label deployed to deride and neutralize the narratives of other groups.

The chapter by Yohannes Ayalew and Atnafu Brhane Ayalew continues the examination of the operation of disinformation during contexts of armed conflict, but turns the focus to the Horn of Africa. They analyse how actors on both sides of the Ethiopian armed conflict use selfies and hashtags as vehicles of disinformation to further their war aims. The authors show how soldiers deploy selfies – photos of themselves allegedly taking control of a strategic town – as part of 'psychological operations' propaganda to support military objectives. The authors unpack the dynamics of how hashtags have been used strategically on social media to amplify the narratives being deployed by protagonists in the war. State actors and their supporters in civil society mobilize around themes such as #UnityForEthiopia and #EthiopiaPrevails while the opposition organize online support using hashtags including #IStandWithTigray and #Tigray Genocide. Many of these campaigns directly target coordinated campaigns of disinformation at English-speaking netizens outside Ethiopia including global agencies and decision-makers. The chapter makes an important contribution in showing how disinformation is used to polarize and divide the population along ethnic lines to support military and political interests. It also shows how disinformation shrinks civic space, impeding open discourse, deliberation and democratic process. The chapter suggests three potential remedies to address disinformation: fact checking, content moderation by social media platforms and criminal sanction by governments.

Whereas the chapters on Mozambique and Ethiopia focus on recent episodes of military conflict, Rutendo Chabikwa's chapter focuses on a historical episode of conflict but which continues to have strong political resonance in contemporary Zimbabwean politics. Chabikwa analyses the coordinated disinformation campaign on Twitter around Gukurahundi: the state-orchestrated massacre of thousands of citizens in the Matabeleland and Midlands provinces between 1983 and 1987. The chapter examines how an issue shrouded in silence by mainstream media and political parties has been raised online by voices seeking to hold the government to account. The chapter illustrates how disinformation strategies are used to reproduce and reinforce the dominant narrative that absolves the ruling party of culpability and blocks accountability. Five major accounts were tracked for more than one year using data scraped from Twitter. The posts from these accounts were then analysed for the work that they do in supporting hegemonic discourse. The analysis reveals how disinformation is used to disrupt accountability claims through three main methods: by disputing historical accounts (historical interjection), by disputing the number of deaths or definition of genocide (semantic rationalization), or by claiming expert support to validate the disinformation posted (miscontructed textual authority). The chapter shows how disinformation actors draw upon history and use the state apparatus to deploy their disinformation practices, manipulate beliefs and defend vested power interests.

The last set of chapters shifts the focus away from military conflict to electoral contests. Nevertheless, like armed conflicts, elections are fundamentally contests over power. As such, the disinformation and power nexus continues to be the leitmotif in this cluster. These chapters indicate that there is a growing role of digital disinformation in elections across the continent: a phenomenon that both scholars and policymakers need to give urgent attention to. Seyoung Jeon, in her chapter, analyses the role of Russian-linked disinformation around elections in the Democratic Republic of Congo, Zimbabwe and South Africa. There has been a lot of analysis of the active role played by Russian-linked actors in coordinated disinformation campaigns during Brexit and the election of Trump, but this chapter is one of the first to analyse claims about Russian disinformation across Africa. The chapter draws on datasets produced by Twitter's Election Integrity Programme of accounts engaged in coordinated inauthentic behaviour online. The chapter analyses these datasets to document the scale and scope of Russian disinformation operations across the three countries. The Russian accounts studied were active around the elections, but in Zimbabwe the number of accounts and tweets were very low and analysis shows them to be responsive to emerging events rather than churning out pre-programmed messaging. In South Africa the volumes were also low and pale in significance when compared to the influence operation mounted by the UK's Bell Pottinger 'Gupta Bots'. In the DRC there were far fewer tweets. Overall, the evidence is that despite claims to the contrary, there was no large or influential Russian disinformation operations in election in any of the three countries.

In her chapter Simone Toussi examines the use of disinformation during Cameroon's 2018 election. She asks what drove the use of election disinformation, what forms it took and what interests were at stake for the electoral process and beyond. Her chapter examines the processes and strategies of disinformation deployed in the electoral period, focusing on the drivers and dynamics of disinformation and their impact on the democratic process. President Biya has held office for over thirty years since 1982 during which time he has often been accused of manipulating citizens' beliefs and behaviour by using foreign companies to deploy disinformation campaigns. The 2018 presidential election period marked a turning point in Cameroon's electoral politics, with more debate and more participation but also more disinformation on digital platforms. The government's disinformation amplified ethnic divisions between francophone and anglophone citizens, manipulating existing tensions to serve the political interests of the ruling party.

Juliet Nanfuka situates the 2021 election disinformation in Uganda in the context of decades of pre-digital disinformation before then analysing digital disinformation since the turn of the millennium. During the 2021 election campaign the Ugandan government petitioned Google to take down the popular YouTube channel of opposition candidate Bobi Wine, without success. Facebook and Twitter did, however, suspend the accounts of a number of government and ruling party officials for orchestrating what it described as a campaign of 'coordinated inauthentic behaviour' designed to manipulate public beliefs and behaviour ahead of election day. This state-coordinated 'lie machine' included the employment of foreign political consultancies, 'keyboard armies' and paid influencers with large social media followings in a coordinated campaign of inauthentic online behaviour. The chapter reveals a sophisticated government machine able to produce and disseminate disinformation designed to manipulate voters' beliefs and behaviours in ways that serve the power interests of the incumbent government.

Edmilson Angelo's chapter on Angola examines the use of political disinformation by the authoritarian political party that has held power in Luanda for more than 40 years. Angelo examines how the state produces and disseminates disinformation to defend its hold on power and its control over the country's lucrative oil and diamond fields. The chapter explores the emergence of an unruly youth voice which is operating outside of establishment parties and media and looks at state disinformation tactics to contain it. The author conducts a digital ethnography of key influencers in Angolan political space around the August 2022 elections. The chapter asks how and why the regime in Angola fabricates and distributes disinformation and examines the (dis)continuities between analogue and digital disinformation. Angelo concludes that young people are not politically disengaged in Angola; rather they are not engaging through legacy media and political parties that fail to represent their interests. Instead, they are politically engaged on social media, communicating contempt for the regime through creative memes and predicted (correctly as it turned out) that they are very likely to vote for opposition candidates in the election, threatening the regime's hold on power in the capital city.

Wambui Wamunyu focuses her chapter on disinformation in Kenya 2022 elections. The country had already experienced three Presidential elections marked by disinformation campaigns in 2013, 2017 and 2022. Cambridge Analytica was one of the foreign political consulting firms employed in Kenya's 2013 campaigns and the campaign served as a testbed for the Brexit and Trump campaigns in 2016. Their tactics reportedly included the use of sponsored posts, attack advertisements aimed at competitors, as well as disinformation on Facebook. It remains the case that domestic and foreign actors use social media and user data to manipulate electoral contests in Kenya and around the world. However, through her research on the 2022 elections, Wamunyu shows that there have been key shifts in the nature of disinformation during elections. The first shift is the growing use of local actors such as social media influencers in disinformation campaigns and the diminishing reliance on foreign disinformation agencies. The second is that the increasing commercialization of disinformation as a service favours those with deep pockets or power over media channels and content creation.

Conclusion

This volume is unique in providing a rich set of diverse case studies analysing the deployment of digital disinformation across ten African countries. By analysing the dimensions and dynamics of specific episodes of disinformation it has been possible to shed light on the drivers of disinformation, a range of actors deploying disinformation, their tactics and techniques, and the gendered, political, economic and military interests that they serve. Analysis across the case studies surfaces important trends and future directions for digital disinformation in Africa including its increasing volume, sophistication and domestication. Although this book is the most extensive collection of case studies of digital disinformation in Africa to date, in truth we have only begun to scrape the surface. It is hoped that this volume provides a platform for research in other countries and other types of disinformation.

The case studies in this collection demonstrate both continuities and discontinuities with disinformation practices in Africa prior to digitalization. The concept of affordances has proven to be a useful way to identify and unpack these qualitative changes. Some things have not changed: disinformation continues to be deployed to manipulate the beliefs and behaviours of citizens in order to serve the interests of powerholders. However, the distinctive affordances of new digital technologies are making possible the micro-targeting and tailoring of messages. Social media affords the ability to message target populations, across any distance, instantly, repeatedly and at low marginal costs. These affordances far exceed what was imaginable just a few decades ago. The continued increase in mobile and internet coverage and uptake across Africa combined with the continuing development of new technologies ensures that disinformation will continue to proliferate.

This collection of case studies powerfully illustrates both similarities and dissimilarities of digital disinformation across Africa when contrasted with studies of disinformation campaigns in the global North. In this respect breaking down disinformation analysis into the four elements of dimensions, dynamics, drivers and directions is helpful analytically. In terms of dimensions of disinformation, we note that the still-low levels of social media use in countries like Mozambique, and lower levels of social media use by some gender, income and rural communities means that the reach and therefore the impact of digital disinformation does not have the same dimensions across all African geographies and demographics. We also note that disinformation actors in African are distinct from those in the most-studied nations in North America and Europe. In Zimbabwe the instigators of disinformation are tightly knit group of dedicated military units and party cadre supported by state-controlled media. This contrasts with state disinformation in Europe and North America, which is often a bought-in service provided by specialist political marketing consultancies.

There is continuity in the drivers of digital disinformation at the highest level of abstraction in that powerholders deploy disinformation to manipulate the beliefs and behaviours of citizens to further the vested power interests. However, in several of the African case studies the incumbent powerholder is a president who has been in power for several decades. In such cases the interests that are served by disinformation are much narrower than, for example, the Brexit campaign in the UK which had to balance the interests of a complex and multi-layered set of interest groups across geographic and class allegiances.

Colonial legacies are another distinctive feature of digital disinformation in Africa. Disinformation was introduced to Africa by colonial powers; it was retained as a tool of power by post-independence administrations; and the current administrations are busy upgrading to a more potent digital form of disinformation operation. The dimensions, dynamics, drivers and directions of digital disinformation in Africa are not a carbon copy of those found in the global North and the differences between countries within Africa are at least as significant. As a result of these discontinuities, we assert that empirical investigation by researchers familiar with local languages, culture, history and politics is essential to any comprehensive analysis of digital disinformation in Africa. It is a mistake to imagine that understandings of disinformation from the United States and Europe can unproblematically be cut and pasted onto other sociocultural and political realities. To avoid this epistemic violence, it is essential to locate studies within the distinct historical context of each country, with roots in colonial relations. In their analysis of disinformation African scholars writing about their own countries are able to draw upon experiential knowledge of the specific cultural and political context of disinformation operations.

This volume is only a first step. Further research is necessary in other African countries, on other topics, and from other perspectives not considered in this book. This volume has focused primarily on digital disinformation directed at political actors, but more research is needed on digital disinformation directed at distorting narratives and policy debates, including those around sexuality and gender, vaccinations, immigration, climate and environment. We have made only modest inroads into considering what is to be done about disinformation. Further research needs to consider at greater length, who needs to do what in order to mitigate or overcome the intentional deployment of lies to manipulate the beliefs and behaviours of citizens in Africa to serve other people's interests. Future empirical studies of disinformation in Africa's fifty-five nations are certain to expose a wide variety of dimensions, dynamics, drivers and direction of digital disinformation.

Bibliography

Baltiwala, S. (2019) *All About Power: Understanding Social Power and Power Structures,* CREA. https://reconference.creaworld.org/wp-content/uploads/2019/05/All-About -Power-Srilatha-Batliwala.pdf.

Benkler, Y., Faris, R. and Roberts, H. (2018) *Network Propaganda: Manipulation, Disinformation, and Radicalization in American Politics.* Oxford: Oxford University Press.

Briant, E. (2020) *Propaganda Machine: Inside Cambridge Analytica and the Digital Influence Industry.* London: Bloomsbury.

CIA (1949) *Special Text No.8 Strategical Psychological Warfare: Operations Manual.* The Ground General School. https://www.cia.gov/readingroom/docs/CIA-RDP78 -03362A000400050001-9.pdf.

De Liedekerke, A. and Zinkanell, M. (2020) *Deceive and Disrupt: Disinformation as an Emerging Cybersecurity Challenge.* Tivoligasse 73a, 1120 Vienna, Austria.

Director of National Intelligence (2022) *U.S. Intelligence Community Budget.* https://www .dni.gov/index.php/what-we-do/ic-budget.

Earle, R. (1997) 'Information and Disinformation in Late Colonial New Granada'. *The Americas,* 54 (2): 167–84, Cambridge: Cambridge University Press.

Freelon, D. and Wells, C. (2020) 'Disinformation as Political Communication'. *Political Communication*, 37 (2): 145–56. doi:10.1080/10584609.2020.1723755. https://www.tandfonline.com/doi/abs/10.1080/10584609.2020.1723755?journalCode=upcp20.

Gaventa, J. (2006) 'Finding the Spaces for Change: A Power Analysis'. *IDS Bulletin*, 37 (6): 23–33.

Gibson, J. (1977) 'The Theory of Affordances'. In R. Shaw and J. Bransford (eds), *Perceiving, Acting, and Knowing*. London: Oxford University Press.

Hayward, C. (1988) 'De-facing Power', *Polity*, 31 (1): 1–22.

Howard, P. (2020) *Lies Machines: How to Save Democracies from Troll Armies, Deceitful Robots, Junk News Operations and Political Operatives*. Yale University Press.

Hutchby, I. (2001) 'Technologies, Texts and Affordances'. *Sociology*, 35 (2): 441–56.

Jemison, M. (2022) 'How Cambridge Analytica Influenced Nigerias Elections'. 20 May. https://www.gatescambridge.org/our-scholars/blog/how-cambridge-analytica-influenced-nigerias-elections/.

Jones, K. (2019) *Online Disinformation and Political Discourse: Applying a Human Rights Framework*. London: Chatham House. https://www.chathamhouse.org/sites/default/files/2019-11-05-Online-Disinformation-Human-Rights.pdf.

Kaminska, I. (2017) 'A Module in Fake News from the Info-wars of Ancient Rome'. *Financial Times*. https://www.ft.com/content/aaf2bb08-dca2-11e6-86ac-f253db7791c6.

Kent, K. S. (2013) 'Propaganda, Public Opinion, and the Second South African Boer War'. *Inquiries Journal/Student Pulse*, 5 (10). http://www.inquiriesjournal.com/articles/781/propaganda-public-opinion-and-the-second-south-african-boer-war (accessed 28 March 2018).

Kuo, R. and Marwick, A. (2021) 'Critical Disinformation Studies: History, Power, and Politics'. *Harvard Kennedy School (HKS) Misinformation Review*. https://doi.org/10.37016/mr-2020-76.

Larry, Madowo. 'How Cambridge Analytica Poisoned Kenya's Democracy'. https://www.washingtonpost.com/news/global-opinions/wp/2018/03/20/how-cambridge-analytica-poisoned-kenyas-democracy/.

Lukes, S. (1974) *Power: A Radical View*. London: Macmillan.

Manqoyi, A. (2018) 'Researching Cannibalising Obligations in Post-apartheid South Africa'. In F. Nyamnjoh (eds), *Eating & Being Eaten*. Bamenda: Langaa Research & Publishing.

McGee, R. (2020) 'Rethinking Accountability: A Power Perspective'. In R. McGee and J. Pettit, (eds), *Power, Empowerment and Social Change*. London: Routledge.

Meta (2020) 'Removing Coordinated Inauthentic Behavior from France and Russia'. https://about.fb.com/news/2020/12/removing-coordinated-inauthentic-behavior-france-russia/.

Mutahi, P. and Kimari, B. (2017) 'The Impact of Social Media and Digital Technology on Electoral Violence in Kenya'. IDS Working Paper 493, Brighton: IDS.

Nixon, R. (2016) *Selling Apartheid: South Africa's Global Propaganda War*. London: Pluto Press.

Norman, D. (1988) *The Design of Everyday Things*. New York: Basic Books.

Nuria Portero Alferez. 'Disinformation as a Destabilising Factor in Libya'. Opinion Paper IEEE 63/2019. enlace web IEEE y/o enlace bie3 (consultado día/mes/año) https://www.ieee.es/Galerias/fichero/docs_opinion/2019/DIEEEO63_2019NURPOR_desinformaLibia_ENG.pdf.

Nyabola, N. (2018) *Digital Democracy, Analogue Politics*. London: Zed.

Ong, J. and Cabanes, J. (2018) 'Architects of Networked Information: Behind the Scenes of Troll Accounts and Fake News in the Philippines'. *Architects of Networked*

Disinformation: Behind the Scenes of Troll Accounts and Fake News Production in the Philippines, 74. https://doi.org/10.7275/2cq4-5396.

Osbourne, M. (2015) 'The Rooting Out of Mau Mau from the Minds of the Kikuyu is a Formindable Task: Propaganda and the Mau Mau war'. *Journal of African History,* 56 (1): 77–97.

Posetti, J. and Matthews, A. (2018) *A Short Guide to the History of 'Fake News' and Disinformation.* https://www.icfj.org/sites/default/files/2018–07/A%20Short%20Guide%20to%20History%20of%20Fake%20News%20and%20Disinformation_ICFJ%20Final.pdf.

Pottier, J. (2002) *Reimagining Rwanda: Conflict Survival and Disinformation.* Cambridge University Press.

Rid, T. (2020) *Active Measures: The Secret History of Disinformation and Political Warfare.* London: Macmillan.

Roberts, T. and Bosch, T. (2023) *Digital Citizenship in Africa: Technologies of Agency and Repression.* London: Zed Books.

Roberts, T. and Mohamed Ali, A. (2021) 'Opening and Closing Online Civic Space in Africa: An Introduction to the Ten Digital Rights Landscape Reports'. In T. Roberts (ed.), *Digital Rights in Closing Civic Space: Lessons from Ten African Countries.* Brighton: Institute of Development Studies. https://opendocs.ids.ac.uk/opendocs/handle/20.500.12413/15964.

Roberts, T., Mohamed Ali, A., Farahat, M., Oloyede, R. and Mutung'u, G. (2021) *Surveillance Law in Africa: A Review of Six Countries.* Brighton: Institute of Development Studies. https://opendocs.ids.ac.uk/opendocs/handle/20.500.12413/16893.

Silverman, C. (2021) 'Why Do A Bunch Of Nigerian Twitter Influencers Want This Alleged Money Launderer To Go Free? They're Being Paid'. *Buzzfeed.* https://www.buzzfeednews.com/article/craigsilverman/nigerian-twitter-campaign-alex-saab.

Toyama, K. (2011) *Technology as an Amplifier in International Development.* Seattle, WA: ACM iConference. https://www.kentarotoyama.org/papers/Toyama%202011%20iConference%20-%20Technology%20as%20Amplifier.pdf.

Tufekci, Z. (2014) 'Big Questions for Social Media Big Data: Representativeness, Validity and Other Methodological Pitfalls'. *Proceedings of the Eighth International AAAI Conference on Weblogs and Social Media.* https://www.aaai.org/ocs/index.php/ICWSM/ICWSM14/paper/view/8062/8151.

Tworek, H. (2020) 'Policy Lessons from Five Historical Patterns in Information Manipulation'. In W. Lance Bennet and S. Livingston (eds), *The Disinformation Age: Politics, Technology and Disruptive Communication in the United States.* Cambridge: Cambridge University Press.

United Nations Human Rights Council (2022) *Role of States in Countering the Negative Impact of Disinformation on the Enjoyment and Realization of Human Rights, A/HRC/49/L.31/Rev.1.* https://documents-dds-ny.un.org/doc/UNDOC/GEN/G22/304/10/PDF/G2230410.pdf?OpenElement.

VeneKlasen, L. and Miller, V. (2002) *A New Weave of Power, People and Politics.* Oaklahoma: World Neighbours.

Wardle, C. and Derakhshan, H. (2017) *Information Disorder: Toward an Interdisciplinary Framework for Research and Policy Making.* https://rm.coe.int/information-disorder-toward-an-interdisciplinary-framework-for-researc/168076277c.

Wasserman, H. and Madrid-Morales, D. (2022) *Disinformation in the Global South.* New Jersey: Wiley Blackwell.

Chapter 2

Digital gendered disinformation and women's civic participation in Africa

Nkem Agunwa

Introduction

Gendered disinformation is an extension of violence against women (Di Meco and Wilfore 2021). It is gradually rolling back the gains of women's rights in Africa and shrinking spaces for women's online and offline participation. Gendered disinformation directly threatens the fight for gender inclusivity and women's ability to engage in democratic processes. It is a tactic to silence critics and exclude women from online civic discourse altogether. According to a study by the Inter-Parliamentary Union (2016) of female lawmakers globally, 41.8 per cent of participants said they have seen degrading or sexual images of themselves circulate on social media.

The weaponization of disinformation against women, mainly online, affects their leadership and political participation opportunities. This chapter defines 'weaponization' as the intentional use of specific narratives, information or tactics to manipulate public opinion to discredit or marginalize certain groups or individuals. It's a strategic deployment of ideas or practices that aims to cause harm or damage to the targeted group, often to gain a political or social advantage. For instance, when weaponizing disinformation, false or misleading information is intentionally spread to sow confusion, create division or discredit a particular individual or group. The chapter will also examine the weaponization of marriage and motherhood, where gendered roles and expectations are used to limit women's participation in public life, reinforcing stereotypes and reducing their agency. Additionally, we'll delve into the weaponization of online spaces and social media platforms, which are manipulated to spread disinformation, harass or intimidate individuals and create an atmosphere of fear and distrust. This chapter aims to clarify and understand the insidious ways gendered disinformation undermines women's agency and civic engagement in Africa with a particular focus on Nigeria and Kenya.

A five-year study by the International Foundation for Electoral Systems (2018) revealed that over 60 per cent of the violent and abusive content targeted at political players in Zimbabwe targets women legislators, who make up barely a third of the country's parliament. In addition, the pervasive low protection of women against sexual and gender-based violence in Africa further heightens the risk that gendered disinformation can cause offline harm. Despite the overwhelming global interest in disinformation, the gendered aspect of this phenomenon receives very little attention (Di Meco 2020). Like every other existential issue, neglecting the gendered dimension makes it incredibly challenging to understand crucial elements necessary to proffer holistic and practical solutions. One significant threat that disinformation poses is its ability to undermine democratic practices (Jankowicz 2017). Gendered disinformation amplified by technology weakens women's voices and erodes women's equal and active participation in civic debates. It undermines the representativeness of democratic institutions and poses a security threat since online attacks can inspire offline violence (Sessa 2022).

This chapter aims to answer three research questions that focus on the impact of gendered disinformation on women's civic participation in Africa. The first question explores the various narratives weaponized to impede women's ability to engage in democratic processes in the continent. The second question delves into the tactics perpetuating gendered disinformation in Africa. Lastly, the third question interrogates how gendered disinformation affects women's civic participation in Africa. By answering these questions, this chapter seeks to shed light on the challenges women face in participating fully in democratic processes in Africa and to provoke further research in this regard.

The chapter aims to gain insights into gendered disinformation by analysing existing research and social media content on Twitter. Although the chapter centres on Africa, the research focuses specifically on Nigeria and Kenya. Using both methods provides a comprehensive understanding of the topic from multiple perspectives.

In terms of contribution to knowledge, while previous works have dealt with gendered disinformation primarily in the global North, there needs to be a deeper analysis of gendered disinformation in Africa, especially as it relates to women's civic participation. This chapter aims to examine the intersection between gendered disinformation and women's civic participation in Africa.

Political participation of women in Africa

The percentage of women in politics in Africa has steadily increased over time. In the last three decades, Africa has had ten substantive and acting female presidents (Watkins 2021). Another significant development is the rise of women parliamentarians across the continent. According to Karma (2022), Rwanda has the highest number of women parliamentarians, with 61 per cent. South Africa, Namibia, Senegal, Mozambique and Ethiopia have more than 40 per cent women representation in parliament. In addition, 65 per cent of the countries in Africa rank above 20 per cent of women's representation in parliament. This is significant for a continent where many still perceive leadership as a masculine attribute. However, cultural barriers, patriarchal structures, sexism and economic inequality continue to hamper women's political participation. A study by Afrobarometer (2021) found that while countries like Rwanda and South Africa have significant women representation, some of the worst performing nations are also on the continent – 8.2 per cent in The Gambia, 7.4 per cent in Benin and 3.6 per cent in Nigeria.

Defining gendered disinformation

Gendered disinformation is an aspect of the broad umbrella of disinformation. Disinformation is the deliberate creation, distribution and amplification of false, inaccurate or misleading information to deceive (Witness 2022). Disinformation is not new, nor are misogyny, sexism and gender stereotypes. What is new, however, is the ease with which digital technology facilitates the coordination, financing and amplification of disinformation, including gendered disinformation (Sessa 2022). Gendered disinformation is the intentional spread of misleading or inaccurate information that draw on misogyny and gender stereotypes (Di Meco 2019). Judson (2021) further states that the end goal of gendered disinformation is to achieve political, economic or social purposes, which often include the use of fake and doctored sexual images, coordinated abuse and caricatures. Gendered disinformation typically frames women as untrustworthy and unintelligent. Alternatively, it pits women against one another or hyper-sexualizes girls and women. For example, a physically attractive woman, regardless of how highly educated she might be, stands the risk of falling under the 'Bimbo' category.

Furthermore, gendered disinformation attempts to portray possessing human emotions, aspirations, priorities and competencies as undesirable attributes for women. This is gendered because the same standards do not apply to men. Although gendered disinformation can target anyone based on their gender, women and gender-diverse people are disproportionately impacted (Di Meco 2019). Women and gender-diverse people who advocate for human rights are often targets of gendered disinformation. It is also used to target voters, activists, government office-holders, political leaders and female public figures (Di Meco 2019). According to a report by Amnesty International (2018), women are specifically targeted when they express strong opinions about race, politics, gender or rape. Judson (2019) ties gendered disinformation directly with identity-based disinformation often used as justification for human rights abuses and entrenches repression of women and minority groups. They further argue that gendered disinformation undermines its targets' digital and political rights as well as their safety and security.

Judson (2019) further describes gender disinformation as a parasite that preys on existing stereotypes. It perpetuates harmful stereotypes about gender identity and is used as an effective tactic to preserve and sustain them and to silence critics and consolidate power. At its core, a gender stereotype is a belief and the holder of that view may draw assumptions about women and/or men who belong to the target group (UNHR 2014). Stereotypes may be harmful, whether they are hostile/

negative or appear to be benign. For instance, the perception that women are more nurturing is the reason why they often shoulder the whole burden of raising children (UNHR 2014). Gendered disinformation draws on traditional stereotypes of women as (a) victims in need of protection, (b) lacking the competency to make informed decisions or lead and (c) only fit to be wives and mothers. Women who do not fit this mould are considered aggressive and not woman enough.

According to Nina Jankowicz (2017), gendered disinformation combines deeply rooted sexist beliefs with the anonymity and accessibility of social media to tarnish women's reputations and drive them away from public life. The framing of women as weak, unintelligent, incompetent and hypersexual are harmful stereotypes that keep women in their place and maintain male dominance. Research by the National Democratic Institute (2021) demonstrates that gendered disinformation has a chilling effect on targeted women as the fear of rebuke forces them to self-censor and, in some cases, completely withdraw from public debate. Gendered disinformation creates a reverberating effect on other women who see what can happen to them if they dare to challenge the status quo. What makes gendered disinformation so effective and, at the same time, elusive is that it plays on socially accepted norms and values, making it difficult to challenge. As a consequence, default methods for countering disinformation, such as fact-checking and verification, prove ineffective in confronting gendered disinformation.

Digital gendered disinformation

Technology has introduced new and more effective tactics to disseminate gendered disinformation, which, in turn, increases the vulnerability of women and gender-diverse people online. The digital era has opened up new spaces for women to express themselves and defend the issues they believe in without having to go through the traditional gatekeepers who often do not prioritize women's issues. However, the weaponization of these digital spaces stifles women's expression. While gendered disinformation is not new, digital technology allows for collective and coordinated anonymous targeting of people with disinformation. The increase in the proliferation and dissemination of disinformation is due to the affordances of digital technologies. Technical affordances are the features of a technology that invite, allow or enable a user to act in a particular way (Roberts 2017). Social media affords users new action possibilities: to create and send text, images and video messages to any number of recipients worldwide instantly. The participatory nature of social media directly contrasts traditional media because it facilitates simultaneous and direct feedback, which propels the speed, scale and anonymity of gendered disinformation.

Furthermore, Jankowicz et al. (2021) identify three defining characteristics of online disinformation: falsity, malign intent and coordination. From this perspective, online gendered disinformation is not undertaken by lone actors seeking to preserve patriarchal structures. Gendered disinformation often takes the form of coordinated efforts that strategically target people who are vocal about issues that threaten the status quo of patriarchal power. Although the tactics of gendered disinformation are often similar across geographical divides – global south and global north – they may have varying outcomes depending on the socio-political setting.

Dominant gendered disinformation narratives in Africa

Weaponization of marriage and motherhood

It is common practice to weaponize marriage and motherhood as gendered disinformation, especially against female public and elected officials (Eggert 2017). For women who are active in public life, marriage is considered a requirement to be worthy of respect and being unmarried or divorced equates to incompetence. Martha Karua, the Kenyan vice-presidential candidate of the major opposition party, Azimio La Umoja, was the target of virulent online attacks based on being a single woman (Wamangu 2022). Despite an impressive two-decade career in politics as a serving lawmaker and cabinet minister, and her work as a magistrate, her suitability to hold the position of Deputy President of Kenya was judged on her ability to be a wife. Even though the marital status of political candidates bears no relevance to their capacity as administrators and serves no public interest, they can influence voter decisions. The digital disinformation targeted at Martha Karua perpetrated the intentional deception that marital status is relevant to political competence and that acting politically is unwomanly, un-African, or immodest.

Martha Karua is far from being the only female politician in Africa against whom such online disinformation has been deployed. Deputy gubernatorial candidates in Nigeria, Funke Akindele (Bassey 2022) and Tonto Dike (Olukomaiya 2022), are repeatedly scrutinized based on being divorced women. By contrast their male counterparts, who are divorced, are not subjected to similar scrutiny. The false claim that divorced women are inept administrators preys on harmful stereotypes that squarely put the onus of responsibility for a marriage's demise on the woman's shoulders. These narratives place an extra burden on female candidates to defend their abilities, a burden their male counterparts do not often have to bear. This distracts from the relevant political issues and does not give room for women politicians and public figures to separate their personal life from their public life.

In a similar tactic, untruths are deployed online against women politicians who are without children or have fewer children. They are portrayed as selfish and unwilling to fulfil their innate obligations of being mothers. This perspective perpetuates the gendered stereotypes that women are primary caregivers and uses digital technology to hound women politicians and force them to address private matters about childbirth. Conversely, women with children are also targeted with false accusations that they are not the biological mothers of their children. Former Nigerian First Lady Patience Jonathan was falsely accused of not being the biological mother of her children with President Goodluck Jonathan (NaijaGist 2012). The attacks would seem a response to silence an active first lady who contributed to political debates in the country, challenging traditional stereotypes that dictate 'a woman should be seen and not heard'. On the other hand, the argument that women's status in any way diminishes their right or ability to participate in political life is an intentional lie designed to close civic space for women in political life. The weaponization of motherhood is a lose-lose situation for female public officeholders, as Eggert (2017) described. These narratives push women out of public life by asserting that a woman without a child may not truly understand the concerns of families and one with a child is too occupied with effectively discharging leadership duties.

Weaponization of gay narratives

Gendered disinformation can intersect with identity-based disinformation as part of a broader strategy to silence critics and consolidate power. In many African countries, same-sex relations are considered by large sections of the population to be taboo and offensive to local cultural values and moral codes. Mob action against same-sex relations is prevalent and sanctioned by some states (Human Rights Watch 2017). As of 2020, thirty-two African nations have made same-sex relationships illegal. In four African countries, the death sentence was imposed as a penalty for same-sex relations (Kamer 2020). This makes any form of gendered disinformation that alleges that a person is gay highly dangerous.

Accusations of being gay or a gender-diverse person are often used to stigmatize vocal people, silence their voices and expose them to offline violence. Winnie Odinga, one of the daughters of Kenyan Presidential candidate, Raila Odinga, faced repeated online accusations of being gay (Celebrity 2022). She is a single woman who has on several occasions asserted herself as heterosexual; however, the gay narratives are constantly pushed forward (Celebrity 2022) and have been viewed as credible because she is an unmarried woman. Being outspoken is still considered a masculine trait that a woman can only appropriate when sanctioned by her husband; therefore, a single vocal woman is considered to lack legitimacy to speak. Importantly, the allegations about her sexuality were amplified online by her father's political opponents, as a way to silence and delegitimize her and, by extension, neutralize her support for her father. This form of gendered disinformation is equally used against heterosexual male politicians with the intention of harming their reputations. For example, in an attempt to politically damage his candidacy, the 2022 Nigerian opposition presidential aspirant Atiku Abubakar faced constant accusations of being gay. Despite the lack of evidence to support this claim, it continues to resurface during every election that Atiku vies for office (Lime 2018). This is relevant because in Nigeria, there is an anti-gay legislation that is punishable by up to 14 days in prison (Lime 2018).

Sexualized distortion

Sexualized distortion has increasingly become a widespread narrative that strips women of their dignity and bodily autonomy. This narrative is perpetuated through distorted videos, screenshots purporting to be from sex tapes and accusations of illicit affairs. This approach thrives on elevating sociocultural norms about women's sexuality and sexual purity. Sexualized content appeals to norms and ideals about how women 'should' behave.

#Room350 was a trending hashtag on Twitter during the 2022 Kenya general elections (Wanz 2022). Room 350 is an alleged room in Western Hotel Nairobi where Deputy President William Ruto allegedly engages in sexual relations with female politicians (Derreck 2022). Top female politicians were accused of sexual involvement with William Ruto to gain political favours (Jill 2022). These claims projected women as incapable of holding public positions without male support. It also delegitimizes the support of women for male candidates they believe in. Furthermore, they force women to publicly address accusations of sexual impropriety, which are inherently challenging to fact-check. For example, Anne Waiguru, the second governor of Kirinyaga County, who took office in 2017, was compelled to respond to a doctored viral photo that depicts her in a sexually intimate setting with William Ruto (Wang'ondu 2022).

Decontextualized narratives

Images can also be stripped of their context in order to distort the truth and achieve political objectives. A photo of Juliana Cherera, the vice chair of Kenya's Independent Electoral and Boundaries Commission, being fed a slice of cake by the Governor of Mombasa surfaced online. The reported photo first appeared online in 2018 and was taken during Julia Cherera's birthday party when she was serving as Governor Joho's chief of staff. The same image resurfaces in 2022 with its context removed and with a new interpretation. The picture was decontextualized and used to falsely allege an intimate relationship between the Commissioner and the Governor. This allegation called into question her independence as a commissioner and was designed to undermine her stand against the outcome of the 2022 presidential election (Gichuhi 2022). Gendered disinformation is deployed strategically to weaken the position of women in authority when they present a challenge to the establishment. Juliana Cherera, in a public statement, pushed back against the photo taken out of context and urged Kenyans to stop sharing the image online (Petra 2022). Despite this, many more users engaged with the decontextualized image online, including on WhatsApp and Telegram (Petra 2022). This is a clear example of the deployment of disinformation for political ends.

Another example is that of Esther Passaris, the Nairobi County representative in the National Assembly of Kenya. Text and audio with alleged sexual connotations were released by the Nairobi County governor, Mbuvi Gideon Kioko, to bring shame and delegitimize her voice (Nyawira 2019). The release of the files came after she publicly criticized the policies of the Nairobi County governor in a heated television debate (Nyawira 2019). Although Passaris pushed back, by claiming the alleged audio and text were mis-contextualized, the digital disinformation fueled online and offline abuse – as it often does – towards a woman who was seen as a threat by a male politician. As this case shows, gendered disinformation goes beyond perpetuating harmful narratives; it is a tactic used to discredit and ultimately silence women's voices. This tactic reinforces the myth that women influence men through their sexuality and do not have legitimate agency to take a political stance.

Tactics for perpetuating digital gendered disinformation

Some common tactics that are used to perpetuate digital gendered disinformation intersect with online gender-based violence. The never-ending virulence of online gender-based violence increases women's susceptibility to gendered disinformation and vice versa. This vicious cycle contributes to the escalating violence against women.

Dogpiling as a tool of gendered disinformation on social media platforms

This involves accumulating and amplifying internet activity from multiple accounts directed towards a particular person or subject (Amnesty International 2018). The technical affordances of social media networks like Twitter make this online mob targeting possible. Though incredibly effective for campaigning, Twitter's quote retweet and hashtag feature and Facebook's share button provide the technical weapons to target individuals and drive gendered disinformation. For example, the feminist coalition, a group of young women activists in Nigeria, came under intense attacks through false allegations made online about their management of the funds raised to finance #EndSARS movement (Kabir 2021). #EndSARS was a movement of young people in Nigeria demanding an end to police brutality. On Twitter, the group became the target of intense accusations of financial misconduct under the hashtag #FemcoGate. Despite the group releasing a financial statement, the false claims persisted (Kabir 2021). These allegations of financial wrongdoing were an attempt to silence them and tarnish their reputation. Even within a social justice movement, women's leadership is considered against the norm. The tools on these social media platforms help to curate and amplify those false accusations.

The impact of shallow fakes on gendered disinformation

This is the use of non-complex technology to alter a piece of content to distort its meaning (Gregory 2022). This form of media manipulation has been used to target women and scare them into silence and is especially prevalent in Africa (Johnson 2019). For example, a sexually suggestive image of Esther Passaris and governor Mbuvi Gideon Kioko appeared online in 2019, right after her vehement criticism of the Governor's policies on a television programme in Kenya. Even though the image was proven to have been manipulated, it was extensively disseminated to delegitimize her stance against the Governor. The pattern that has become evident is that women often face these attacks when they criticize oppressive powers. Their risk exposure minimizes if they remain quiet or do not participate in political debates.

To identify the perpetrators, Ms. Passaris announced on Twitter that she would provide a cash prize of $10,000 to anyone who could identify the people responsible for the photoshopped image. Despite being in violation of Twitter's community standards, this fabricated picture continued to circulate on the platform forcing Ms. Passaris, the target, to bear the burden of finding the perpetrators. In this case not only was Ms. Passaris the victim of gendered disinformation, she also had to bear the burden of policing it online. The responsibility for ensuring a safe space for all users, particularly the most vulnerable should arguably fall on social media platforms.

Deepfakes and their effect on women's political participation

This emerging form of audio-visual manipulation allows people to create realistic simulations of someone's face, voice and actions (Adger and Glick 2021). The technology needed to make non-consensual sexual deepfakes is now more easily accessible and does not require any specific technical knowledge, as the technology does the heavy lifting for them. In most cases it only requires a simple digital device, as some of the applications used to make deepfakes are now available on mobile app stores. This represents a potentially dangerous trend given how easily 'deepnudes' can be distributed online. These 'deepnudes' are particularly difficult to take down, especially when they are shared on encrypted messaging platforms like WhatsApp.

Although the use of deepfakes against women is not widely prevalent in African countries, it has been used in other parts of the world to humiliate and silence women who speak up against injustice. Furthermore, the accessibility of the technology through open AI tools allows for unparalleled volume, variance and personalization. This can cause psychological harm and discourage women from participating in politics, leading to a significant gender gap in political representation. For example, the journalist Rana Ayyub was a victim of a deepfake porn plot that devastated her. This virulent attack came soon after she campaigned for justice for an eight-year-old girl in India who was raped over days and then murdered (India Today 2018). What is most troubling about deepfakes is that they do not need to be convincing to cause harm. All that's required is for the subject to be recognizable, mainly in unfavourable circumstances such as sexually explicit videos.

The tactics described earlier can be employed to perpetuate online gendered disinformation and serve the purpose of silencing women's political voices. This has potentially severe outcomes that include shrinking civic space for women and ultimately discouraging women's online civic participation. These tactics are made possible by the incentivization of scandalous materials by social media platforms, the underinvestment in adopting and enforcing platform community standards, especially outside of the global North and a lack of technologies that enable in-app verification. Effective self-regulation by technology platforms would mitigate the irresponsible deployment of technology that exposes vulnerable groups to attacks. In addition, an investment in authenticity and provenance infrastructures that make it easier for users to track the source and edit of any media would provide a standardized mechanism for addressing disinformation in general.

Effects of gendered disinformation

Gendered disinformation can violate a range of women's rights: the right to live free from violence, participate in community life, or exercise freedom of political opinion, association and speech. These are fundamental human rights guaranteed to all citizens in constitutions, international conventions and domestic laws. Violating these rights leads to emotional distress and trauma, damages community and family relationships and negatively impacts a person's standing in the community. It may result in them withdrawing from political participation. Additionally, there is a tremendous cost to society because women are increasingly being pushed out of public life. Those who are already there leave because they believe it is no longer bearable or safe for them, and those who stay frequently avoid interacting with the public on social media (Judson 2021). When women occupy a public office or express strong ideas in public debates, their presence challenges the status quo of male dominance. This often makes them the target of coordinated disinformation efforts that can cause rejection, exclusion and ultimately withdrawal from public discourse.

In 2020, the electoral commission in Uganda declared the election 'scientific' (Mumbere 2020). The declaration meant that campaigns were entirely conducted online. However, according to a study on the elections in Uganda by Pollicy (2021), women politicians utilized social media far less than their male counterparts. For example, Twitter experienced low online engagement rates of women candidates during the campaign period. According to a report by Pollicy (2021), the reduced online presence of female politicians during the election period in Uganda can be attributed, at least in part, to the gendered disinformation they encountered on various digital platforms. A similar pattern is repeated in Zimbabwe where a five-year-long study by the International Foundation for Electoral Systems (2018) revealed that over 60 per cent of the violent and abusive content targeted at political players targets women legislators who make up barely a third of Zimbabwe's parliament. This underscores the pervasive problem of gendered disinformation and highlights the need for more inclusive and equitable online spaces.

Gendered disinformation makes it difficult for women in politics to engage the electorate on serious issues, as the focus is shifted away from their experience and expertise and instead placed on moral judgments. The resultant effect is an undue scrutiny of the competency of women in leadership. On Facebook, a manipulated photo of Thuli Madonsela, a former public protector in South Africa, was circulated portraying her in a dress made out of the flag of the apartheid regime in South Africa (Dube 2019). This crudely manipulated image, characterized her as untrustworthy and supportive of the apartheid regime – neither of which was true. As a black woman, this was designed to damage her political reputation and drive a wedge between her and her community/constituency. Similarly, the circulation of photoshopped nudes of the only female presidential aspirant in the 2017 Rwandan election, Diane Shima Rwigara, undermined her electoral bid (Rwigara 2017) and effectively served as a warning sign to other women who seek to contest for political office.

A woman's marital status, sexuality or personal life is not in any way relevant to their political competence. Women's lives are regulated by radically different expectations and standards than men's, notwithstanding the changing legal and social landscape. Gendered disinformation weaponizes gender roles to shrink women's agency and legitimize violence against those who do not conform. The weaponization of motherhood, marriage and sexualized narratives are targeted efforts to ridicule and promote violence against women who dare to speak up. Further, due to the prevailing conservative sexual mores in many communities, accusations of sexual affairs are particularly damaging. They reduce women to the object of male gratification, and their achievements are attributed to favours from powerful men.

Conclusion

In this chapter, I have considered three related research questions. Firstly, I explored the dominant narratives weaponized to impede women's ability to engage in the democratic processes in Africa. I showed that such narratives include traditional ideas about marriage and motherhood, false accusations of belonging to sexual minority groups and false accusations of sexual impropriety. The research found that these narratives are used to silence women critics who are perceived as threatening to the status quo and who hold strong political views. This reverberating effect extends beyond the intended target and leads to political apathy among women across the countries examined: Nigeria and Kenya. Second, I analysed online tactics deployed to perpetuate gendered disinformation in Africa. Such online tactics include dog piling, shallow fakes and deepfakes. These tactics have potentially devastating outcomes that shrink civic space for women and ultimately have a chilling effect. Further, the technical affordances of social media make online mob targeting highly effective. Lastly, I interrogated the effects of gendered disinformation on women's civic participation in Nigeria and Kenya. I argued that such effects include unequal participation of women in civic participation, stigmatization and a culture of online violence against women in politics. The analysis of cases, technologies and techniques in this chapter demonstrate the intentional deployment of lies to serve patriarchal interests. Gendered disinformation is designed to preserve male dominance of the political realm. Although women have fundamental human rights to participate in political life, disinformation is deployed to diminish their ability to exercise those rights. It is essential to social justice that women, members of the LGBTQ community and all marginalized groups can exercise, defend and expand these rights offline and online. Corporate platforms, national and regional legislatures and civil society organizations must end gendered digital disinformation and secure an open and inclusive civic space offline and online.

Bibliography

Adjer, H. and Glick, J. (2021) 'Just Joking! Deepfakes, Satire, and the Politics of Synthetic Media'. *Co-Creation Studio*. https://cocreationstudio.mit.edu/just-joking/ (accessed 22 March 2022).

Amnesty International (2018) '#Toxictwitter Violence And Abuse Against Women Online'. *United Kingdom: Amnesty International*. https://www.amnestyusa.org/wp-content/uploads/2018/03/Toxic-Twitter.pdf.

Barometer, A. (2021) 'Africa Women's Political Participation Women's Political Participation'. https://www.idea.int/sites/default/files/publications/womens-political-participation-africa-barometer-2021.pdf (accessed 5 September 2022).

Bassey, E. (2022) 'Running Mate: Funke Akindele Unfit for Leadership – Uche Maduagwu The Nation Newspaper'. *The Nation*. https://thenationonlineng.net/running-mate-funke-akindele-unfit-for-leadership-uche-maduagwu/ (accessed 5 September 2022).

Celebrity (2022) 'Winnie Odinga Dragged Out of the Closet'. *Kelebrity*. https://kelebrity.com/drama/aoko-drags-winnie-odinga-out-of-the-closet (accessed 5 September 2022).

Derrick, K. (2022) 'Kenyans React as Blogger Reveals DP William Ruto Sleeps with Women in Room 350 at Bubba Lounge on the Second Floor of Weston Hotel'. *Kossy Derrikent*. https://www.kossyderrickent.com/2022/01/kenyans-react-as-blogger-reveals-dp.html (accessed 5 September 2022).

Di Meco, L. (2019) '#Shepersisted Women, Politics & Power In The New Media World'. *The Wilson Centre*. https://static1.squarespace.com/static/5dba105f102367021c44b63f/t/5dc431aac6bd4e7913c45f7d/1573138953986/191106+SHEPERSISTED_Final.pdf (accessed 16 September 2022).

Di Meco, L. (2020) 'Why Disinformation Targeting Women Undermines Democratic Institutions'. *Power 3.0: Understanding Modern Authoritarian Influence*. https://www.power3point0.org/2020/05/01/why-disinformation-targeting-women-undermines-democratic-institutions/ (accessed 5 September 2022).

Di Meco, L. and Wilfore, K. (2021) 'Gendered Disinformation is a National Security Problem'. *Brookings Institution*, 8 March. https://www.brookings.edu/techstream/gendered-disinformation-is-a-national-security-problem/ (accessed 5 September 2022).

Dube, T. (2019) 'No, Thuli Madonsela Did Not Pose in an Apartheid-era Flag with F. W. de Klerk — It's a Forgery'. *Fact Check*. https://factcheck.afp.com/no-thuli-madonsela-did-not-pose-apartheid-era-flag-fw-de-klerk-its-forgery (accessed 5 September 2022).

Eggert, N. (2017) 'Female Politicians and Babies: A Lose-Lose Situation?'. *BBC News*, 2 August. https://www.bbc.com/news/world-40800687 (accessed 5 September 2022).

Gichuhi, G. (2022) 'No, KTN News Didn't Tweet that Kenyan Electoral Commission Vice Chair's Bank Account has been Frozen – Screenshot Fake'. *Africa Check*. https://africacheck.org/fact-checks/meta-programme-fact-checks/no-ktn-news-didnt-tweet-kenyan-electoral-commission-vice (accessed 23 November 2023).

Hannie Petra (2022) 'Juliana Cherera Asks Kenyans to Stop Circulating her Photos with Azimio Leaders'. *Mpasho*. https://mpasho.co.ke/politics/2022–08–18-juliana-cherera-asks-kenyans-to-stop-circulating-her-photos-with-azimio-leaders/ (accessed 16 September 2022).

HM Government (2019) 'Gender and Countering Disinformation'. https://assets .publishing.service.gov.uk/government/uploads/system/uploads/attachment_data/ file/866353/Quick_Read-Gender_and_countering_disinformation.pdf (accessed 16 September 2022).

Human Rights Watch (2017) '"Tell Me Where I Can Be Safe" | The Impact of Nigeria's Same Sex Marriage (Prohibition) Act'. *Human Rights Watch*. https://www.hrw.org/ report/2016/10/20/tell-me-where-i-can-be-safe/impact-nigerias-same-sex-marriage -prohibition-act.

India Today (2018) 'I Was Vomiting: Journalist Rana Ayyub Reveals Horrifying Account of Deepfake Porn Plot'. *India Today*. (accessed 12 May 2023).

International Foundation for Electoral Systems (2018) 'New Assessment of Violence Against Women in Elections in Zimbabwe | IFES - The International Foundation for Electoral Systems'. *www.ifes.org*. https://www.ifes.org/publications/new-assessment -violence-against-women-elections-zimbabwe (accessed 16 September 2022).

Inter-Parliamentary Union (2016) 'Issues Brief'. *Inter-Parliamentary Union*. http://archive .ipu.org/pdf/publications/issuesbrief-e.pdf (accessed 16 September 2022).

Jankowicz, N. (2017) 'How Disinformation Became a New Threat to Women'. *Coda Story*. https://www.codastory.com/disinformation/how-disinformation-became-a-new-threat -to-women/ (accessed 5 September 2022).

Jankowicz, N., Hunchak, J., Pavliuc, A., Davies, C., Pierson, S. and Kaufmann, Z. (2021) 'Science and Technology Innovation Program AuthorsMalign Creativity How Gender, Sex, And Lies Are Weaponized Against Women Online Science and Technology Innovation Program'. https://www.wilsoncenter.org/sites/default/files/media/uploads /documents/Report%20Malign%20Creativity%20How%20Gender%2C%20Sex%2C %20and%20Lies%20are%20Weaponized%20Against%20Women%20Online_0.pdf.

Jill, P. and Jill, P. (2022) 'Robert Alai's Source Confirms DP Ruto's Infamous Room 350 is Legit'. *KenyaReports*. https://www.kenyareports.com/robert-alais-source-confirms-dp -rutos-infamous-room-350/ (accessed 5 September 2022).

Johnson, A. (2019) 'Report on a One-Day Expert Workshop on Understanding Deepfakes and Other Forms of Synthetic Media in Sub-Saharan Africa Organised by Witness in Collaboration with the Centre for Human Rights, Faculty of Law, University of Pretoria'. In *witness.org*. New York: witness. https://blog.witness.org/wp-content/ uploads/2020/02/witness-south-africa-deepfakes-workshop-report.pdf (accessed 24 April 2023).

Judson, E. (2021) *Gendered Disinformation: 6 Reasons Why Liberal Democracies Need to Respond to This Threat | Heinrich Böll Stiftung | Brussels Office - European Union*.

Kabir, A. (2021) 'Feminist Coalition (FemCo) Archives'. *Premium Times Nigeria*.https:/ /www.premiumtimesng.com/tag/feminist-coalition-femco (accessed 23 November 2023).

Kamer, L. (2020) 'African Countries where Homosexual Activity is not Criminalized 2020'. *Statista*. https://www.statista.com/statistics/1269852/countries-where-same-sex-acts -between-adults-in-private-are-legal-in-africa/ (accessed 11 June 2023).

Karma, L. (2022) 'Criminalization of Homosexuality in Africa 2020'. *Statista*. https:// www.statista.com/statistics/1269999/criminalization-of-same-sex-relations-in-africa/ (accessed 17 November 2022).

Lime, A. (2018) 'A Year in Fake News in Africa'. *BBC*. https://www.bbc.com/news/world
-africa-46127868 (accessed 20 April 2022).

Mumbere, D. (2020) 'Inside Uganda's Proposed "Scientific Election" | Analysis'. *Africanews*.
https://www.africanews.com/2020/06/24/inside-ugandas-proposed-scientific-election
-analysis/.

NaijaGist (2012). 'Is Dame Patience The Mother of President Jonathan's Children? –
NaijaGists.com – Proudly Nigerian DIY Motivation & Information Blog'. *NaijaGist*.
https://naijagists.com/is-dame-patience-the-mother-of-president-jonathans-children/
(accessed 22 June 2023).

National Democratic Institute (2021) 'Addressing Online Misogyny and Gendered
Disinformation: A How-To Guide'. *National Democratic Institute*. https://www.ndi.org
/sites/default/files/Addressing%20Gender%20%26%20Disinformation%202%20%281
%29.pdf (accessed 5 September 2022).

Nyawira, L. (2019) 'Passaris Hits Back at Sonko over Hotel Invite Allegation'. *The Star*.
https://www.the-star.co.ke/news/2019-06-10-passaris-hits-back-at-sonko-over-hotel-
invite-allegation/ (accessed 5 September 2022).

Olukomaiya, O. (2022) 'Meet two Nollywood Divorcees Who are Deputy Governorship
Candidates - P.M. News'. *PM News*. https://pmnewsnigeria.com/2022/07/20/meet
-two-nollywood-divorcees-who-are-deputy-governorship-candidates/ (accessed 5
September 2022).

Pollicy (2021) 'Amplified Abuse'. *Pollicy*. https://archive.pollicy.org/amplified-abuse/
(accessed 16 September 2022).

Robert, T. (2017) '1 Participatory Technologies: Affordances for Development'. In *IFIP
Advances in Information and Communication Technology*. International Conference
on Social Implications of Computers in Developing Countries, 1–8. United Kingdom:
Institute for Development Studies. https://doi.org/10.1007/978-3-319-59111-7_17.

Rwigara, D. S. (2017) 'Opinion | I Wanted to be Rwanda's First Female President. Then
Fake Nude Photos Appeared Online'. *Washington Post*, 2 August. https://www
.washingtonpost.com/news/global-opinions/wp/2017/08/02/what-happened-when
-i-tried-to-run-to-become-rwandas-first-female-president/ (accessed 5 September
2022).

Sam Gregory (2022) 'Shallowfakes are Rampant: Tools to Spot Them Must be Equally
Accessible'. *The Hill*. https://thehill.com/opinion/technology/3616877-shallowfakes
-are-rampant-tools-to-spot-them-must-be-equally-accessible/ (accessed 5 September
2022).

Sessa, M. G. (2022) 'What is Gendered Disinformation? | Heinrich-Böll-Stiftung | Tel
Aviv – Israel'. *Heinrich-Böll-Stiftung*. https://il.boell.org/en/2022/01/26/what-gendered
-disinformation (accessed 16 September 2022).

UNHR (2014) 'Gender Stereotypes and Stereotyping and Women's Rights'. *UNHR*. https://
www.ohchr.org/sites/default/files/Documents/Issues/Women/WRGS/OnePagers/
Gender_stereotyping.pdf (accessed 5 September 2022).

Wamangu, S. (2022) 'Uproar as UDA MP Attacks Martha Karua on Her Marriage, Looks'.
Kenyans.co.ke. https://www.kenyans.co.ke/news/76146-uproar-uda-mp-attacks-martha
-karua-her-marriage-looks (accessed 5 September 2022).

Wang'ondu, W. (2022) 'No Amount of Intimidation Will Make Me Abandon
Ruto – Waiguru'. *The Star*. https://www.the-star.co.ke/counties/central
/2022-03-31-no-amount-of-intimidation-will-make-me-abandon-ruto-waiguru/
(accessed 5 September 2022).

Wanz, D. (2022) 'KOT and Why Room 350 is Trending - Kenyan Bulletin'. *Kenyan Bulletin.* https://kenyanbulletin.com/2022/01/06/kot-and-why-room-350-is-trending/ (accessed 5 September 2022).

Watkins, J. (2021) 'List of Female Africa Presidents – Updated July 2021 | Africa Faith and Justice Network'. *afjn.org.* https://afjn.org/list-of-female-africa-presidents-updated-july -2021/ (accessed 5 September 2022).

Witness (2022) 'Misinformation and Disinformation Tip Sheet in Elections'. *Witness.* https://library.witness.org/product/misinformation-and-disinformation-in-elections -africa/ (accessed 16 September 2022).

Chapter 3

Disinformation on a shoestring

Examining the anatomy and strategies of the pro-state network in the Zimbabwean Twitterverse

George Hamandishe Karekwaivanane

Introduction

In August 2020, the hashtag #ZimbabweanLivesMatter unexpectedly went viral on Twitter worldwide. The hashtag was launched to critique the repression, human rights abuses and economic mismanagement perpetrated by the Zimbabwean government on its citizens. At its peak, the hashtag was used in more than 700,000 tweets a day. To counter this powerful public criticism, pro-government actors on Twitter launched a counter-campaign to regain the political initiative. This chapter uses the state's coordinated digital disinformation campaign to defuse the power of the #ZimbabweLivesMatter campaign as a window to examine the anatomy, goals, strategies and tactics of the pro-government network on Twitter.

Several factors helped to make the hashtag popular across the world. The first was the support it quickly got from bands like Morgan Heritage, which has a quarter million followers on Twitter, and from celebrities like the British Ghanaian rapper Fuse ODG and South Africa DJ Tira. In some cases, people created fake accounts with the names of prominent people like the recently inaugurated Malawian President Lazarus Chakwera. These accounts were used to tweet to support the campaign, which helped give the hashtag further velocity. Another important factor is that the campaign was launched a few months after the murder of George Floyd in America, which resulted in the #BlackLivesMatter hashtag going viral worldwide. This triggered several localized efforts that challenged different forms of racism and oppression against black people in other parts of the world. Building on the momentum of the larger global campaign, #ZimbabweanLivesMatter quickly resonated with Twitter users worldwide.

One of the key responses of pro-government accounts was to try to minimize the significance of the social media campaign. They argued that social media was inconsequential in Zimbabwean politics and that government opponents could fulminate as much as they wanted on social media – however, the ruling party operated on the ground where it mattered. At one level, this argument made sense, alluding as it did to the reality of the digital divide in Zimbabwe and the fact that 'Zwitter' – the name for Zimbabweans on Twitter – were a small minority of the electorate and many of them were abroad. It was also a thinly veiled reference to the fact that ZANU PF had complete control of the arms of state power.

However, the irony of this comment would not have escaped keen observers of the debates on Zimbabwean social media. Since 2018, the government devoted substantial energy to developing its capacity to influence debates about Zimbabwe on social media. Following the November 2017 coup d'état that removed President Mugabe from power after thirty-seven years, the new government led by Emmerson Mnangagwa devoted substantial resources towards taking on opposition and civil society voices on social media platforms. A key area where they focused their efforts was Twitter. The pivotal moment was during the run-up to the 2018 elections when Mnangagwa exhorted ZANU PF members to get on social media and engage the opposition online. His specific phrase was 'Varakashei', which means thrash them or brutalize them in Shona. As a result, the ZANU PF cyber-army and pro-ruling party voices on Twitter became known as 'Varakashi' or those who thrash/brutalize. In the run-up to the elections, the government allegedly recruited social media officers who would defend the government on Twitter and put out its narrative. There were other efforts to recruit pro-government voices on Twitter in 2019 that were coordinated by a key figure in the pro-government account analysed in this chapter.

The phenomenon of the 'Varakashi' has been receiving increasing attention in the scholarly literature. Studies have examined their origins, their 'Twitter wars' with opposition supporters or their role in the 2018 elections (Chibuwe 2020; Moyo 2019; Munoriyarwa and Chambwera 2020). This chapter builds on this literature and takes it forward by focusing on uncovering the network's architecture and operation. Whereas other studies have treated the Varakashi as a homogenous group, I see them as a network of different types of accounts. I disaggregate the different kinds of actors in the network and examine this pro-government cyber army's goals, strategies, tactics and impacts. In my efforts to disaggregate the Varakashi, I found that a more productive way of understanding the network was to look at the division of labour in the efforts to peddle disinformation. In doing so, I was able to identify five main groups of actors: (a) the agenda setters, (b) the amplifiers, (c) the pseudo-news organizations, (d) astroturf accounts and (e) invisible tech-savvy people.

In thinking about disinformation in Zimbabwe, I am guided by the definitions put forward by scholars like Howard, Ong and Cabanes (2018) and the European Union Code of Practice on Disinformation (2018), which are discussed in more detail in the introduction. The ideas put across in these different texts are combined and summarized by W. Lance Bennet and Steven Livingston, who define disinformation as 'intentional falsehoods or distortions, often spread as news, to advance political goals such as discrediting opponents, disrupting policy debates, influencing voters, inflaming existing social conflicts, or creating a general backdrop of confusion and informational paralysis' (Lance Bennet and Livingstone 2020: 3). The value of this definition lies in its comprehensiveness and the way it captures the multiple goals of disinformation campaigns, especially in the Zimbabwean context.

This chapter also examines the connections between disinformation and the exercise of power in Zimbabwe. I argue that the Zimbabwean government's Twitter operation can be characterized as 'disinformation on a shoestring'. This phrase adapts Sara Berry's notion of 'hegemony on a shoestring' (Berry 1992). She uses the phrase to explain how British colonial officials sought to exercise authority over large expanses of territory colonial Africa in a context where they had limited financial and human resources. They sought to resolve the fundamental question of how to assert power across a broad, expansive area when you have limited resources. In many ways, the Zimbabwean government is grappling with this problem. In a world where digital platforms are becoming an important way of communication and coordinating resistance to power, how can an under-resourced government use a digital platform like Twitter to defend and assert its power? Part of its answer, so far, has been to build a rag-tag cyber army of Varakashi. In this chapter, I provide an outline of this cyber army as well as its core strategies and tactics.

Methodology

In my research of the pro-government disinformation network in Zimbabwe, I employed qualitative and quantitative methods. The primary method I used was digital ethnography (Pink et al. 2016). Over four months, between August and November 2020, I regularly monitored the online debates around the hashtag #ZimbabweanLivesMatter and associated ones and made ethnographic notes in a research diary. I also used NodeXL social network analysis software to collect 18,000 tweets that contained the hashtag #ZimbabweanLivesMatter at a time. I used the software to analyse several aspects of online conversations, such as determining the most influential accounts, popular phrases, the dominant sentiment and the relations between the different accounts. NodeXL was particularly useful in visually depicting the online crowds convoked by the hashtag. I also used NodeXL graphs to track the reach of government counter-messaging through hashtags like #WhenZimbabweMatters.

In addition, I used Botometer to determine whether any of the Twitter accounts were automated, that is bots. During my research, I found no automated accounts in the pro-government network. This was confirmed by analysing the tweets of the most prolific accounts. The content and the posting patterns of these accounts indicated that they were managed by human beings, many of whom were fluent in local languages. The Google reverse image search function allowed me to identify which accounts in the network were using stolen images for their profile pictures. In all, I identified around seventy-one pro-government accounts that were actively tweeting in support of the government. Of those accounts, I primarily focused on thirty-two that tweeted more than thirty times a day. Table 3.1 breaks down the accounts according to the average number of daily tweets. I have defaulted to

Table 3.1 Twitter Accounts in the Network and Their Posting Frequency

Average number of tweets a day	Number of accounts
30–50	13
50–70	7
70–100	6
Over 100	6

referring to them as accounts. This is because it is not uncommon for one person to run many accounts in such networks. In addition, just because the profile picture is of a woman, one cannot assume that the person operating the account is that woman (or even a woman at all).

Concerning ethics, my research has been guided by a number of principles. First, my search for online material on Twitter was guided by material posted using hashtags. Hashtags are used on Twitter to signal one's participation in a wider debate. In addition, by using a hashtag, individuals expect that a wider group of people interested in that particular discussion will read their tweets. I used this to decide which tweets I would subject to closer analysis. I have anonymized the majority of the accounts that I studied and have also chosen not to quote directly from any tweets in order to maintain that anonymity. The few accounts I mention specifically are public-facing ones, such as the accounts of journalists, government officials and diplomats.

Historical background to disinformation in Zimbabwe

The use of disinformation for political purposes has a long history in Zimbabwe that can be traced at least as far back as the origins of the colonial state (Beach 1974). One justification for the colonization of Zimbabwe was the myth that the Ndebele were a kingdom of warriors who predated over the Shona chieftaincies. Therefore, the British needed to step in and protect them. This false narrative was spread by travel writers and other colonial agents and was used to legitimize colonial occupation. This illustrates how colonial rule in Zimbabwe was partly enabled by disinformation. Later examples of the use of disinformation during the colonial period include the efforts to manipulate news about the anti-colonial war in the 1970s. This disinformation was meant to avoid stoking anti-colonial sentiment within the black population and to prevent panic and demoralization within the white population. It was often joked within the white community that the settler government treated them like mushrooms that are 'kept in the dark and fed bullshit' (Godwin and Hancock 1993).

The colonial government's disinformation efforts were based on its control over a broad portfolio of government-owned newspapers and television and radio broadcasting services. After independence in 1980, the new government inherited control of this information apparatus. One example of a period during which this information control apparatus was used is during the massacres in Matabeleland in the mid-1980s. The government put out a false version of events that concealed its role in killing thousands of citizens in Matabeleland and exaggerated the culpability of the dissidents for the disturbances in the region. Another critical period during which the government used its control of the information ecosystem was during the post-2000 period when the state-controlled media was awash with pro-ruling party propaganda and international news organizations were shut out of the country. This propaganda often contained falsehoods about the opposition and other perceived enemies of the government. Repressive laws were passed to control media organizations, and journalists who criticized the state were harassed, intimidated and sometimes jailed.

The spread of mobile telephony and the emergence of social media began to break the government's control over information. Opposition and civil society activists quickly became proficient in using social media as it afforded them a rare opportunity to circumvent government-controlled media and communicate with their constituencies. Platforms like Facebook, Whatsapp and Twitter fast became spaces where they actively tried to spread their message. For much of the period when Robert Mugabe was in power (1980–2017), the government focused primarily on controlling legacy media. However, following the November 2017 coup that deposed Mugabe, the Mnangagwa administration began actively trying to control the information on social media.

There are a few key points from this brief historical overview. The first is that the colonial occupation of Zimbabwe was legitimized through disinformation. Second, over time, the colonial state developed an elaborate disinformation apparatus that produced information products targeted at different demographic groups depending on their race and class. Third, this apparatus was inherited by the new government at independence, and it built on these capabilities and expanded them extensively. The rise in social media platforms and the way that they empowered individuals to disseminate information outside of the control of the government posed a new challenge to the government. The Varakashi were part of the government's answer to this challenge. The rest of this chapter examines how the government used its cyber army to meet this challenge. I begin by examining the different elements of the government network, then I turn to an analysis of the tactics and strategies that they used. Finally, I examine the 'disinformation on a shoestring' that was implemented by the Zimbabwean authorities.

Disaggregating the pro-government network

In the course of observing the online interactions on Twitter, it became clear that different types of accounts were part of the pro-government network on Twitter. These can be usefully divided according to the division of labour among them. The first set of accounts can be classified as the agenda-setters who were at the apex of the hierarchy and disseminated the key political messages. The rest of the accounts in the network took their cues from these accounts. There were only a handful of accounts in this category, and they were often senior government officials. In a few instances, they were influencer accounts with a large following and commented on Zimbabwean politics. It was common for accounts in this category to do tweet threads from time to time as a way of disseminating key ideas.

The second category of accounts could be characterized as amplifiers. These were either sock puppet accounts that had recently been set up, or accounts belonging to real people who had agreed to be part of the project of defending the government on social media. An assessment of the tweets by many of these accounts revealed that their two main activities were retweeting and replying. In other words, they were either amplifying pro-government tweets by retweeting them or trolling government critics on Twitter by responding to their tweets. Their standard approach was to monitor accounts of specific categories of people perceived as government opponents. These included opposition politicians, journalists, civil society activists and Western embassies. When the person or organization tweeted, they responded aggressively/derisively. They also 'mentioned' or tagged other network members in these replies. The 'mention' alerted the other accounts, and they descended upon the initial tweet and joined in the debate/argument. This practice of 'mentioning' each other made it clear that the different accounts were aware of each other and were coordinating their actions. It also made it easier to identify accounts in the pro-government network.

I found dozens of this category of accounts, many of which used 'stolen' photos. Some literature on troll armies notes that the accounts usually have pictures of national symbols such as flags, soldiers or other similar features. However, in the case of the Varakashi, there was no single trend. An examination of the accounts shows that, for the most part, they were attempting to pass themselves off as ordinary Zimbabweans. Many of the names on the accounts were ones you would expect to see in Zimbabwe. However, the photos were taken from a range of different websites. In many cases, there is a catfishing logic to the choice of photographs. Many of these photographs are of fashion models or minor celebrities. In other cases, they used stock photos that can be traced using a Google reverse image search. A handful of accounts that were in this category were either restricted or suspended by Twitter during the time I was doing my research. Twitter has since shut down a few of the most influential/prolific accounts.

The next set of accounts in the network were pro-government pseudo-news organizations. These organizations often have Twitter accounts, which they use to push out positive news stories on government development projects that are picked up and amplified. There had the name ZOOM (Zimbabwe Open Online Media) and then the name of a city: for example, ZOOM Bulawayo or ZOOM Harare. These pseudo-news organizations tweeted stories about successful government development and infrastructural projects, or statistical data about a successful agricultural season. In some cases, the photos of infrastructural projects were taken from other countries. The pseudo-news organizations role was, therefore, to generate the 'evidence' of good governance that was deployed by pro-government accounts to challenge any criticism of the government on Twitter. Consequently, these pseudo-news organizations were among the most commonly retweeted or mentioned news sites by the pro-government cyber troops. This is not as sophisticated as the multi-platform disinformation operations that other international actors launch. However, what is clear is that there was an attempt to build up a network that involves coordinated action between different types of actors in the network.

The next category is the mass astroturf accounts with formulaic alpha-numeric names and often no profile photographs. They generally tweeted infrequently but followed people of interest. In some cases, dozens of such accounts were often set up on the same day, suggesting that someone was deliberately setting up batches of accounts. During the time that I was conducting my digital ethnography, I was not able to detect any major activity involving these accounts. However, some government critics claimed that whenever they criticized key pro-government personalities, they were soon assailed by attacks from these accounts.

The final group in the network was the invisible tech-savvy people. What was clear from observing all the memes, images and videos posted by the pro-government accounts is that a group of technologically savvy people worked behind the scenes to produce all this material. They were carefully curating and falsifying embarrassing photos of journalists, activists and opposition politicians and which they then put out to discredit them. A clear example of this group of people's work was the mini-documentary widely circulated by pro-government accounts to dispute the true claims made by three female opposition party leaders that government agents had abducted and tortured them. (I discuss this case in more detail later.) The documentary combined different photographs and video clips from a range of sources, such as closed-circuit camera footage from a Harare supermarket. These were used to produce a false sequence of events that was supposed to disprove the abduction claims made by the three leaders. Having discussed the different categories of accounts, I will now turn to the tactics and strategies deployed by the actors in the network.

Common strategies and tactics

A useful framework to use as a starting point for thinking about the strategies and tactics employed by the pro-government network on Twitter is Ben Nimmo's 4 D framework, which emerged from his study of Russian disinformation (Nimmo 2015). Nimmo argued that the Russian disinformation operations had four main goals – to dismiss, distort, distract and dismay. The Digital Forensic Research Lab (DFRLab) provide the following explanation of the four Ds:

Dismiss – 'if you do not like what your critics say, insult them'.
Distort – 'if you do not like the facts, twist them'.
Distract – 'if you are accused of something, accuse someone else of the same thing'.
Dismay – 'if you do not like what someone else is planning, try to scare them off'(DFR Lab 2019).

A fifth D, that is 'Divide', has since been added to this framework by MisinfosecWG, a working group set up by the research community Credibility Coalition. They point out that disinformation operations also aim to sow the seeds of division. Based on my own research on Zimbabwe, a sixth D should be added to the framework *viz* 'Disrupt'. This refers to the use of disinformation to disrupt important conversations in the public sphere before they develop and the participants in those conversations gain critical mass. These six Ds provide a useful framework for thinking about the activities of the pro-government network. In the rest of this section, I will use this framework to examine three examples of the activities of the accounts: (a) their efforts at counter-messaging, (b) their use of gaslighting and gendered disinformation and (c) their efforts to target Twitter accounts of local Western embassies.

A key objective for the accounts in the network was to counter government criticism online. This was achieved through several strategies, one of which was character assassination or spreading malicious rumours about someone in order to destroy their credibility. One target was the journalist Hopewell Chin'ono, who has a large following on social media and regularly exposes and criticizes government corruption and malfeasance. Accounts in the network falsely claimed he was wanted on criminal charges in the UK. In addition, they falsely claimed that he was involved in assisting people to get US visas fraudulently. Yet others accused him of being a US spy. These lies were an attempt to distract public attention from the corruption revelations made by Chin'ono. Another tactic was to try and sow the seeds of division in the opposition by regularly tweeting false rumours about clashes between senior members of the strongest opposition party and suggesting that a split was imminent. There was never any real evidence offered to back these rumours up, and this was a clear attempt to divide the opposition and to distract attention from critiques of the government.

Unsurprisingly, the troll army used inflammatory language in their engagement with perceived enemies on Twitter. For some accounts, vulgar language and insults were their primary mode of engagement. One account that regularly used inflammatory language, for example, called the US ambassador a 'son of a bitch'. In addition, accounts in the network took to calling the US ambassador, who was an African American, 'thug'. This pejorative nickname drew on negative stereotypes about African Americans and gangs. They also regularly resorted to misogynistic or homophobic language. This corresponds closely to Nimmo's argument that one of the primary goals of disinformation is to dismiss. In other words, by making *ad hominin* attacks on government critics, they were trying to dismiss the content of the criticism and focus on attacking the character of the people making the criticism. The use of inflammatory language was also useful in disrupting debates. The basic rationale behind these efforts was 'if you can't win a debate or do not like the direction it is taking, disrupt it'. For example, if someone posted a tweet critiquing a specific government action, such as a constitutional amendment that concentrated power in the hands of the president, the accounts in the network would reply to the original post with false claims peppered with expletives and insults directed at the original poster. These insults would predictably offend and provoke people into exchanging insults with the pro-government accounts. The ultimate result was that instead of debating the constitutional amendment and devising ways to challenge it, the discussion descended into a festival of insults. They effectively hijacked online discussions by using insults and falsehoods.

One of the common strategies that was employed by members of the network was counter-messaging, and this took many forms. However, at its heart was an effort to try and challenge the core message of the campaign and introduce an alternative interpretation or even hashtag. One key example was the attempt by a senior government official outlined as follows. Within days of the #ZimbabweanLivesMatter hashtag going viral, the presidential spokesperson introduced their own hashtag, #WhenZimbabweMatters. The argument behind this counter-hashtag was that the country's opposition politicians and civil society activists were creating a false impression that there is a crisis in Zimbabwe in order to get Zimbabwe on the agenda at the impending Southern African Development Community's security troika meeting in August 2020. The social network analysis graph that emerged from an analysis of the tweets that had this hashtag is presented in Fig 3.1. The shape of the graph shows that the counter-hashtag constituted a broadcast network. This refers to a network structure that 'is dominated by a hub and spoke structure, with the hub often being a media outlet or prominent social media figure, surrounded by spokes of people who repeat the messages generated by the news organization or personality' (Smith et al. 2014). In this case, the hub was the presidential spokesperson, while the spokes led to the other accounts in the pro-government network that sought to amplify the message.

The limited traction the account gained is clear from the limited number of accounts that interacted with the hashtag. This is in clear contrast with the graph for the main hashtag #ZimbabweanLivesMatter, which resonated much more and went viral. This is clear from Figure 3.2, which shows the thick lines of interactions and the dense clusters of people who were having conversations around the hashtag.

A common practice that was used by accounts in the network is 'gaslighting' in the sense that they vigorously denied that the government had done certain things despite the fact that there was clear evidence that it had done so. In doing so, they sought to manipulate the populace into doubting their understanding of events because of the constant drumbeat of messages. This practice falls into the third D of disinformation viz 'distort: if you do not like the facts, twist them' (DFRLab 2019). A prominent example of this related to the abduction of three female opposition leaders, Joanna Mamombe, Netsai Marowa and Cecilia Chimbiri. The three had led a youth protest by Movement for Democratic Change – Alliance against the government's decision to declare a lockdown without providing support for those whose livelihoods had been negatively affected by it. The three women were arrested for violating lockdown restrictions. While in police custody, they were taken by masked assailants and driven to a remote area outside the city, where they were tortured and sexually assaulted. *The Guardian* report carried the following excerpt of their experiences:

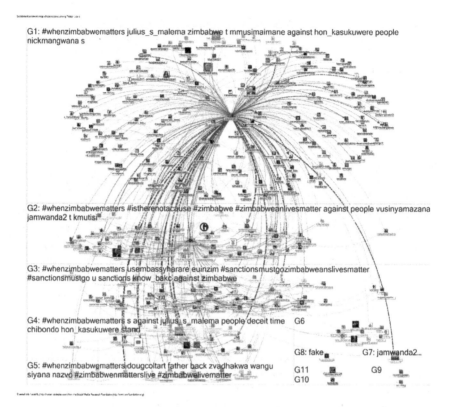

G1: #whenzimbabwematters julius_s_malema zimbabwe t mmusimaimane against hon_kasukuwere people nickmangwana s

G2: #whenzimbabwematters #istherenotacause #zimbabwe #zimbabweanlivesmatter against people vusinyamazana jamwanda2 t kmutisi

G3: #whenzimbabwematters usembassyharare euinzim #sanctionsmustgozimbabweanslivesmatter #sanctionsmustgo u sanctions know_back against zimbabwe

G4: #whenzimbabwematters s against julius_s_malema people deceit time chibondo hon_kasukuwere stand   G6

G5: #whenzimbabwematters dougcoltart father back zvadhakwa wangu siyana nazvo #zimbabwenmatterslive #zimbabwelivematter

G8: fake   G7: jamwanda2...

G11   G9
G10

Figure 3.1 #WhenZimbabweMatters NodeXL social network graph – 5 August 2020. *Source*: author.

Joana Mamombe, one of the youngest Zimbabwe Members of Parliament, described how they were forced to march and sing protest songs. 'They were pouring water on us. They beat us if we stopped. They made us drink each other's urine. They were fondling Cecilia' Mamombe, 36, told reporters at a private Harare hospital where she is receiving treatment. (*The Guardian* 2020)

The following excerpts of Chimbiri's accounts were reported by the *Newsday*:

'They were taking turns to suck my boobs. They forced a gun into my anal passage. They forced us to drink urine. They beat us under our feet, (and on) my back. They were also beating us with bare hands' said a visibly shaken Chimbiri. 'But most of all, they violated me. They sexually assaulted me. They asked me if I had labia minora, and I thought they wanted to rape me. They went on to force the barrel of their gun and a stick up my anal passage.' She said they were forced to sing non-stop and beaten every time they stopped, and they nicknamed her Dolly Parton. (*Newsday* 2020)

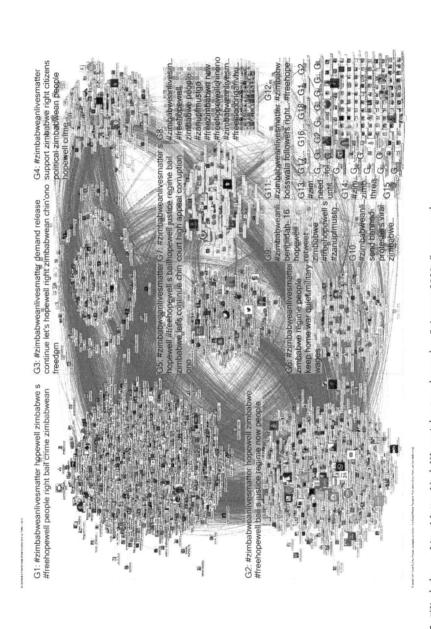

Figure 3.2 #ZimbabweanLivesMatter NodeXL social network graph – 5 August 2020. *Source:* author.

After being tortured, the three women were left in the remote area and were later rescued and taken to hospital for treatment. Photographs and video evidence of the women being rescued and recounting their harrowing ordeal were widely circulated in the news media and on social media platforms. It should be pointed out that abductions are a common practice of the Zimbabwean government in punishing and intimidating critics, and in 2020 alone, more than seventy government critics were abducted (Human Rights Watch 2021).

Despite the widespread evidence of the abduction and torture, the government proceeded to arrest the three for faking an abduction. The pro-government network soon began tweeting in support of the government's position that the three women had faked an abduction. There was a continuous drumbeat of tweets providing different false theories of where they could have been. A short 'documentary' was released, putting forward 'evidence' supposedly disproving the abduction claims. Ahead of the release of the fake video, the Permanent Secretary for Information tweeted:

> We presented 3 scenarios over the alleged abduction of Joanna Mamombe et al. 1 – There was no abduction 2 – Third Force did it 3 – MDC and anti-ED characters within the establishment did it. We will release irrefutable evidence that there was no abduction. Scenario 1 is correct.

The tweet was using a subtle disinformation tactic of putting up several alternative explanations for an event. Although he claimed that a particular 'scenario' was correct, he was also casting doubt on the idea that the government had perpetrated the abduction by suggesting that there are several 'plausible' scenarios that explain the events.

The tweet is an example of the role played by the 'agenda setters' in the network. The different pro-government accounts in the network took their cue from the tweet and began proposing multiple alternative scenarios to dispute the claim by the three women that they had been abducted by assailants who were working with the state. The false alternative theories often employed sexist tropes that objectified the women or falsely portrayed them as sexually immoral. For example, one account claimed that Mamombe was captured on video with her boyfriend on the day she claimed to have been abducted. Another account fabricated a story that Mamombe had fought with her boyfriend because she was unfaithful to him, a story that had no basis in fact. There was, therefore, a gendered dimension to the disinformation. Not only was the pro-government network gaslighting, they were also drawing on misogynistic stereotypes in order to advance their cause. The accounts also challenged anyone who expressed sympathy with the women or objected to their treatment/persecution by the government. They also doubled down on the narrative that people who faked abductions and tried to tarnish the government's image deserved to be prosecuted. In keeping with cyber-armies in other parts of the world, the pro-government account falsely claimed they were trying to 'set the record' straight in the face of falsehoods being peddled by opposition politicians. The goal here was not to persuade people about a specific alternative version of events, but simply to throw as many possible accounts that people would doubt that the three women had been abducted.

The online onslaught on the three women did not end with the accusations of faking an abduction. They faced several court appearances and were arrested by police while they were in their lawyer's car on the way to appear at a police station in fulfilment of their bail conditions. This was a typical example of the weaponization of the legal system, and the use of prosecution is a form of persecution (Karekwaivanane 2017). Digital disinformation in Zimbabwe should, therefore, not be viewed in isolation. It is part of the wider tools of repression that are used by the Zimbabwean government to silence dissent. This is clear in the way that law was used to persecute Mamombe. She developed a mental health illness as a result of the abduction and had to be hospitalized. This resulted in her failure to appear in court. The prosecutor refused to accept that she was unwell and requested a warrant for her arrest. Consequently, she had to be driven to court in an ambulance, and her doctor had to testify that she genuinely required treatment. However, the prosecutor rejected her doctor's account and applied to the court that she be taken into custody for two weeks and examined by government doctors. The court granted this application, and Mamombe was committed to the Chikurubi Maximum Prison for a psychological examination.

On Twitter, the pro-government accounts took up the charge of challenging her medically evidenced claims that she was suffering from mental illness. The state-owned daily newspaper *The Herald* contributed to the disinformation campaign by reporting that an investigating officer had video 'evidence' that 'proved' that she was not suffering from a mental illness. A senior official in the Ministry of Information tweeted a link to this article. This trend was an example of the ways that digital disinformation in Zimbabwe often involves cooperation between 'legacy media' and 'new media'. In addition, it highlights the reality that digital disinformation is happening in a wider information ecosystem.

One of the accounts in the network posted a CCTV video of Mamombe shopping in a supermarket in Harare. The accompanying comment made a sexist insinuation she and the man she was with probably had sex later that day. It further made a sexist comment about how she was walking and used that to cast doubt on her claim that she was suffering from a mental illness. On the same day, another prominent account posted photos of her in a morning gown accompanied by sexist commentary. The basic claim by the network of accounts was that she had faked an abduction and was now faking mental illness. What was clear from all the photographs of her being posted on Twitter was that she was under surveillance. The images from this surveillance were being curated and drip-fed to the public through the network of pro-government accounts. The relentless online and offline harassment of Mamombe and the harmful impact this had on her mental health is in some ways reminiscent of the experience of James Le Mesurier, the founder of the Syrian 'White Helmets' who committed suicide in 2019. Le Mesurier had been the victim of a relentless disinformation campaign to destroy his reputation and organization. This had a severe impact on his mental health, and he ultimately committed suicide by jumping out a window at his home. While disinformation is often thought of in terms of its wider impacts on large groups of people such as electorates, the case of Mamombe throws into sharp relief the personal consequences that disinformation can have.

In addition to the gaslighting and gendered disinformation discussed earlier, another key preoccupation of accounts in the network was trying to combat criticisms of the government by Western diplomats on Twitter by targeting their accounts. Some of the main targets were the Twitter accounts of the EU, UK and US embassies in Zimbabwe. Government officials presented their actions as being self-defence against attacks by Western embassies and groups that were critical of the government, which they alleged were funded by Western governments. These allegations are difficult to verify, and the architects of disinformation operations often claim they are 'setting the record straight'. However, it should be added that the Snowden leaks revealed that from 2011 the British 77th Brigade ran an information operation against the Mugabe government. It is not clear what the nature of the operation was, how long it ran for and whether there have been other operations since. This does not vindicate the Zimbabwean government. Rather, it shows that digital information operations are increasingly becoming part of the cut and thrust of contemporary international relations.

Perhaps the highest profile example of this connection between disinformation and international relations was the statement in May 2020 by Robert O'Brien, the National Security Advisor to President Donald Trump. This statement was made in the aftermath of the tragic killing of George Floyd by a policeman. O'Brien claimed that Zimbabwe was one of the countries using social media operations to take advantage of the national divisions over race and undermine America's standing in the world (https://mobile.twitter.com/ABC/status/1267088602342797314). O'Brien promised that there would be a proportionate response to these acts. The grounds for making this allegation were never made clear. However, it does suggest that the impact of the rag-tag network of pro-government accounts should not be underestimated.

The goal in targeting the accounts of diplomats appears to be the neutralization of their influence on Zimbabwean issues on Twitter by drowning out their criticisms of Zimbabwe with criticisms of their own countries. An example is when the UK Ambassador to Zimbabwe tweeted a message of solidarity with Mamombe, Marowa and Chimbiri following their abduction. Within a short time of the post going online, several accounts in the pro-government network descended upon the tweet with tirades of different kinds. One of the pro-government accounts derided the ambassador as 'a condescending old woman with a colonialism hangover'. This use of insult is consistent with the first D of disinformation discussed earlier that is Dismiss. Rather than deal with the accusation, they chose instead to insult the ambassador. Another account asked why Julian Assange was in jail in the UK. This was an attempt to distract attention from the criticisms of the treatment of the three opposition politicians by pointing to alleged abuses by the UK government. In this case, the target was not just the Ambassador. But it was also Zimbabweans who followed the ambassador's account. The goal appears to be to drown out her voice and to flood the thread with other views.

Any tweets by Western embassies that challenged the government's human rights violations typically got responses framed in this anti-neocolonial discourse. These responses were usually accompanied by photographs or videos of black people being treated in violent, humiliating or dehumanizing ways by white people. For example, one account posted a photograph of white children standing next to a caged black boy who appeared to be their pet. Another account posted a drawing of slaves being led into the hold of what appears to be a slave ship. Another account posted a link to a documentary about alleged CIA assassinations of foreign leaders. These were emotive images designed to associate the Western embassies with the historical abuse of black people. The goal was to strike particular emotional chords for Zimbabwean readers. Many of these replies to the original tweet were couched in anti-neocolonial discourse and tried to challenge any claims of moral superiority on the part of the United States of America. This was a pre-emptive move aimed at neutralizing the potency of their criticism of the Zimbabwean government. This anti-neocolonial discourse on Twitter was consistent with the larger narrative that the government has been advancing in state-owned newspapers, television and radio since 2000. The core claim has been that the sanctions and the criticism of the Zimbabwean government were part of neo-colonial efforts to implement regime change in the country and put in place opposition leaders who are Western stooges. This 'regime change agenda' was framed as being part of a long history of racist attempts to dominate African people that included slavery and colonialism. What was happening in this case was that this rhetoric was being re-purposed for social media using a cyber army that targeted Western diplomats and tried to drown out the voices on platforms like Twitter.

Disinformation on a shoestring

Digital disinformation operations come in different shapes and forms. Some governments pay for a complete suite of services from public relations firms, many of which are based in the West (Howard 2020). These firms implement well-choreographed digital operations. Other governments depend on the in-house services of the intelligence or the military. In other cases, governments with limited resources may try to put together a rag-tag cyber army by drawing upon a range of resources from government officials in charge of information dissemination, intelligence officials and political supporters who are active online. These types of operations are often scaled up at critical times, such as elections or social unrest and scaled back down after those periods. The Zimbabwe case, at least up to late 2020, falls into this group. This was an under-resourced government running a cyber-army on the cheap. It was essentially a case of 'disinformation on a shoestring budget'.

Nevertheless, this does not mean this kind of operation is not effective in some respects. They were very effective in shutting down important conversations and making the public sphere toxic and polarized. They were vigilant in their monitoring of criticisms of the government on Twitter and swiftly pounced on the critics. In addition, they hounded certain opposition figures, sometimes with devastating results for individuals. They also have substantial reach and appear to be doing more than just annoying embassy staffers in charge of the social media account. As shown earlier, the Varakashi have managed to get the attention of national security personnel in the White House.

Notwithstanding these observations, the pro-government network lacked the ability to act in a coordinated way that would have been present in a campaign managed by a PR firm. This is clear in their flatfooted response to the #ZimbabweanLivesMatter. The lack of a centralized formal structure also meant that over time, tensions emerged within the network. One individual who was active in recruiting members of the cyber army in 2018 publicly criticized a senior government official, and this resulted in a very revealing exchange. Through their public exchange, it became clear that the individual in question was being paid to assist the government's online operations. In another incident, a prominent account that was part of the agenda setters publicly criticized the former Minister of Foreign Affairs for being too tolerant of the US ambassador and the embassy's perceived interference in the country's internal affairs. This internal tension was a key characteristic of the network.

Conclusion

The chapter has examined the disinformation efforts of a network of pro-government accounts that form part of the larger government cyber army commonly known as Varakashi in Zimbabwe. Unlike previous studies that have treated the Varakashi as a homogenous group, I have disaggregated the network of Twitter accounts that form part of this rag-tag cyber army by focusing on the division of labour among them. I argued that there are five main categories of actors in the network: agenda setters, amplifiers, pseudo-news organizations, astroturf accounts and the invisible techies working behind the scenes. In examining the tactics and strategies used by the pro-government network, I have adopted and elaborated the framework originally developed by Ben Nimmo. I have thus employed the six Ds of disinformation (dismiss, distract, distort, dismay, divide and disrupt) to analyse the key examples of digital disinformation. Ultimately, I argue that in the period under study, Zimbabwe offers a case of disinformation on a shoestring budget. This represented the efforts of a government with limited means to take on its various perceived enemies on social media. This approach had mixed results. On the one hand, it was able to challenge local and foreign government critics with a measure of success. On the other, there were clear problems with internal cohesion within the rag-tag cyber army.

Bibliography

Beach, D. N. 'The Shona and Ndebele Power'. Unpublished paper, Henderson Seminar No. 26, University of Rhodesia – Department of History.

Bendiek, A. and Schulze, M. (2019) *Disinformation and Elections to the European Parliament.* (SWP Comment, 16/2019). Berlin: Stiftung Wissenschaft und Politik -SWP- Deutsches Institut für Internationale Politik und Sicherheit.

Berry, S. (1992) 'Hegemony on a Shoestring: Indirect Rule and Access to Agricultural Land'. *Africa: Journal of the International African Institute,* 63 (3): 327–55.

Chibuwe, A. (2020) 'Social Media and Elections in Zimbabwe: Twitter War between Pro-ZANU-PF and Pro-MDC-A Netizens'. *South African Journal for Communication Theory and Research,* 46 (4): 7–30.

DFR Lab (2019) 'Disinfo Bingo: The 4 Ds of Disinformation in the Moscow Protests Applying the 4 Ds of Disinformation Formula to Assess the Kremlin's Propaganda Surrounding the Moscow Protests'. *The Medium,* 24 September. https://medium .com/dfrlab/disinfo-bingo-the-4-ds-of-disinformation-in-the-moscow-protests -6624d3d677e6 (accessed 22 June 2022).

Freelon, D. and Wells, C. (2020) 'Disinformation as Political Communication'. *Political Communication,* 37 (2): 145–56.

Godwin, P. and Hancock, I. (1994) *Rhodesians Never Die: The Impact of War and Political Change on White Rhodesia c 1070–1980.* Harare: Baobab Books.

Howard P. N. (2020) *Lie Machines: How to Save Democracy from Troll Armies, Deceitful Robots, Junk News Operations, and Political Operatives.* New Haven, CT: Yale University Press .

Human Rights Watch (2020) 'Zimbabwe: Events of 2020'. https://www.hrw.org/world -report/2021/country-chapters/zimbabwe.

Jones, K. (2019) *Online Disinformation and Political Discourse: Applying a Human Rights Framework.* London: Chatham House. https://www.chathamhouse.org/sites/default/ files/2019–11–05-Online-Disinformation-Human-Rights.pdf (accessed 22 June 2022).

Karekwaivanane, G. H. (2017) *The Struggle Over State Power in Zimbabwe.* Cambridge: Cambridge University Press.

Kuo, R. and Marwick, A. (2021) *Critical Disinformation Studies: History, Power, and Politics. Harvard Kennedy School (HKS) Misinformation Review.* https://misinforeview .hks.harvard.edu/article/critical-disinformation-studies-history-power-and-politics/.

Lance Bennet, W. and Livingston, S. (2020) 'A Brief History of the Disinformation Age: Information Wars and the Decline of Institutional Authority'. In W. Lance Bennet and S. Livingston (eds), *The Disinformation Age: Politics, Technology, and Disruptive Communication in the United States,* 3–40. Cambridge: Cambridge University Press.

Lukito, J. (2020) 'Coordinating a Multiplatform Disinformation Campaign: Internet Research Agency Activity on Three U.S. Social Media Platforms, 2015–2017'. *Political Communication,* 37: 238–55.

Moyo, C. (2019) 'Social Media, Civil Resistance, the Varakashi Factor and the Shifting Polemics of Zimbabwe's Social Media "War"'. *Global Media Journal: Africa Edition,* 12 (1): 1–36.

Munoriyarwa, A. and Chambwera, C. (2020) 'Tweeting the July 2018 Elections in Zimbabwe'. In M. Ndlela and W. Mano (eds), *Social Media and Elections in Africa,* Vol. 1, 75–96. Cham: Palgrave Macmillan.

Newsday (2020) 'MDC Official Recounts Abduction Ordeal', 16 May. https://www.newsday .co.zw/2020/05/mdc-official-recounts-abduction-ordeal/ (accessed 22 June 2022).

Nimmo, B. (2015) 'Anatomy of an Info-war: How Russia's Propaganda Machine Works, and How to Counter it'. 19 May. https://www.stopfake.org/en/anatomy-of-an-info-war -how-russia-s-propaganda-machine-works-and-how-to-counter-it/ (accessed 22 June 2022).

Nimmo, B. 'The 4D Model of Disinformation, Coursera Lecture'. https://www.coursera
.org/lecture/russian-invasion-of-ukraine-teach-out/ben-nimmo-the-4d-model-of
-disinformation-campaigns-bR7uH (accessed 22 June 2022).

Ong, J. C. and Cabanes, J. V. A. (2018) *Architects of Networked Disinformation: Behind
the Scenes of Troll Accounts and Fake News Production in the Philippines.* University of
Massachusetts Amherst Communication Department Faculty Publication.

Pink, S., Horst, H., Postill, J., Hjorth, L., Lewis,T. and Tacchi, J. (2016) *Digital
Ethnography: Principles and Practice.* London: Sage.

Smith, M. A., Rainie, L., Shneiderman, B. and Himelboim, I. (2014) *Mapping Twitter Topic
Networks: From Polarized Crowds to Community Clusters.* Pew Research Center. http://
www.pewinternet.org/2014/02/20/mapping-twitter-topic-networks-from-polarized
-crowds-to-community-clusters (accessed 22 June 2022).

The Guardian (2020) 'Zimbabwean MDC Activists "Abducted and Sexually Assaulted"'. 17
May. https://www.theguardian.com/world/2020/may/17/zimbabwean-mdc-activists
-abducted-and-sexually-assaulted (accessed 22 June 2022).

The Independent (2019) 'James Le Mesurier Death: Co-founder of White Helmets Besieged
by Funding Worries and Russian Propaganda Campaign Against Him'. 15 November.
https://www.independent.co.uk/news/world/europe/james-le-mesurier-death-white
-helmets-syria-russia-propaganda-a9204896.html (accessed 22 June 2022).

Tworek, H. (2020) 'Policy Lessons from Five Historical Patterns in Information
Manipulation'. In W. Lance Bennet and S. Livingston (eds), *The Disinformation Age:
Politics, Technology, and Disruptive Communication in the United States*, 169–89.
Cambridge: Cambridge University Press.

United Nations Human Rights Council (2022) *Role of States in Countering the Negative
Impact of Disinformation on the Enjoyment and Realization of Human Rights, A/
HRC/49/L.31/Rev.1.* https://documents-dds-ny.un.org/doc/UNDOC/GEN/G22/304/10
/PDF/G2230410.pdf?OpenElement (accessed 22 June 2022).

Wardle, C. and Derakhshan, H. (2017) *Information Disorder: Toward an Interdisciplinary
Framework for Research and Policy Making.* https://rm.coe.int/information-disorder
-toward-an-interdisciplinary-framework-for-researc/168076277c (accessed 22 June
2022).

Chapter 4

Disinformation, social media networks and terrorism in Mozambique

Narratives, strategies and practices

Dércio Tsandzana

Introduction

In October 2017, violent conflict erupted in the Cabo Delgado region of Mozambique following the discovery of large reserves of natural gas. The United States of America labelled the main armed group responsible for the violence the 'Islamic State in Mozambique' and classified them as a terrorist organization. Despite the relatively low levels of 21 per cent internet connectivity and 9 per cent social media use in Mozambique (Hootsuite 2023), digital disinformation is being actively used as a weapon in the conflict. Although access to the internet is still limited in Mozambique, it is still vital to study how disinformation manifests itself in the country's information ecosystem.

This chapter is one of the first studies of disinformation in Mozambique. Specifically, this chapter aims to investigate the link between the spread of digital disinformation and terrorist attacks in Mozambique. To answer this question, I propose three complementary questions: (i) What are the causes of digital disinformation in Mozambique? (ii) Who are the main disinformation actors in the country? (iii) What tactics are used to deploy disinformation and to combat it?

In terms of structure, I begin by presenting the historical context of conflict and terrorism in Mozambique. This is followed by a review of the existing literature on disinformation and terrorism and a discussion of my research methodology. I then present a series of examples of the disinformation deployed by combatants, journalists and criminal gangs, as well as government responses, before drawing some tentative conclusions.

Historical and political context

Mozambique has been plagued by long periods of conflict for more than half a century. Mozambique's independence from Portugal in 1975 was the result of an armed anti-colonial struggle. This was followed by a civil war that ended with

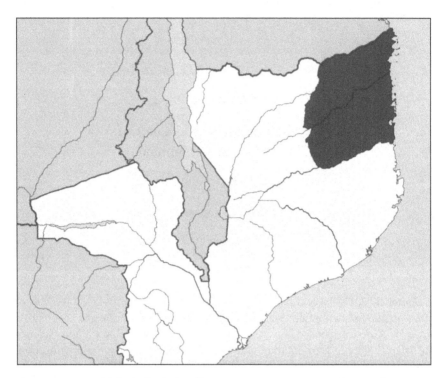

Figure 4.1 Map of Cabo Delgado (Profoss, creative commons, November 2011).

the signing of a peace agreement in 1992. During that time, Frelimo exercised tight control over media until the advent of social media. However, in 2013 there was a resurgence of armed conflict in the central region of the country led by the opposition party RENAMO. The efforts to end this insurgency included the signing of a new peace agreement in 2015 and another in 2019.

The latest round of conflict began in October 2017 in the northern province of Cabo Delgado which is the area shaded dark grey in Figure 4.1. Verified facts about the causes and actors in the conflict are difficult to come by. During these attacks, the port town of Mocimboa da Praia was seized in August 2020. Sources from January 2023 indicate that over 1 million Mozambiquan civilians were internally displaced by the conflict (OIM 2023). On 24 March 2021, the insurgents seized the town of Palma, leading to an exodus of civilians to the provincial capital Pemba. Fighting continued sporadically in 2022, and fear and uncertainty continued to dominate the region. The UN Refugee Agency UNHCR (2022) has estimated that more than 900,000 people were internally displaced due to escalating violence. According to Armed Conflict Location & Event Data Project (ACLED)/Cabo Ligado – a conflict observatory – more than 3,000 people have been killed already since the attacks began in October 2017.

Several explanations have been offered about the causes of the conflict (Chichava 2020). One explanation maintains that the Islamic State is behind the attacks and intends to occupy the gas production areas in Mozambique. In March 2021, the United States designated Ahlu Sunaa Wal Jammah, a group allegedly operating in Cabo Delgado alongside Tanzanian fighters, as a terrorist organization. The US administration labelled the group Islamic State in Mozambique. However, the International Crisis Group has argued that although ISIL has contact with the insurgents in Mozambique and has provided some finance, it does not exert command and control authority over the group.

In addition, some reports indicate that the insurgents are primarily Muslims from the coastal zone of Cabo Delgado, recruited by local fundamentalist preachers who have claimed that the imposition of Sharia, or Islamic law, would bring equality and everyone would share in the wealth from the newly discovered gas reserves. The message and the promise of jobs and money have led many young men to join the insurgency, and it has gained support in local communities.

There has been little scholarly and policy research on digital disinformation and its relationship to terrorism in the country. However, there are cases of information propagation on social media networks with intentions to create fear, loot property or create panic. The first attack was in 2017 on Mocimboa da Praia, the only city and port in this northern zone. A central challenge for researchers trying to understand the conflict has been the lack of access to information and the dissemination of controversial data and disinformation about the conflict. Therefore, this chapter seeks to trace the general state of access to 'correct information' and the use of social media networks in times of terrorist insurgency in Mozambique.

In general, one of the main debates that has created controversy and acts of disinformation is the alleged involvement of international Islamic terrorist groups in the attacks in Cabo Delgado. When the insurgents entered Palma on 24 March 2021, they were attacking a rapidly growing town with significant foreign investment and more than 1,000 foreign workers linked to the gas industry. Just two weeks before, the United States had labelled the insurgents as 'ISIS-Mozambique' and designated it as a Foreign Terrorist Organization (FTO). Four days after the attack, the Islamic State group-aligned Amaq news agency issued a statement claiming that its fighters had attacked Palma and destroyed government offices and banks.

Despite claims that the Islamic State is behind the attacks and intends to occupy the gas production areas in Mozambique, Habibe, Forquilha and Pereira have argued that neither the perpetrators nor the origins of the violence have been clearly identified (Habibe, Forquilha and Pereira 2019). In addition, the exact political identity, ideology and demands of the extremists remain unknown. However, there are indications that the extremists have some known demographic characteristics (Matsinhe and Váloi 2019).

Morier-Genoud (2020) argues that the insurgents probably switched to armed jihadism due to the growth and radicalization they experienced as a result of the repression they suffered from mainstream Muslim organizations and later the Mozambican state. This perspective is at odds with the US Department of State alternative, which connects the insurgents to the Islamic State. However, before discussing the case of Mozambique further, it is important to explain how disinformation acts in times of extreme conflict.

Disinformation in Mozambique: The legal framework and its implementation

Concern about the impact of disinformation on democratic society has stimulated an enormous amount of research into the types of disinformation, the data-driven mechanisms that underpin its distribution, its impact on democracy and how to tackle its spread (Ó Fathaigh et al. 2021). Increased concern about disinformation has stimulated new laws and regulations. Mozambique has a law that restricts disinformation: the 1991 Press Law (under review since 2021) stipulates that any media outlet or journalist disseminating disinformation can be punished with the corresponding penalty for defamation. This includes penalties such as revocation of the journalism licence or deportation in case of foreign journalists. In May 2022, Mozambique's Parliament approved a new anti-terror law that imposes severe prison sentences for convicted terrorists and anyone spreading disinformation about the country's insurgency. The law provides for up to twenty-four years in prison for those found guilty of terrorism offenses. Civil society organizations and activists have criticized the law because of its excessive penalties and the possibility of its use to violate the rights of freedom of expression and access to information.

Analyses of the influence of the internet on the recruitment of youth and the spread of terrorism in the country have shown that disinformation is one of the main challenges. However, there has been no evidence to support the idea of youth recruitment through digital media. For example, Feijó (2020) analysed how some messages circulating on social networks could have created pockets of terrorism in Cabo Delgado while Tsandzana (2020) has demonstrated that there is no clear link between terrorist recruitment and digital platforms.

Disinformation in conflict settings

The introduction to this volume has discussed the definition of disinformation in detail. Therefore, I will not rehash that literature here. Suffice it to say that I understand disinformation as fabricated or deliberately manipulated audio or visual content, even if it can also be described as intentionally created conspiracy theories or rumours – it can also be defined as information that is false and deliberately created to harm a person, social group, organization or country (Wardle and Derakhshan 2018). I will, however, focus on the scholarly literature on the connections between conflict and disinformation.

It is often said that the truth is the first casualty of war. This adage holds true in the case of Mozambique, where the absence of reliable information has created a vacuum in which disinformation has been able to thrive. As Schmid (2004) noted, terrorism can be defined as the calculated use of violence or the threat of violence to inculcate fear, intended to coerce or intimidate governments or societies. This is done in order to pursue political, religious or ideological goals (Schmid 2004). In this chapter, I focus on terrorist acts perpetrated by non-state actors who deliberately attack civilian and military targets to advance their political aims.

In his analysis of digital terrorism, Byman (2018) argues that online disinformation aids terrorist organizations in two main ways: propaganda and recruitment. Byman recommends that to counter the exploitation of the internet by malign agents and states, social media companies should develop emergency protocols. According to Byman, digital media is used by terrorists to spread messages that can destabilize society and try to recruit new members to their factions. In general, disinformation can serve several purposes in a conflict context.

Piazza (2021) explains that online disinformation aids terrorist recruitment by radicalizing individuals. The author also argues that disinformation helps to ferment, reinforce and enhance personal and group grievances. It is designed to be incendiary, regardless of how ridiculous the claims may be. It also plays to existing prejudices held by its consumers, deepening their sense of outrage and grievance and whetting their appetite for militant action.

Piazza (2021) also explains that online disinformation drives a range of adverse and potentially dangerous outcomes. For example, online disinformation consumption fosters citizen distrust of mainstream, non-partisan media and other sources of authoritative information. In addition, the literature on terrorism and the internet (Johnson 2018; Deibert 2019) argues that individuals who frequent websites and social media communities featuring disinformation have been found to exhibit higher levels of political extremism and radicalization. This literature argues that the internet and social media communities aid in radicalizing individuals and enhance terrorist groups' ability to recruit members, plan and execute attacks and publicize their activities.

In theory, social media provides anyone with a social media account the potential to instantly reach a global audience of millions. This poses major challenges to democracy and civil rights (Unver 2017). Disinformation is among these challenges. In the not-so-distant past, 'a propagandist eager to spread disinformation had to have a printing press to publish books containing false information, an airplane from which to drop leaflets, or a television channel via which disinformation could be broadcast to masses' (Ruohonen 2021: 2). Although access to the media has been democratized, the ability to influence a large audience requires other elements: a network of followers (social capital), a compelling narrative, other people to boost your message (retweet, like) – access is significant, but it is not a sufficient condition for change.

Internet and terrorism: A perfect combination?

Powerful new technology makes manipulating and fabricating content relatively simple and affordable. Social networks can dramatically amplify falsehoods peddled by states, populist politicians and dishonest corporate entities if they are shared by an uncritical public. People may take as credible content that is endorsed by their social networks and uncritically accept information which corresponds with their pre-existing beliefs (UNESCO 2018). In general, most discussions about the concept of disinformation typically focus on the role of nation-states like Russia and China (*The New York Times* 2019; *The Guardian* 2019). But violent non-state actors, including terrorist groups, also rely on disinformation, and some groups have developed sophisticated disinformation capabilities. This chapter focuses on disinformation produced by non-state actors and the response of the Mozambique authorities to counter it.

The insurgents in Cabo Delgado have been labelled as terrorists by the United States, and their online communications labelled disinformation by the Government of Mozambique. This chapter focuses on digital disinformation produced by non-state actors to spread terror in Mozambique. I contend that the objectives of these actions can vary, but are almost always some combination of spreading fear and terror, recruiting new followers to the cause, radicalizing individuals and confusing and distracting public safety officials in order to use up their finite resources.

As noted by UNODC (2012), one of the primary uses of the internet by terrorists is to disseminate digital propaganda. This propaganda generally takes the form of multimedia communications providing ideological or practical instruction, explanations, justifications or promotion of terrorist activities. These may include virtual messages, presentations, magazines, treatises, audio and video files and video games developed by terrorist organizations or sympathizers. Nevertheless, what constitutes terrorist propaganda, as opposed to legitimate advocacy of a viewpoint, is often a subjective assessment. Further, disseminating propaganda is generally not, in and of itself, a prohibited activity. The promotion of violence is a common theme in terrorism-related propaganda. In fact, the broad reach of content distributed via the internet exponentially increases the audience that may be affected.

The lack of accurate information about the causes of a conflict and the perpetrators of violence creates a context conducive to continued violence because there is no one to hold accountable. Government, media and civil society all blame one another for the silence, claiming there is no information. Civil society has accused the executive arm of the government of failing to protect the media, while the government has labelled the media a vector for the dissemination of disinformation. As a result, activists and human rights defenders launched a campaign on social media networks in 2018 to raise awareness of the conflict, denouncing human rights abuses and using hashtags and short publications to highlight the humanitarian crisis. It is important to note that since 2021, the Southern African Development Community Mission in Mozambique (SAMIM) and the Rwandan and Mozambican defence forces have been intervening in the country to support Mozambique, together with International Cooperating Partners and multilateral agencies of the United Nations.

In the case of Mozambique, the ruling Frelimo party, which has been in power since 1975, controls the public sphere. In terms of disinformation, although there is not much documented evidence, it is known that Frelimo has already come out publicly to denounce the existence of disinformation around terrorism circulating in social networks. For example, in 2021, the President of Mozambique, Filipe Nyusi, alleged that digital platforms promoted disinformation. However, while Frelimo appears to denounce these acts, it also exercises its power through the executive government that creates laws to curtail the freedoms of expression and press around terrorism and creates platforms that dictate what is true or not about terrorism. This power relationship is shown to dominate one political actor against the rest of society. This situation represents a context where the government appears to be fighting disinformation but is at the same time using it as a tool to exert political control/influence.

Methodology

An important question in the Mozambican context is whether there is a link between the spread of digital disinformation and terrorist attacks in Mozambique. To answer this question, I adopt an approach based on digital ethnography (Dawson 2019). There is no specific hashtag to follow about terrorist disinformation in Mozambique, so my focus has been to search for examples that arise in the digital space, especially social networks, which illustrate how these tools are used to promote disinformation in the country. To this end, my approach is based on publications by Mozambican and foreign citizens telling the narratives of the conflict in Cabo Delgado, either on Twitter or Facebook.

I admit that such reality makes my analysis limited, as I discuss a problem – terrorism – for which there is no consensus about its origins and causes in Mozambique (Feijó 2020). For this reason, I have chosen to combine the analysis of online data (Rogers 2015) and the local sociopolitical context of Mozambique to explain the reality studied. I have conducted digital ethnography following particular users over an extended period to filter and assess posts on disinformation and evidence of propaganda or recruitment. This type of work always brings challenges. One challenge I had to grapple with was how to present examples that clearly reflect the disinformation promoted on digital platforms while still preserving the anonymity of the actors who published such information on platforms like Twitter or Facebook.

To do this research, I have tracked online publications to understand how digital social media networks have been used to disinform people and spread terrorism in Mozambique. To collect the data, I have adopted a search through specific hashtags such as #Mozambique #CaboDelgado #MocimboaDaPraia and #Palma, as many of the publications that were made contained at least these references between September 2020 and May 2021. Even though my main analysis focuses on that period, some examples have emerged in 2022. I also used the names of key actors, such as the President of the Republic #FilipeNyusi, to find his virtual speeches about social media and terrorism in Mozambique. Likewise, the search for media reports was fundamental. Table 4.1 summarizes the posts that I analyse in this chapter.

Table 4.1 Research Design – Number of Posts Analysed in the Chapter

Source	Actors	Action	Date
Twitter (two posts)	Politicians	Denouncing disinformation	May 2021
	Diplomats	Defending their country	May 2021
	Journalists	Promoting disinformation	April 2021
Facebook (two posts)	Ordinary citizens	Denouncing disinformation	March 2021
	Non-identified actors	Broadcasting false videos	September 2020
	Digital firefighters	Denouncing disinformation	April 2021
TV Channels (2 videos)	Media companies	Reporting disinformation	April 2021

The analysis focuses on two social networks (Twitter and Facebook), using a qualitative analysis between September 2020 and May 2021. I have chosen this period because it was during that moment when one of the biggest attacks in Cabo Delgado took place, precisely in the District of Palma (24 March 2021), whose international repercussions gained new impetus with the diffusion of photos and videos whose veracity was questionable. In addition, I divided the analysis into three categories, one promoted by actors with links to politicians, the second by journalists and another based on ordinary citizens, especially activists. One of these categories will focus on disinformation to promote recruitment to terrorism and disinformation as a tool to manipulate the reality about what is happening on the ground. I have chosen to discuss whether there is a link between the spread of digital disinformation and terrorist attacks in Mozambique. In this chapter I have analysed seven cases chosen from a more extensive set of cases.

Accessing the internet and social media networks in Mozambique

Mobile phone and internet use levels are low in Mozambique by regional standards, especially in rural areas. Fifty-two per cent of the country's population owns a mobile phone, 21 per cent have access to the internet, 11 per cent use Facebook and less than 1 per cent use Twitter (Hootsuite 2023). According to the Alliance for Affordable Internet (A4AI 2017), although the government and regulator have introduced much-needed reforms, further efforts to reduce the price of broadband for all – especially for the significant number of citizens living under the poverty line – are needed.

This figure means that Twitter's advertising reach in Mozambique was equivalent to 0.2 per cent of the total population. These modest figures raise the question of whether social media networks can be considered an effective medium for disseminating disinformation in the country. Based on my observations, despite the difference in use between the two social networks, the spread of information around terrorism is increasingly present. A key difference is that on Facebook, there are more local actors, while on Twitter, the profile of users who talk about terrorism in Mozambique is international, especially journalists and diplomats.

Although the internet enables connection across the country, it is increasingly being seen as a technological risk, especially in the face of the rapid spread of

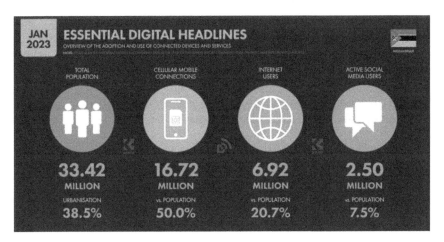

Figure 4.2 Access to the internet in Mozambique (DataReportal, 2022).

rumours, disinformation and hate speech. Mobile internet is also frequently used for services like banking and mobile money. Despite their importance to ordinary Mozambicans, these mobile services have been a target for the government. For example, they have been accused of being sources of terrorist financing in Cabo Delgado (Global Voices 2021).

Hootsuite (2023) noted that according to GSMA Intelligence, mobile connections in Mozambique were equivalent to 50 per cent of the total population in January 2023. In addition, the number of mobile connections in Mozambique increased by 1.4 million (+9 per cent) between 2022 and 2023. However, only a fraction of those with a mobile phone connection would have been targeted by digital disinformation.

Digital disinformation and terrorism in Mozambique: Dynamics and tactics

This section examines whether there is a link between the spread of digital disinformation and terrorist attacks in Mozambique, highlighting the motives, tactics and responses. My analysis builds on the existing literature (Byman 2018) and extends it by identifying additional categories of disinformation: (a) disinformation for propaganda; (b) disinformation for recruitment; (c) disinformation for criminality; (d) disinformation for journalist prestige. In addition, I identify the following government responses: (a) expanded online narrative; (b) fact-checking site; and (c) digital firefighters.

Case one: French armoured vehicles

The first example of disinformation occurred in May 2021 and relates to the entry of foreign armed forces to support Mozambique in 2021. A Twitter user posted images of what they claimed were 'French made armoured personnel carriers' and implied that France was involved in the conflict. The tweet suggested that there was a political dimension to the intervention of Western countries in the fight against terrorism in Mozambique. It made a connection with the future intention of gas exploration in Northern Mozambique, especially by the French company Total Energies which has a presence in the region. The tweets presented here capture the French ambassador's response to the false tweet in May 2021:

> @User: Pictures of French made Acmat TPK-420 BL armored personnel carriers of the Mozambican police.
>
> @French Ambassador: Not French. My advice: look better! ☺

Tweet 1: French ambassador denies circulation of combat vehicles in Mozambique (May 2021)

In the brief tweet on 20 May 2021, the French Ambassador refuted the claims that the vehicles were evidence of the presence of French troops in Mozambique. In this example, the French Ambassador demonstrated that the vehicles were not from France. The Mozambican armed forces later confirmed this information, proving that there was no evidence that these vehicles belonged to the French army.

This reality is in line with what the literature has shown, as contemporary disinformation tactics attest to for a constant variation of the media (Tumber and Waisbord 2021). All sides in the conflict, 'terrorists', the government of Mozambique, local and foreign civil society and the US government have used online platforms to project their version of events and perspective of priority issues. As Von Clausewitz points out, a 'great part of the information obtained in war is contradictory, a still greater part is false, and by far the greatest part is of a doubtful character' (Crilley and Chatterje-Doody 2021).

Case two: Claimed army violence

In September 2020 another case marked the landscape of terrorism disinformation in the country. In that period, Mozambique's Defence Minister Jaime Neto said that a video showing people dressed in army uniforms beating and killing a naked woman was a sign of misinformation. The video caused social outrage after it was circulated on social media. In the video, a group of men wearing army uniforms surround a woman, one hits her in the head and body with a stick several times before others shoot.

The video was shared by unidentified individuals, and it was quickly claimed that they were soldiers from the Mozambican armed forces. The same video was later shared on Twitter by an account associated with the Islamic group (@ASWJ), indicating that the uniformed men killing civilians were the government forces. It is worth noting that the source of the video was unknown, as were the individuals in the video and the cause of the violence they perpetrated. However, the public perception is that the video was real. The Islamic insurgents exploited the video for their own political purposes, while the state was forced to defend itself from the allegations.

Additionally, the information shared at the time indicated that it was information created to provoke fear or discredit the work done by the Mozambican armed forces, given that the terrorists had also worn the same uniform as the Mozambican military to create confusion about their identity. This strategy had been used to obtain profits or spread terrorist practices in the country. One of the examples to illustrate that situation was the dissemination of a video showing the murder of a woman by armed men believed to be terrorists but wearing the uniform of the Mozambican armed forces. This video was released in September 2020. Other videos of beheadings were also shared in the same circumstances.

Case three: Criminal gangs

On 28 June 2022, local media reported that the Mozambican police in the northern province of Cabo Delgado had arrested two men who staged fake terrorist attacks in villages in Ancuabe district from 5 June 2022. Using digital platforms like Facebook to spread their intentions, the men posed as terrorists and looted goods from the residents. The two men were accused of spreading messages on digital platforms about possible attacks in the region. According to the police, the messages contained terms such as #attacks and #terrorism. However, the evidence about this was not shared by the police.

The fact that they spread disinformation in order to steal people's belongings shows how the broader context of terrorism can be used as a means of accumulation. As a result, the Police Commander said that investigations were underway to find out whether the individuals detained had any genuine connection with the Islamist terrorists. In addition to that a weekly update (June 2022) on the Cabo Ligado's website stated that Mozambique featured strongly in IS official media in the last week of June 2022, as seven incident reports were produced, and three photo reports. 'Mozambique Province' actions were also featured on a full-page infographic in *Al Naba* magazine – a weekly publication that has been published by the Islamic State's Central Media Office since 2014. The newspaper's first edition was released in May–June 2010, and on 17 October 2015, it began publishing an official weekly newsletter.

There wasn't similar media coverage of activities in the Facebook content produced by IS supporters that was targeted at East Africa (Ayad et al. 2022). These examples seem to be digital disinformation, as the intention was to create fear and manipulate the actual situation on the ground. The target audience was people connected to the Twitter account of *Al Naba* magazine which @Jasminechic00 regularly shared. Equally, local Mozambicans could also be among the targeted audience. It is part of my definition of terrorism for propaganda, not necessarily for recruitment. In addition, Cabo Ligado's website also mentioned that while official IS reporting from the ground has accelerated and been given prominence, this is not reflected in unofficial information pages on Meta's Facebook platform that target East Africa. Facebook clearly remains an active conduit for IS disinformation, noted Cabo Ligado (2022).

Case four: The Palma siege

In March 2021, some media outlets claimed that Palma was besieged by terrorists. *CBS News* called it an 'ISIS militant siege' with hundreds of foreign workers cowering in fear – an unspecified number of individuals died. The UK's *Daily Mirror* newspaper called it 'ISIS terror' and a 'jihadist massacre'. The UK's *Times* newspaper had earlier headlined: 'ISIS militants attack town housing foreign workers in Mozambique'. But on the same day, before some of the newspaper headlines were published, the ISIS claim was debunked.

However, Jasmine Opperman, the Africa analyst at the ACLED, who has been following the insurgency in Mozambique's Cabo Delgado province closely, showed on her Twitter account that the videos and photos were not from Palma, but from Mocimboa da Praia, 65 km to the south. Considering what Jasmine Opperman said, I note that the presumed intention of ISIS in this context was politically to create fear and tension, as well as to share the image according to which the situation was out of control and that the Government of Mozambique did not have the capacity to contain the attacks.

This came at a time when Mozambique was preparing to start gas exploitation in that part of the country. This led to reports that the intention of the attack was to stop that activity and benefit the terrorist network economically with the natural resources, as Cabo Delgado was considered a natural resource trafficking zone. After the attack in Palma, President Nyusi stated that there were people who published content to disinform the population about terrorism, calling for such actors to be denounced and punished, as noted by *TV Miramar* – the first private television linked to Brazil and based in Maputo – on 16 April 2021.

What can be distilled from these examples of digital disinformation is that international terrorist organizations like ISIS are putting out disinformation to exaggerate their military capabilities – the main example has been the publication of seizure of weapons and vehicles of war that belong to the armed forces of Mozambique. This is done through Twitter accounts and shared permanently by other accounts like @DelgadoCabo and @JVDW19.

Second, it would appear that disinformation has been promoted for economic gain – some citizens promote messages about attacks on social networks to take advantage of them and loot goods from the population. This occurred in Ancuabe district, as discussed in Case 3 earlier. Third, there is a perception within the upper echelons of the political establishment that disinformation about terrorism in Mozambique is a dangerous phenomenon that needs to be contained.

Although Byman (2018) argues that online disinformation aids two of the three terrorist group processes which are facilitated by the internet – propaganda and recruitment – the evidence from Mozambique only partly backs this argument. To date, there is no evidence that disinformation has been used as a means of recruitment (Tsandzana 2020). In addition, it is interesting to note that discussions about terrorism in Mozambique on Twitter are mostly carried out in English, a language that is not widely used within Mozambique. This suggests that the debates on the platform about terrorism and disinformation have their roots and repercussions beyond Mozambique – we can argue the existence of an international dimension to the phenomenon.

Case five: Attack on Mueda

This case is taken from TVM, a public television outlet based in Maputo, Mozambique, which is Mozambique's public national broadcaster. The government provides the majority of the operating funding for television; advertisers and other commercial sources provide the remaining funds.

> They are attacking Mueda, in Cabo Delgado. There is no communication, no network. There are people decapitated along the roads in Mueda. The atmosphere is horrific. I refuse to publish photos . . . (Translated from Portuguese)

TV Illustration 1: 'On social media, internet user agitates people claiming Mueda was under attack' (TVM – public television – April 2021)

This was information that was not verified by the author. Mueda is one of the districts in Cabo Delgado province that has been the target of terrorist attacks. In TV illustration 1, it is noted that the country's main media outlet (TVM) is used as a medium to clarify (or manipulate) acts of disinformation on terrorism in Mozambique. This is interesting because it shows that traditional media such as television are not disconnected from what is happening in the social networks.

Likewise, in the case of Mozambique, it is a means that the government has found to use the public media to promote its own narrative that does not jeopardize its fight against terrorism in the country. It later became evident that no attack had taken place in Mueda. The journalist who reported about the attack was based in Lisbon; however, he later stated that it was disinformation intended to politically demoralize those fighting against terrorism in Mozambique.

Case six: Journalistic disinformation

There are no scholarly references about disinformation by journalists in Mozambique, but in 2020 the Mozambican President, Filipe Nyusi, expressed concern over what he called the prevalence of a wave of disinformation and public manipulation of the situation of terrorism in Cabo Delgado. At the time, the Mozambican statesman considered that this was one of the factors threatening national unity and that it should be fought. In his speech, Nyusi directly targeted some media outlets and even alleged that they were serving the interests of terrorists (VOA 2020). On 11 April 2023, as part of the celebration of the Mozambican Journalist Day, it was noted that the widespread use of social media and the advent of digitalization have been contributing to the dissemination of false news, requiring journalists to have the ability to verify facts. This is what Case 6 discusses.

> This photo has been circulating on social media since last week. For those who believe that this is a photo from the theatre of operations in Cabo Delgado, it is important to clarify that it is a photo taken in Gorongosa (Sofala) during a reportage on a forest ranger manoeuvre a few years ago.
>
> Obviously, the Defence and Security Forces (FDS) would not let a journalist cover a battle without a bulletproof vest . . . I mean, the FDS would not let a journalist cover anything, looking at what happened to the other journalist . . . (Translated from Portuguese)

Facebook post 1: Internet user denounces a wrong photo about the conflict in Cabo Delgado (March 2021)

In this case (Facebook post 1), one of the users denies that the photo was made during a terrorist attack in Cabo Delgado, mentioning that it is part of another conflict that was taking place at the time in central Mozambique – in Sofala province. The information shared by the TVM's journalist (Brito Simango) was later confirmed to be accurate by military officials, and it was then deleted from Facebook. The post highlighted that the journalist was there to promote his image and gain some individual political prominence, since it was not the truth of the reported fact.

This action can be described as intentional because the author (journalist) made the post, but with the knowledge that it does not represent the context described. The journalist who was part of the forest ranger manoeuvres later shared the photograph on his Facebook, falsely claiming that it was from the anti-terrorist efforts.

Disinformation and the government's cyber reaction

The Mozambique government has three main countermeasures to address disinformation: (a) increasing its own online engagement; (b) establishing a fact-checking site to rebut false claims; (c) deploying digital firefighters to counter disinformation and amplify government narratives online. I will examine each response in turn.

Increasing its own online engagement

In November 2020, President Nyusi challenged the Mozambican Armed Forces (FADM) to restore normalcy to conflict-affected parts of the country. Notably, he attacked the use of social media to spread disinformation in Cabo Delgado. 'We lament the growing trend towards disinformation and the attempts to manipulate public opinion by inventing facts, which are then publicized by using the platforms provided by social media', Nyusi said. After the President's pronouncement, the State Information Office created a platform called *Credível* (credible in English) to monitor the online publication of information.

The office stated that the verification platform sought to ensure the authenticity of content disseminated by the press or on social networks. Access to the platform is free, and citizens can share content to this page and quickly expect a response from the person who created the information confirming its veracity. However, so far Credível's inner workings remain secret – there is no public data on how the website is managed or which state entity is responsible.

Establishing a fact-checking site to rebut false claims

On Credível's website news article are given 'truth' or 'lie' stamps that signify the organization's judgement of the claim in the article. These stamps also demonstrate how the government manages its own narrative about the insurgency. I suggest that the government is weaponizing the issue of disinformation to allow it to control information about terrorism, using *credivel* to exercise the power to authorize what is true and what is false.

It is important to note that Nyusi's warning against misleading online propaganda came roughly two weeks after the launch of a new Frelimo (ruling party) website, called Frelimo 1962. This site was established by Defesa MZ, the same organization that in 2020 set up a website called Notícias de Defesa, which publishes news about the war in Cabo Delgado, alongside official statements from the Mozambican ministries of the interior and defence.

The government promotes these two platforms but also uses them to spread the government's own narrative about the conflict while still using and criticizing other social media users (Global Voices 2021). An interesting aspect about how the information is managed on these platforms, websites and social media accounts is that they all seem to have links to the ruling party Frelimo. Moreover, it is important to note that while the political power is concerned about terrorism disinformation, these political actors show some interest in monitoring the circulation of information that directly or indirectly jeopardizes their political stability.

In addition to that, there is a Twitter account (@DefesaNoticias) which is used as the main source of information about the achievements of the Mozambican Armed Forces (FADM). It also serves as a medium to deny any information which is deemed to be wrong. An interesting aspect about this account is that it only publishes in English. This suggests that the information that is shared by this Twitter account is targeted at a non-Mozambican audience such as journalists and diplomatic representatives (embassies).

Deploying digital firefighters to counter disinformation

One of the features of the response to disinformation about terrorism in Mozambique is how 'digital firefighters' – social media gurus and digital influencers – are mobilized to support the government's actions and promote messages that condemn those who allegedly publish disinformation about the conflict in Cabo Delgado. In other words, 'digital firefighters' is a Mozambique-specific term to refer to citizens that are identified by the political actors to occupy and control the virtual media landscape in support of the government's actions (Global Voices 2021).

Most of them are influential individuals with numerous followers on social media platforms. Nobody knows how many there are, but unconfirmed information indicates that they are paid by political actors (Zitamar News 2020). One example is a distinguished professor and media commentator who is linked to the ruling party. In 2020, he suggested on Facebook that journalists reporting on the attacks should be silenced by the military, police and secret services and that 'extra-judicial' methods be used if necessary. The professor added that news stories about the conflict 'demoralise those who have the duty to defend our country and glorify its attackers'.

> The lady in the picture, is part of the consortium – ACLED, where we have Mediafax (Group Mediacoop), Zitamar Newss (Tom Bowker) and CIA. She was one of those who reported the fake news / alleged attack on Palma and Mueda.

> Unfortunately, the international media has these energumen [fanatical groups] sources of information to report about the terrorist attacks in Cabo Delgado. We always denounce that there are Mozambicans, anchored in journalism and but, who are at the service of foreign agendas . . . (Translated from Portuguese)

Facebook post 2: Denouncing publications on terrorism in Mozambique (April 2021)

One of the strategies used by the 'digital firefighters' is to associate the authors of publications that disinform about terrorism as people who are unpatriotic or who are politically at the service of external countries. In Facebook post 2, such individuals are referred to as 'anti Mozambique'. The alleged attack in Palma (Facebook post 2) did not take place and this was later confirmed by the Mozambican armed forces. The denunciation of the false claim about the attack made by one of the 'digital firefighters' suggested that the foreign journalist was in the service of foreign entities like the CIA who want to control the exploitation of natural resources in Cabo Delgado.

Case seven: Attack on Afungi

In April, a user shared a tweet about the tense situation in Palma. The tweet referred to a supposed attack that was later revealed to have never occurred. This episode happened precisely on the day of the attack in Palma, where there was no communication between that area and the rest of the country because of that attack.

> @User 1: Dear followers, please the disinformation on Palma and Afungi circulating is simply astonishing. Just ask yourself how the person got the

information, with communication towers down. How many can claim to have access now?

@User 2: True! I can see many eager to report that Afungi has been attacked since the PMC and Total left. For us Mozambican each attack is felt the soul. It's breath-taking. Heart-breaking. May God save from both the jihadists and fake news!

Tweet 2: Illustration of a case of disinformation on Twitter (April 2021)

The aforementioned illustration reveals that terrorism does not have borders. The spread of disinformation in Palma is directly linked to natural gas exploitation in Cabo Delgado province. This is because the main gas exploitation infrastructures are in Palma, many allegations have always indicated that terrorists wanted to occupy the facilities in order to dominate the gas market. Thus, spreading disinformation opens space for terrorists to act and profit from Palma gas. In other words, there is an economic motive to spread disinformation about Palma. In fact, the objective of terrorists is to have control of the billions of dollars in future gas profits. Conflict or war is a tactic to secure that objective. Terrorism is a tactic of war and propaganda is a tactic of war. Disinformation is a tactic of propaganda, and all have the same political and economic objective.

Conclusion

This chapter set out to examine the link between digital disinformation and terrorist attacks in Mozambique. It was noted that the absence of reliable information has created a vacuum in which disinformation has been able to thrive. Trying to verify online claims, often made anonymously, about inaccessible locations, in the fog of war about on-going conflict is extremely challenging. There are almost no existing studies on which to build, but this study has shown that disinformation is taking place, that there are multiple sources and forms of disinformation and that the government response is taking shape. The chapter began by locating the study in a historical context of repeated conflict and in the contest for control over narratives, territory and oilfields.

The historical, political and economic context is central to any analysis of Mozambique's emerging forms of disinformation. Although internet and social media use levels are relatively low in Mozambique, all sides in the conflict have found reasons to contest narratives online. The chapter has documented examples of disinformation that seek to further the interests of specific actors in the conflict. Drawing on Byman's framing (2018), several examples of disinformation that served the propaganda interests of insurgents were found. However, no examples of disinformation to further recruitment were identified.

Disinformation is deployed by insurgents, criminal gangs and journalists to serve a range of interests. The types of disinformation identified include false claims of military action (battles, sieges), false attacks, criminal gangs and manipulated videos. The chapter also identified three kinds of digital responses to disinformation by the Mozambican government: increasing its own online engagement, establishing a fact-checking website to rebut false claims and deploying digital firefighters to counter disinformation.

It illustrates that all disinformation is a reflection of power relationships: powerholders trying to influence the beliefs and behaviours of others. A key limitation of this research relates to the challenges of verifying truth claims in conflict zones. The fact that this is a relatively new and ongoing conflict adds to the fog of war. Nevertheless, this preliminary study has established the existence of several types of disinformation, which will provide a foundation for further research.

Bibliography

Alliance for Affordable Internet – A4AI (2017) *Mozambique Affordability Report Highlights*. https://a4ai.org/research/affordability-report-2017/.

Ayad et al. (2022) *Under-Moderated, Unhinged and Ubiquitous: Al-Shabaab and the Islamic State Networks on Facebook*. Beirut: Institute for Strategic Dialogue (ISD).

Byman, D. (2018) *An Intelligence Reserve Corps to Counter Terrorist Use of the Internet (AEGIS Paper Series)*. Hoover Institution.

Cabo Ligado Weekly (2022) June (20–26). https://www.caboligado.com/monthly-reports/cabo-ligado-monthly-october-2022 (accessed 10 August 2023).

Chichava, S. (2020) 'Os primeiros sinais do "Al Shabaab" em Cabo Delgado: Algumas histórias de Macomia e Ancuabe'. *IDeIAS*, 129: 1–3.

Crilley, R. and Chatterje-Doody, P. (2021) *Government Disinformation in War and Conflict*. London: Routledge.

DataReportal (2022) *Digital in Mozambique*. https://datareportal.com/reports/digital-2023-mozambique.

Dawson, C. (2019) *A-Z of Digital Research Methods*. London: Routledge.

Deibert, R. (2019) 'The Road to Digital Unfreedom: Three Painful Truths About Social Media'. *Journal of Democracy*, 30 (1): 25–39.

Feijó, J. (2020) 'Assimetrias no acesso ao estado: Um terreno fértil de penetração do jihadismo islâmico?'. *Observador Rural*, 93: 1–22.

Global Voices (2021) *Mozambican Government Reacts to Conflict by Imposing its Own Digital Narratives*. https://globalvoices.org/2021/12/14/mozambican-government-reacts-to-conflict-by-imposing-its-own-digital-narratives/ (accessed 11 August 2022).

Habibe, S., Forquilha, S. and Pereira, J. (2019) *Radicalização Islâmica no Norte de Moçambique: O Caso de Mocímboa da Praia*. Maputo: IESE.

Hootsuite (2023) *Digital in Mozambique*. Kepios . https://datareportal.com/reports/digital-2023-mozambique (accessed 14 August 2023).

International Organization for Migration – IOM (2023) *Conflict Displacement*. Maputo: Cabo Delgado.

Johnson, J. (2018) 'The Self-Radicalization of White Men: "Fake News" and the Affective Networking of Paranoia'. *Communication Culture & Critique*, 11 (1): 100–15.

Matsinhe, D. and Váloi, E. (2019) *The Genesis of Insurgency in Northern Mozambique, Institute for Security Studies*. Pretoria: ISS, Institute for Security Studies.

Morier-Genoud, E. (2020) 'The Jihadi Insurgency in Mozambique: Origins, Nature and Beginning'. *Journal of Eastern African Studies*, 14 (3): 396–412.

Ó Fathaigh, R., Helberger, N. and Appelman, N. (2021) 'The Perils of Legally Defining Disinformation'. *Internet Policy Review*, 10 (4): 1–25.

Piazza, J. (2022) 'Fake News: The Effects of Social Media Disinformation on Domestic Terrorism'. *Dynamics of Asymmetric Conflict*, 15 (1): 55–77.

Rogers, R. (2015) *Digital Methods*. Cambridge: MIT Press.

Ruohonen, J. (2021) 'A Comparative Study of Online Disinformation and Offline Protests'. *ArXiv*: 1–11.

Schmid, A. (2004) 'Terrorism – The Definitional Problem'. *Case Western Reserve Journal of International Law*, 36 (2): 375–420.

The Guardian (2019) 'Facebook Removes Africa Accounts Linked to Russian Troll Factory'.

The New York Times (2019) 'Russia Tests New Disinformation Tactics in Africa to Expand Influence'.

Tsandzana, D. (2020) 'Jovens, redes sociais da Internet e radicalização em Moçambique: Itinerários e ambiguidades'. In D. do Rosário, E. Guambe and E. de Salema (org.), *Democracia Multipartidária em Moçambique*, 299–314. Maputo: EISA.

Tumber, H. and Waisbord, S. (2021) *Media, Disinformation, and Populism: Problems and Responses*. London: Routledge.

UNESCO (2018) *Journalism, 'Fake News' & Disinformation, Handbook for Journalism Education and Training*. Paris: UNESCO – United Nations Educational, Scientific and Cultural.

UNHCR (2022) UN Refugee Agency UNHCR, End of Year Report.

UNODC (2012) *The use of the Internet for Terrorist Purposes*. New York: UNODC – United Nations Office on Drugs and Crime.

Unver, H. (2017) 'Digital Challenges to Democracy: Politics of Automation, Attention, and Engagement'. *Journal of International Affairs*, 71 (1): 127–46.

VOA (2020) *Filipe Nyusi acusa parte da imprensa de manipular informações sobre a guerra em Cabo Delgado*. https://www.voaportugues.com/a/filipe-nyusi-acusa-parte-da-imprensa-de-manipular-informa%C3%A7%C3%B5es-sobre-a-guerra-em-cabo-delgado/5676048.html (accessed 9 August 2022).

Wardle, C. and Derakhshan, H. (2018) *Information Disorder: Toward an Interdisciplinary Framework for Researchand Policy Making*. Strassbourg Cedex: Council of Europe.

Zitamar News (2020) *Nyusi Supporters Call for 'Extrajudicial' Measures to Silence Cabo Delgado Journalists*. https://www.zitamar.com/nyusi-supporters-call-extrajudicial-measures-silence-cabo-delgado-journalists/ (accessed 8 August 2022).

Chapter 5

On selfies and hashtags

Disinformation during armed conflict in Ethiopia

Yohannes Eneyew Ayalew and Atnafu Brhane Ayalew

This chapter considers the ways in which various actors effectively deploy selfies and hashtags as disinformation tools, which in turn pose a serious threat to the lives of civilians during the armed conflict in northern Ethiopia. Evidently, disinformation was spiked in its intensity during the armed conflict in the Northern Ethiopia between 2021 and 2022. Although the pattern, driver and audience of disinformation vary, its impact on political and social conversations is profound. Disinformation can help foment polarization, division and hatred and *sometimes* armed conflicts in Ethiopia. Internet penetration in Ethiopia is still low with an estimated 23.5 million people using the internet out of a population of over 120 million people. However, digital disinformation has a real-life impact in the context of the northern Ethiopian conflict.

This chapter poses the following questions: First, whether and to what extent disinformation has been a factor in the war in northern Ethiopia? Second, what changes to platform practices, regulation or law are needed to reduce the harm caused by disinformation? To answer these questions, this chapter uses a mixed method approach. It employs qualitative and doctrinal methods through a document analysis and reports of fact-checking organizations. It focuses on some case studies in Ethiopia and will analyse these through the lens of international human rights law. We applied the social media analytics tool Crowdtangle to assess how popular hashtags reach broader audience online. The chapter also examines three regulatory responses to deal with disinformation: information correction, content moderation and criminal sanction.

This chapter is divided into five sections. Section 1 reviews the existing scholarship on disinformation in Ethiopia. In Section 2 we examine the disinformation war in northern Ethiopia, focusing on the role of selfies and hashtags. The various regulatory responses put in place in Ethiopia, including legal and non-legal responses of disinformation, will be examined in Section 3. Finally, Section 4 summarizes the major findings and makes some recommendations on how to better protect Ethiopian citizens from disinformation, both off and online.

A brief background of the legislation and definitions of disinformation in Ethiopia

Ethiopia has a long history of criminalizing disinformation for the best part of a century. During the early days of the reign of Emperor Haile Selassie, spreading false information without adducing a source was considered a criminal act under the 1930 Imperial Order (Woldekirkos 2009). The Penal Code of 1957 would later become the first modern codified legislation that criminalized the spreading of false information.

While the spread and pattern of disinformation in Ethiopia is substantial, research on the subject remains very limited and patchy. Given that the phrase 'fake news' has become a cliché in the media and is part of the daily vocabulary for politicians, this chapter uses the concept of 'disinformation'. Although a number of attempts have been made to define disinformation, none of them have offered a universally accepted definition for the term 'disinformation'. In this chapter, we consider disinformation as 'Information that is false and deliberately created to harm a person, social group, organization or country' (Wardle and Derakhshan 2017; Howard 2006, 2020; Freelon and Wells 2020). This definition underlines the importance of the mental element (*mens rea*) in that the disseminator deliberately plans to sow false information. This mental (intention) element distinguishes disinformation from misinformation (Ibid).

The Ethiopian Hate Speech and Disinformation Prevention and Suppression Proclamation No.1185 (2020) defines disinformation as 'speech that is false, is disseminated by a person who knew or should reasonably have known the falsity of the information and is highly likely to cause a public disturbance, riot, violence or conflict' (Proclamation 2020, art 2(3)). However, this definition is broad and subjective which likely impinges the legality requirement of international human rights (Ayalew 2020; Feldstein 2021). In addition, concerns are growing over the issue of how one knows a given statement is false. Furthermore, who determines that a speech is false? Is it the attorney general, the courts or fact checkers? During Parliamentary deliberation, the Ethiopian deputy attorney general gave an answer to these questions by remarking that 'We know a statement is fake through evidence.' This suggests that it is for courts to determine this (Ayalew 2020). Second, the definition of disinformation under the Proclamation lacks precision as it fails to define what constitutes 'knew or should reasonably have known the falsity of the information'. Yet Article 29 of the Constitution of Ethiopia does not, by its terms, limit the freedom of expression to 'truthful information'; rather, it applies to 'information and ideas of all kinds'. Accordingly, the Proclamation violates the aforementioned constitutional provision.

It must be noted that disinformation is a growing problem in Ethiopia. Although its patterns, actors and audiences vary across different periods in Ethiopia, disinformation impedes citizens' ability to exercise their constitutionally guaranteed human rights and freedoms. It impacts the integrity of elections and the public's confidence and trust in democratic institutions in any society. Simply put, disinformation erodes the public's confidence in institutions and the rule of law and is an affront to democracy. The UN Special Rapporteur on freedom of opinion and expression expressed her concerns on the impacts of disinformation online in a 2021 report. She observed that as: 'When it interacts with political, social and economic grievances in the real world, disinformation can have serious consequences for democracy and human rights' (UN disinformation report 2021, para 2).

In recent times, viral disinformation has fuelled violence and armed conflict in Ethiopia. Online campaigns through hashtags have fed into an already explosive situation in a country with a history of ethnic polarization. This has been exacerbated by inflammatory messages that sow fear and confusion and further ignite tensions (AFP 2021).

The armed conflict in northern Ethiopia is being supported by online campaigns. According to various fact-checking organizations, supporters of both belligerents (government and Tigrayan People's Liberation Front (TPLF)) were spreading various forms of disinformation (Ayalew and Yimer 2021). For example, some users posted a viral video from the Nagorno-Karabakh conflict between Armenia and Azerbaijan to break the news that the Ethiopian government forces were scoring triumphs in the battle. The other instance of disinformation was when both government and TPLF supporters took to social media with various competing hashtags, such as #EthiopiaPrevails and #TigrayPrevails. These duelling hashtags sought to promote their own narratives to gain support and influence the international community (Wilmot et al. 2021).

The (disinformation) war in northern Ethiopia: Contexts and patterns

Ethiopia is a sovereign country found in East Africa and is the largest and second most populated country – next to Nigeria – in Africa. Historically Ethiopia is the oldest polity that preserved its civilization from foreign domination and successfully defended its sovereignty from colonial rule (Tibebu 1996). Ethiopia is also dubbed as the 'museum of people' because it is the home of more than eighty ethnic and tribal groups. However, since 1995, the country has been organizing the federation on basis of ethnicity and is divided into nine regional states. One of the reasons disinformation is especially dangerous in Ethiopia is that society is already deeply divided along ethno-nationalistic lines.

From 1995 to 2018, Ethiopia was ruled by a political coalition called the Ethiopian People's Revolutionary Democratic Front (EPRDF). Within the coalition the Tigray People's Liberation Front (TPLF) was the dominant party and had more influence on the 'deep state' (security, intelligence and economy) of the country than parties from Amhara, Oromia and the Southern Nations, Nationalities and People's region. Major ethnic groups in Ethiopia include the Oromo and Amhara, who were at the heart of the protests that led to Ethiopia's tortuous transition to democracy in 2018. In 2018, Prime Minister Abiy Ahmed took power and dissolved the EPRDF collective and fused it into a single party called 'Prosperity Party'. However, TPLF refused to join the newly formed party due to its acute disagreement on the role of previous coalitions and were left out in the process. Long-simmering political tensions with ethnic undertones were brought to a boil in November 2020, with the outbreak of war in northern Ethiopia. The immediate cause of the outbreak was the unprovoked attack on the Northern Command of the Ethiopian National Army by the TPLF forces. As will be clear from the following paragraphs, the war in northern Ethiopia was not only a kinetic one but also involved information warfare, with disinformation used as a central weapon.

Before delving into trends and drivers of disinformation during armed conflict, it is important to briefly set out the context of the conflict in northern Ethiopia. In many modern armed conflicts, a legitimate question is asked as to who starts the war and whether the war is just or not. In the case of the war in northern Ethiopia, there is a disagreement as to who started the conflict. According to a joint probe report of the UN Office of the High Commissioner for Human Rights and Ethiopian Human Rights Commission, the war broke out due to the Tigray People's Liberation Front's unprovoked offensive against the Northern Command of the Ethiopian Army on 3 November 2020. Following this, Ethiopian Prime Minister Abiy Ahmed ordered a military offensive against TPLF forces on 4 November 2020 (Joint report 2021, para 76). Of course, knowing the *casus belli* (who or what started the war) has many implications. For instance, the law on the use of force forbids the use of force as provided under Article 2(4) of the UN Charter. It also constitutes a crime of (internal) aggression despite the joint investigation finding that the war was a non-international armed conflict, or a conventional civil war (Joint report 2021, para 37). While the pretext for the outbreak of the war is the assault of the Northern command by TPLF forces, the fundamental bone of contention is structural problems including disagreement over nation building, the squandered political transition and abortion of the transitional justice are the major factors at play that form the prelude to the armed conflict.

Importantly, the full extent of the human rights and humanitarian casualties of the war in northern Ethiopia is not yet fully reported. It is not the aim of this chapter to establish individual criminal responsibility of persons implicated in those crimes; rather, this chapter makes a reference to contrasting examples to illustrate how various forms of disinformation, mainly selfies and hashtags, are deployed by the supporters of the warring parties.

In addition to kinetic warfare, the civil war in northern Ethiopia was fought online through various forms of disinformation. Before the outbreak of the war, a flurry of disinformation and propaganda in the form of labelling, demonization and military parade was deployed by both the federal government and Tigrayan People's Liberation Front (TPLF) forces. For example, TPLF forces were briefing news organizations that they possessed one of the largest stocks of heavy weaponry in Africa and claimed to have more than 250,000 active combatants (a claim that was not confirmed by fact-checking organizations). Nevertheless, the growing role of disinformation in fuelling polarization and violence has regained increasing traction after the war broke out in northern Ethiopia on 3 November 2020.

Initial discourses on social media were limited to a polarized exchange of ideas and skewed narratives as to who started the war and the attacks of the Northern Command of the Ethiopian National Army. In the midst of the armed conflict in Ethiopia, Frances Haugen, a whistle-blower and former employee of Facebook, made significant revelations (Horwitz, 2021). Her revelations helped to shed light on how social media platforms (and mainly Facebook) have been involved in spreading unregulated content including disinformation in Ethiopia and beyond.

It must be noted that disinformation is not an isolated incident in the context of the war in northern Ethiopia; rather, it is an inter-connected pattern and process between different actors to win battles and terrorize the civilian population. Sympathizers of belligerents have used various strategies of disinformation that Phillip Howard has described as 'lie machines'. These comprise of people and the technologies for deliberately disseminating the falsehoods they come up with (Howard 2020). Of course, lie machines put information technology into service for a political ideology (and for instance, defeating the enemy in the northern Ethiopian conflict) by generating computational propaganda through device networks, social media algorithms and personal data. Ultimately, disseminators of disinformation (be it government, political parties, insurgent or rebel groups or private actors) effectively use social media and internet technologies to manipulate or shape public opinion (Bradshaw et al. 2021). To this end, selfies and hashtags were among the various strategies of disinformation and propaganda used by the supporters of belligerents in the course of the armed conflict in Ethiopia, as the next subsections present.

Selfies

The saying 'a picture is worth a thousand words' is a commonly cited adage in multiple cultures. It means that complex and multiple ideas can be conveyed by a single still image. In addition, it conveys its meaning or essence more effectively and powerfully than a mere verbal description. This adage is particularly pertinent in the digital age when disinformation or propaganda disseminated via images or selfies reaches millions of people in real time with visual effects that can be more potent than the text (Michael et al. 2020). When disinformation is disseminated through images, its credibility is higher than textual disinformation (Hameleers et al. 2020). This is because the use of visuals in disinformation is likely to be motivated by the premise that images are a direct representation of reality and as such are perceived as more credible than more abstract forms of communication such as words (Messaris and Abraham 2001). While social media platforms have improved the accessibility of visual messages, visual communication as a propaganda tool has a long history (Bagchi 2016). According to the theory of normative conduct, individuals get motivated by what most people do since people often follow the actions of the majority by mimicking behaviour (Ittefaq 2023). Thus, it follows that when war correspondents and supporters of belligerents take selfies to spread falsehoods, there is a high incidence of disseminating disinformation by individuals and civilians.

Given poor digital media literacy skills, social media users in Ethiopia are exposed to fake images or real images with manipulated or doctored content. Bad actors can thus easily publish fake visual content or propaganda to deceive or influence their viewers, inflicting cognitive stress, exploiting prior beliefs in conflict situations or similar contexts, or influencing individuals' decisions and actions (Shen et al. 2019).

As shall be shown in the following, propagandists and sympathizers of warring parties were spreading various forms of propaganda through visual selfies and images to create an atmosphere of fear, panic and terror among the civilian population in various towns of northern Ethiopia. These selfies and images might not be false in a strict sense; rather they are sometimes framed and presented sensationally in a manner that could reasonably terrorize and intentionally deceive the civilian population; in the latter case, they may amount to disinformation. In this sense, propaganda resembles disinformation since the communicator intentionally distributes incorrect information to achieve a certain (e.g. winning battles and scoring political points as shown Figures 5.1 and 5.2) goal (Marwick and Lewis 2017). Crucially, propaganda and disinformation are usually motivated by ideology, money and/or status and attention or a combination of one or more of these categories (Jack 2017;

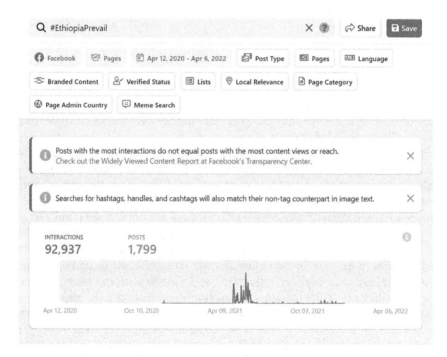

Figure 5.1 Ethiopia prevail campaign. *Source*: authors.

Caplan and Boyd 2018) To some extent, both propaganda and disinformation converge and cover common grounds. Nevertheless, propaganda is a discrete concept. According to Taylor (2003: 6), propaganda is 'the deliberate attempt to persuade people to think and behave in a desired way'. This implies propaganda at least involves some effort at persuasion while the message is not necessarily false and intentional like disinformation. For example, TPLF combatants and frontline paramilitaries posting selfie images allegedly showing TPLF forces conquering Wollo University, Dessie, in the Amhara region. This was followed by a digital geo-location analysis by 'Ethiopia Map' and posts on its Twitter and Telegram pages.

While the pattern and extent of propaganda vary considerably, government supporters and activists also used selfie images/videos to assert victory over TPLF forces in the Amhara region. For example, an individual (whose name is withheld for anonymity) who initially identified as an activist later became associated with a paramilitary group, supporting the allied Federal, Amhara and Afar forces. This person utilized their personal Facebook account, boasting over 38,000 followers, to stream a live selfie video. In the video, he made assertions that the allied forces were making significant progress against TPLF forces in Borru Meda, located on the outskirts of Dessie in the Amhara region, despite the fact that TPLF was scoring a victory against government forces. Nonetheless, the said activist using selfie-video claimed that the government forces were winning (the picture is withheld by authors for anonymity). It must be noted that these claims of the government were not fact checked either.

On 6 August 2021, a Twitter account named Ethiopia Map took on Twitter and posted that TPLF forces were allegedly claiming to have captured the oldest Ethiopian town, Lalibela, after combatants and non-combatants posted a selfie-like picture in front of Nib International Bank Lalibela branch (the picture is withheld by authors for anonymity). On 13 August 2021, Ethiopia Map's Telegram Channel posted selfie pictures portraying TPLF forces standing in front of the Commercial Bank of Ethiopia Nefas Mewucha branch and Nefas Mewucha Polytechnic College (Ibid.).

While these selfies seem to be accurate evidence of events on the ground, none of these pictures have been fact-checked by independent fact checking organizations. It should be noted that the propaganda and disinformation disseminated through selfies on social media has had a real-life impact on civilians in the northern Ethiopia conflict (Zelalem and Guest 2021).

In the course of the northern Ethiopian conflict, many civilians left their homes in the Amhara region and were displaced due to orchestrated propaganda and deception campaigns by the supporters of TPLF (and sometimes by government sympathizers), who used selfies and manipulated images on Facebook, Twitter and Telegram to spread panic and terror as well as concern over cities falling under the control of rebels. Strictly speaking, in Ethiopia, using selfie images to persuade adversaries and cause panic and terror against the civilian population would fall in the ambit of propaganda and not disinformation, unless such acts cross the legal threshold of disinformation under Article 2(3) of the Hate Speech and Disinformation Prevention and Suppression Proclamation No.1185 (2020). The legislation defines disinformation as 'speech that is false, is disseminated by a person who knew or should reasonably have known the falsity of the information and is highly likely to cause a public disturbance, riot, violence or conflict'. The next section presents how hashtags are deployed as means of disinformation in the context of the northern Ethiopian conflict.

Hashtags

Hashtags on social media have helped to amplify political narratives of politicians and their supporters (Egbunike 2018). Undeniably, hashtags have the potential to create a bandwagon effect as some users on social media repeat online claims without questioning their authenticity (Keller et al. 2020; Linvill and Warren 2020). However, hashtags have played an instrumental role in shaping narratives and spreading falsehoods and coordinating disinformation in relation to the northern Ethiopia conflict. Technically, hashtags can be used to identify posts shared by a large number of users using identical terms or identifiers. When it comes to the northern Ethiopian conflict, there are two antagonistic camps that were vying for narrative control in the digital space. The first camp is a pro-government group, and the second camp is the TPLF supporters' group.

The pro-government group comprises Ethiopian government officials, a coalition of Pan-Ethiopian diaspora advocacy, individuals and organizations. For this group, the unprovoked attack of the Northern Command of the National Defense Forces by TPLF is the common rallying cause to stand for national unity. Thus, state actors and networks of non-government supporters launched their own campaigns to influence international audiences and counter-competing narratives by supporters of TPLF. For the pro-government camp, their common cause revolves around national unity and seeks to promote a concept of Ethiopian 'unity' that Abiy has pursued since forming the Prosperity Party. The most commonly used hashtag campaigns in pro-government circles include #UnityForEthiopia, #EthiopiaPrevails and #NoMore (Wilmot et al. 2021).

Our Crowdtangle analysis shows that the #EthiopiaPrevail hashtag attracted more than 92,000 interactions on Facebook between 12 April 2020 and 6 April 2022. This hashtag reached its climax when Ethiopian forces claimed victory over the TPLF forces and gained control of major towns in Tigray.

The second camp comprises Tigrayan activists and TPLF supporters in the diaspora who want to control the narrative in the digital space. Since the war broke out in early November 2020, Tigrayan activists began using Twitter and Facebook to create and promote hashtags such as #StopTheWarOnTigray, #TigrayGenocide and #IStandWithTigray (Wilmot et al. 2021). These campaigns were responsible for large volumes of tweets and posts in November 2020, during the earliest stages of the conflict.

Some of the hashtags seem to be disseminated in a coordinated manner to influence international policymakers. There are pre-planned standby hashtags

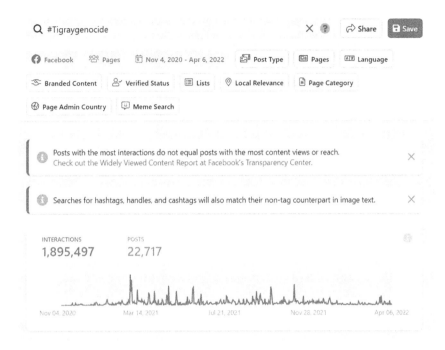

Figure 5.2 The hashtag #TigrayGenocide has attracted close to 2 million interactions on Facebook between 4 November 2020 and 6 April 2022. *Source*: authors.

and list of actors to be tagged. For example, a Tweet posted by the Twitter user 'Stand With Tigray', who has almost 50,000 followers. According to the account biography Stand With Tigray Inc is a US-registered 501(c)(3) non-profit organization whose mission is to raise global awareness and end the atrocities in Tigray using advocacy campaigns. This account appears to be orchestrating a coordinated online campaign to influence international policymakers. The Tweet lists a series of hashtags that followers can use to aggregate their posting alongside a list of campaign targets for the messaging including several UN agencies and powerful individuals (Source: https://twitter.com/SWTigray/status /1339078254410387457).

Take for example, in a Tweet posted on 6 September 2021 this Twitter user used #MaikadraMasacare hashtag. The hashtag disseminated the false claim that the Maikadra massacre was committed against Tigrayans, when in fact it was perpetrated against Amhara civilians (Joint report 2021, ¶ 113; #StandWith Tigray https://twitter.com/SWTigray/status/1434701336604561415).

From the outset, some sympathizers and political analysts were using different techniques to hoodwink the public and aggrandize the military might of TPLF. For instance, Tigrayan campaign participants and operators spread some unverified rumours which may amount to deliberate deception and disinformation. Some of these rumours were first posted by TPLF-officials. A prominent example of the spread of disinformation early in the conflict is the rumour that the Tekeze dam was bombed in early November, which appears to have originated with TPLF leader Debretsion Gebremichael on Tigrai Television, which could have been an intentional effort to spread a false narrative. Yet, there was no evidence the dam was bombed, as confirmed by fact-checking bodies like HaqCheck, and the claim was later found to be false (Reuters 2020).

In the middle of the conflict, war correspondents and supporters of the government were also misleading the public by providing false accounts of military triumphs (breaking) news and coordinated hashtags (Ayalew and Yimer 2021). Moreover, pro-government groups promoted hashtag campaigns at times sharing slogans, government statements and government-backed fact checks. They also spread media reports that supported their narrative of the conflict, as well as content that accused Tigrayan activists of being part of a massive TPLF disinformation campaign (Wilmot et al. 2021).

The disinformation war and hashtag campaigns by both camps is aimed at getting maximum attention and 'trending' on Twitter, thus winning control of the political narratives in the digital space. Specifically, both camps have created click-to-tweet (i.e. a free link generator that allows users to share pre-made content through their Twitter account) campaigns to ensure hashtags such as #TigrayGenocide and #NoMore trended. A key goal for both sides has been to have their narratives influence international actors and supporters. To counter this manipulation, Twitter suspended and disabled its 'trend service' in Ethiopia from 6 November 2021.

The following is a Twitter Safety Statement issued on 6 November 2021:

> Given the imminent threat of physical harm, we've also temporarily disabled Trends in Ethiopia. Alongside continued efforts to disrupt platform manipulation, we hope this measure will reduce the risks of coordination that could incite violence or cause harm.
> (Source: https://twitter.com/TwitterSafety/status/1456813765387816965?s=20)

Although Twitter claimed that removing Trends in Ethiopia could help 'reduce the risks of coordination that could incite violence or cause harm', this does not appear to have worked. When one examines the volume of English-language conversations on Twitter about the conflict before and after Trends were removed, there is no discernible change in the volume of tweets or the prevalence of disinformation and hate speech. This suggests that the Twitter intervention did not work as intended (Brown and Knight 2022).

Regulatory approaches to prevent disinformation in Ethiopia

Disinformation undermines the enjoyment of human rights and fundamental freedoms (Jones 2019). According to Kate Jones (2019), disinformation impinges on a broad range of human rights such as the right to freedom of thought and

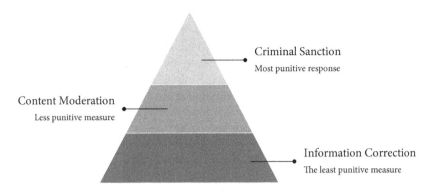

Figure 5.3 Regulatory responses on disinformation. *Source*: authors.

opinion, the right to privacy, the right to freedom of expression and the right to vote in elections. This implies that disinformation disempowers individuals, robbing them of their autonomy to search, receive and share information and form opinions (UN Disinformation report 2021, para 84).

Regulating the threats of disinformation requires multi-dimensional, multi-stakeholder responses that are well grounded in human rights law. In addition, as Irene Khan suggests, it requires the proactive engagement of states, companies, international organizations, civil society and the media (UN Disinformation report 2021, para 87). In particular, encouraging independent journalism and building robust public information regimes are important antidotes to disinformation. In the Ethiopian context, there are some normative hopes to foster independent media; however, public information regimes are still feeble and insufficient.

In regard to regulation, there are at least three approaches to tackling disinformation. These are information correction, content moderation and criminal sanction (Helm and Hitoshi 2021) While information correction and content moderation are inherently non-punitive actions, criminal sanctions are punitive measures that could entail penal reasonability for breaching a legal provision on disinformation.

Information correction

Information correction is the least intrusive mechanism to alleviate the dangers of disinformation and propaganda in the digital space. Technically, information correction does not directly interfere with false or misleading information or access to it; instead, it creates a designated digital platform where the falsity of a particular content is publicly announced (Helm and Hitoshi 2021). This approach is premised upon the idea that the best mechanism to deal with disinformation is through a free flow of information in the 'marketplace of ideas' and individuals are presumed to be rational thinkers who seek out truth when they find falsehoods or problematic content. Thus, instead of severe criminal sanctions, correcting falsehoods through information correction is paramount in a democratic society (Helm and Hitoshi 2021).

Social media platforms such as Twitter and Facebook have adopted information correction initiatives on their own, specifically by labelling content deemed to be 'synthetic' or 'manipulated'. For example, this approach was widely used on Facebook when users posted problematic content about Covid-19.

In Ethiopia too, information correction regimes could thrive if the government facilitates the free flow of information by setting up a regular press briefing and allowing independent fact-checking bodies. One of the contributing causes to the rise of disinformation in Ethiopia is the government's unwillingness to inform the public in a timely fashion about what is going on in the country. Part of the problem is the absence of an independent institution to provide timely and up-to-date information to the public. Following widespread criticism, in October 2021 the government set up an institution called 'Government Communication Service' which is meant to provide and facilitate access to information in the country. It is too early to assess the overall performance of the Government Communication Service, but there are reasonable grounds to believe that this institution is not living up to the public's expectations. During the height of the armed conflict in northern Ethiopia, it gave irregular, intermittent press briefings and statements to journalists and the general public. Indeed, the government seems to be reluctant to facilitate the free flow of information through formal channels. Ironically, the government sometimes leaks or communicates important information through informal channels on social media such as using paid and pro-government activist(s).

In addition, the growing dominance of the government in fact-checking services is a stumbling block for effective information correction. When the war started, the government established a body named State of Emergency Fact Check and later renamed it Ethiopia Current Issues Fact Check. While the country's sovereignty and territorial integrity by then were at stake, it's also important to note that government-led fact-checking casts doubt on the impartiality and neutrality of the service. In effect, the government was seemingly restricting independent fact-checking and access to verified information.

Nonetheless, information correction is not a silver bullet for tackling disinformation. The key flaw of this mechanism for tackling disinformation is that psychological biases may make people resistant to information correction, particularly where disinformation is consistent with their existing beliefs or cultural outlook.

Content moderation

Compared to information correction, content moderation is a more intrusive mechanism of regulation to deal with disinformation. Content moderation is an intricate process by which a team of content moderators reviews content that internet users have flagged as inappropriate or false. This can be done manually or through artificial intelligence (AI), and any false content is taken down or blocked

(UN Special Rapporteur content moderation report 2018, A/HRC/38/35, paras 32–38).

Through content moderation, social media platforms can play a significant role in the elimination of disinformation on their sites (Marsden et al. 2020). However, content moderation is a challenging undertaking. This is because of the fact that online communities and moderators walk the tightrope between overuse and underuse, as well as aggressive curation and insensitive curation (Grimmelmann 2015; Klonick 2018; Ayalew 2021). To put it another way, when platforms are aggressive and hypersensitive about removing potentially harmful content like disinformation, particularly in the absence of any oversight, due process and accountability mechanisms, they may end up restricting free speech (Kaye 2019; York 2021).

The African Commission on Human and Peoples' Rights (ACHPR) in its 2021 landmark resolution expressed its concerns about the challenges of content take-downs by algorithms which may negatively impact relevant evidence of human rights abuse or discrimination against particular populations (ACHPR/Res. 473 (EXT.OS/ XXXI) 2021, para VI; Salau 2020). This argument is compelling because social media platforms are overly relying on algorithms to flag problematic content. One possible explanation for the absence of effective content moderation is the perceived lack of linguistic capability of social media platforms to interpret content posted in indigenous African languages (Zaugg 2020; Ayalew 2021).

They are several additional challenges with content moderation by social media companies in Ethiopia. These include insensitivity towards local contexts, for example, language and culture, a low number of content moderators who are fluent in local Ethiopian languages, partiality towards certain content and an over-reliance on algorithmic methods (Ayalew 2021).

While the full extent of the war in northern Ethiopia is yet to be recorded, platforms should undergo an ongoing due diligence assessment of how their services and products are causing harm and offline violence to civilians in Ethiopia. Importantly, the Oversight Board suggested Meta undertake a due diligence assessment in Ethiopia after unverified information was contested on Facebook (Decision 2021–014-FB-UA, 2021). It ruled that 'Meta should commission an independent human rights due diligence assessment on how Facebook and Instagram have been used to spread hate speech and unverified rumours that heighten the risk of violence in Ethiopia'. The Board also highlighted that Meta needs to assess and review the success of measures it took to prevent the misuse of its products and services in Ethiopia. Interestingly, the Oversight Board underscored that such an assessment should review Meta's language capabilities in Ethiopia and whether they are adequate to protect the rights of its users.

Criminal sanctions

The final approach to deal with disinformation is criminal sanction. Indeed, criminal sanction is an effective regulatory response due to its deterrent effect, based on the premise of criminal law, against the dissemination of such news in the first place (Helm and Hitoshi 2021). Certainly, criminal sanction can be justified when the legal basis for imposing it is well-grounded in international human rights law. This is particularly true when it is tailored in a way that specifically, and with sufficient precision, addresses the legitimate interests of national security, public order, public health or morals, as provided under Article 19(3) of the ICCPR and Article 29(6) of the Ethiopian Constitution (UN Human Rights Committee 2011).

Previously, dissemination of intentional false rumours was addressed in Article 479 of the 1957 Penal Code which stipulated that 'Whoever spreads alarm among the public: (b) by deliberately spreading false rumours concerning such happenings or general disturbances, or imminent catastrophe or calamity; is punishable with simple imprisonment or fine.' A similar corresponding provision is found under Article 485 of the 2004 Revised Criminal Code of Ethiopia.

In addition, Article 480 of the 1957 Penal Code which was later amended by Article 486 of the 2004 Revised Criminal Code criminalizes inciting the public through false information. Article 486 reads:

> Whoever, apart from crimes against the security of the State (Arts 240, 257 (e) and 261 (a)): a) starts or spreads false rumours, suspicions or false charges against the Government or the public authorities or their activities, thereby disturbing or inflaming the public opinion or creating a danger of public disturbances is punishable with simple imprisonment or fine, in serious cases, with rigorous imprisonment not exceeding three years.

However, this provision has been repealed by Article 9 of the Hate Speech and Disinformation Prevention and Suppression Proclamation No 1185/2020. While the Proclamation repealed the spreading of false information under Article 486, it is unclear why the Proclamation left Article 485 which criminalizes causing alarm or panic among the public through false information.

A criminal provision on causing alarm to the public through panic or terror is reminiscent of the colonial legacy of sedition and public alarm laws. According to the African Commission on Human and Peoples' Rights 2010 Resolution, criminal defamation, false news and libel laws are repressive laws and are sometimes invoked in connection to national security (ACHPR/Res.169(XLVIII)). In *Agnès Uwimana Nkusi and Saïdati Mukakibibi v. Rwanda*, the African Commission upheld: 'Criminal defamation and insult laws not only violate article 9 of the African Charter but impede development in open and democratic societies.' To this end, we suggest that Ethiopian authorities repeal Article 485 of the 2004 Criminal Code on causing public alarm, which has roots in colonial times (although Ethiopia was never formally colonized) and replace it with a law that is in line with international human rights law.

Reverting to the substantive provision of the Ethiopian Disinformation Prevention Proclamation No.1185/2020, it criminalizes the dissemination of disinformation. Article 5 provides that 'Disseminating of any disinformation on public meeting by means of broadcasting, print or social media using text, image, audio or video is a prohibited act.' Thus, the law forbids dissemination of disinformation through any means including offline and online mediums. In terms of criminal liability, Article 7(3) outlines what the perpetrators of disinformation could face. Consequently, the law provides 'Any person who commits acts proscribed under Article 5 shall be punished with simple imprisonment not exceeding one year or a fine not exceeding 50,000 birr.'

Specifically, Article 7(4) of the Proclamation has a stern criminal provision that includes both imprisonment and hefty fines when the crime of disinformation is committed through a social media account having more than 5,000 followers or through a broadcaster. Thus, if the offence of disinformation has been committed through a social media account having more than 5,000 followers or through broadcasters, the person responsible for the act will be punished with imprisonment not exceeding three years or a fine not exceeding 100,000 birr (3,000 USD). This punishment may go higher in grave cases if violence or public disturbance occurs due to the dissemination of disinformation. In such cases, the punishment will be rigorous imprisonment ranging for a period between two years and five years, as stipulated under Article 7(5).

It is bizarre to see the 5,000 followers' standard as a threshold; the move seems to be novel and arbitrary. It is unclear whether it is based on Facebook's friendship limit or comparative experience. Unlike Egypt where the law obliges personal social media accounts with 5,000 followers to come under Law on the Organisation of Press, Media and the Supreme Council of Media 2018, the 5,000 standard in Ethiopia is stricter and is aggravating grounds for a charge rather than a starting point.

Moreover, the fine is large compared to the fines for ordinary crimes in the Criminal Code. Also, given the modest income of many social media writers, this law could lead to self-censoring of free speech on the internet and could force some to reduce their followers to avoid punishment. The Proclamation would have a chilling effect on freedom of expression on the internet. It stipulates that if the offense of disinformation was committed through a social media account with more than 5,000 followers, the person responsible for the act shall be punished with simple imprisonment not exceeding three years, and/or a fine not exceeding 100,000 birr (3,000 USD). This is an instance where journalists and activists could be targeted for having 5,000 followers and found to have committed a crime of disinformation. Ultimately, this would have the effect of chilling freedom of expression online in Ethiopia.

However, there are some potential defences that absolve criminal responsibility under Article 6 of the Proclamation. Accordingly, a speech will not be considered as disinformation and its dissemination is not prohibited if it is part of: (1) an academic study or scientific inquiry, (2) a news report, analysis or political critique, (3) artistic creativity, performance or other forms of expression, (4) religious teaching. Furthermore, a certain speech will not be considered disinformation and prohibited if a reasonable effort has been made under the circumstances by the person making the speech to ensure the veracity of the speech or if the speech is more inclined to political commentary and critique instead of being a factual or news report.

In practice, nonetheless, the Disinformation Prevention and Suppression Proclamation is being applied against journalists such as Yayesew Shimelis and Bekalu Alamrew. Shimelis was arrested and charged in April 2020 for allegedly violating the Hate Speech and Disinformation Prevention and Suppression Proclamation by disseminating disinformation. The charge relates to a Facebook post that suggested the government had prepared 200,000 burial places in response to Covid-19, a claim that the Ministry of Health found to be false. Alamrew, who is an Ethiopian journalist employed by the YouTube broadcaster Awlo Media Center, was arrested on 4 November 2020. The charge was disseminating false news in connection with an unspecified media report which alleged that the federal government and National Army were directly involved in the killing of 200 ethnic Amharas. However, an Amnesty International probe found that fifty-four Amharas were brutally massacred in Wollega in November 2020 by suspected members of the Oromo Liberation Army. Thus, the claim by the journalist that the government was responsible seemed to be false, even though other investigative reports argue that the government was complicit. He was granted bail and released after being detained for over two weeks. Given their cases are being litigated and pending, we will not comment on the merits of the case (CPJ, 2020).

Conclusion

Disinformation continues to pose serious regulatory and institutional challenges in Ethiopia. The chapter has demonstrated how selfies and hashtags are telling examples of disinformation used by the supporters of belligerents to spread their disinformation campaigns and narratives in the course of the armed conflict in Ethiopia. While a selfie image or video in a strict sense resembles propaganda, it may be used to spread disinformation. Similarly, a hashtag may be deployed in a click-to-tweet/post form to deliberately circulate falsehoods about the conflict in Ethiopia.

Nevertheless, regulating disinformation is a delicate exercise since it requires striking a balance between protecting freedom of expression and corresponding interests, such as public safety and security. The chapter has argued that a multidimensional and multi-stakeholder response that is well grounded in human rights law and the proactive engagement of States, companies, international organizations, civil society and the media is an important mechanism to minimize disinformation, both offline and online. While social media platforms do not have a direct responsibility for third party content in their websites, they are expected to respect and protect human rights, in particular, to conduct due diligence to meaningfully 'identify, prevent, mitigate and account for' actual and potential human rights impact throughout the company's operations and to provide for, or cooperate in, the remediation of adverse human rights impacts associated with their business as per the UN Guiding Principles on Business and Human Rights (UNGPs) (UNGPs 2011, Principle 17). Flowing from this, we suggest that social media platforms should redouble their efforts to implement non-punitive measures such as information correction and content moderation and to train their algorithms in different Ethiopian languages which, in turn, effectively help stamp out disinformation (Chonka et al. 2022).

While Ethiopia has enacted criminal legislation on disinformation, we suggest the government repeal Article 485 of the 2004 Criminal Code on causing public alarm as it has roots in colonial times, undermines freedom of expression and is out of step with international human rights law.

In addition, civil societies should redouble their fact-checking and digital literacy efforts and redirect resources to support such initiatives. Thus far, fact-checking efforts in Ethiopia are being undertaken by a handful of individuals and civil society organizations with limited resources and staff. Therefore, supporting fact-checking and digital literacy initiatives is paramount to fighting disinformation. Going forward, governments and social media companies should support studies and research on the real-life impact of disinformation on human rights in Ethiopia. More specifically, future studies should focus on disinformation and algorithmic bias in content moderation. In addition, more attention should be given to human rights due diligence of social media platforms in Ethiopia and improving tech-friendly systems in the fight against disinformation in the digital ecosystem.

Bibliography

AFP (2021) 'Ethiopia's Warring Sides Locked in Disinformation Battle'.<https:// www.france24.com/en/live-news/20211222-ethiopia-s-warring-sides-locked-in -disinformation-battle> (accessed 22 December 2021).

Ayalew, R. and Solomon, Y. (2021) 'Does Social Media Intensify the Conflict in Northern Ethiopia?'. *Addis Zeybe*. Addis Ababa, Ethiopia.

Ayalew, Y. E. (2020) 'Assessing the Limitations to Freedom of Expression on the Internet in Ethiopia Against the African Charter on Human and Peoples' Rights'. *African Human Rights Law Journal*, 20: 315–45.

Ayalew, Y. E. (2021) 'From Digital Authoritarianism to Platforms' Leviathan Power: Freedom of Expression in the Digital age Under Siege in Africa'. *Mizan Law Review*, 15 (2): 455–92.

Bagchi, D. (2016) 'Printing, Propaganda, and Public Opinion in the age of Martin Luther'. *Oxford Research Encyclopedia of Religion*: 1–25. https://oxfordre.com/religion/view/10 .1093/acrefore/9780199340378.001.0001/acrefore-9780199340378-e-269.

Bradshaw, S., Bailey, H. and Howard, P. N. (2021) *Industrialized Disinformation: 2020 Global Inventory of Organized Social Media Manipulation*. Oxford: Oxford Internet Institute, 8.

Brown, M. A. and Knight, T. (2022) *Trendless Fluctuation? How Twitter's Ethiopia Interventions May (Not) Have Worked*. Austin, TX: Tech Policy Press (accessed 28 May 2022).

Caplan, R. and Danah, B. (2018) 'Who's Playing Who? Media Manipulation in an Era of Trump'. In Zizi Papacharissi and Pablo J. Boczkowski (eds), *Trump and the Media*, 49. Cambridge, MA: The MIT Press.

Chonka, P., Diepeveen, S. and Haile, Y. (2022) 'Algorithmic Power and African Indigenous Languages: Search Engine Autocomplete and the Global Multilingual Internet'. *Media, Culture & Society*, 45 (2): 246–65, at 258.

Committee to Protect Journalists (CPJ) (2020) 'Ethiopian Journalist Bekalu Alamrew Arrested, Accused of Disseminating False News'. November 10. New York, NY (accessed 28 July 2022).

Egbunike, N. (2018) *Hashtags: Social Media, Politics and Ethnicity in Nigeria*. Lagos, Nigeria: Narrative Landscape Press.

Feldstein, S. (2021) *The Rise of Digital Repression*. Oxford University Press, 177–211.

Freelon, D. and Wells, C. (2020) 'Disinformation as Political Communication'. *Political Communication*, 37: 145–56.

Grimmelmann, J. (2015) 'The Virtues of Moderation'. *Yale Journal of Law & Technology*, 17 (42): 47.

Hameleers, M., Powell, T. E., Van Der Meer, T. G. L. A. and Bos, L. (2020) 'A Picture Paints a Thousand Lies? The Effects and Mechanisms of Multimodal Disinformation and Rebuttals Disseminated via Social Media', *Political Communication*, 37: 281–301.

Helm, R. K. and Hitoshi, N. (2021) 'Regulatory Responses to "Fake News" and Freedom of Expression: Normative and Empirical Evaluation'. *Human Rights Law Review*, 21: 302–28.

Horwitz, J. (2021) 'The Facebook Whistleblower, Frances Haugen, Says She Wants to Fix the Company, Not Harm It'. *The Wall Street Journal*, The Facebook Files Article 9 (accessed 28 April 2022).

Howard, P. N. (2006) *New Media Campaigns and the Managed Citizen*. Cambridge: Cambridge University Press.

Howard, P. N. (2020) *Lie Machines: How to Save Democracy From Troll Armies, Deceitful Robots, Junk News Operations, and Political Operatives*. New Haven, CT: Yale University Press, 15.

Ittefaq, M., Kamboh, S. A. and Abwao, M. (2023) 'COVID-19 Vaccine Selfie: A Modest Endeavor to Increase Vaccine Acceptance'. *Psychology & Health*, 38: 209–13.

Jack, C. (2017) 'What's Propaganda Got to Do With It?'. *Data & Society: Points*, January 5 (accessed 26 May 2022).

Jones, K. (2019) *Online Disinformation and Political Discourse: Applying a Human Rights Framework*. London: Chatham House.

Kaye, D. (2019) 'Speech Police: The Global Struggle to Govern the Internet'. *Columbia Global Reports*, 112–26.

Keller, F. B., Schoch, D., Stier, S. and Yang, J. (2020) 'Political Astroturfing on Twitter: How to Coordinate a Disinformation Campaign'. *Political Communication*, 37: 256–80.

Klonick, K. (2018) 'The New Governors: The People, Rules, and Processes Governing Online Speech'. *Harvard Law Review*, 131: 1598.

Linvill, D. L. and Warren, P. L. (2020) 'Troll Factories: Manufacturing Specialized Disinformation on Twitter'. *Political Communication*, 37 (4): 447–67.

Marsden, C., Meyer, T. and Brown, I. (2020) 'Platform Values and Democratic Elections: how can the law Regulate Digital Disinformation?'. *Computer Law and Security Review*, 36: 1–18.

Marwick, A. and Lewis, R. (2017) 'Media Manipulation and Disinformation online'. *Data and Society Research Institute*, 1–104 (accessed 26 May 2022).

Messaris, P. and Abraham, L. (2001) 'The Role of Images in Framing News Stories'. In Stephen D. Reese, et al (eds), *Framing Public Life: Perspectives on Media and Our Understanding of the Social World*, 215. Mahwah, NJ : Lawrence Erlbaum Associates.

Report of the Ethiopian Human Rights Commission (EHRC) and Office of the United Nations High Commissioner for Human Rights (OHCHR), Joint Investigation into Alleged Violations of International Human Rights, Humanitarian and Refugee

Law Committed by all Parties to the Conflict in the Tigray Region of the Federal Democratic Republic of Ethiopia, 3 November 2021.

Report of the Special Rapporteur on the promotion and protection of the right to freedom of opinion and expression, Irene Khan, 'Disinformation and freedom of opinion and expression' (UN disinformation report) A/HRC/47/25, 13 April 2021, para 87.

Report of the UN Special Rapporteur on the promotion and protection of the right to freedom of opinion and expression, David Kaye, A/HRC/38/35, The regulation of user-generated online content, 2018, para 53.

Reuters Staff (2020) 'Ethiopia Denies Bombing Tigray's Tekeze Power Dam'. *Reuters*, 13 November (accessed 28 May 2022).

Salau, A. O. (2020) 'Social Media and the Prohibition of 'false News': Can the Free Speech Jurisprudence of the African Commission on Human and Peoples' Rights Provide a Litmus Test?'. *African Human Rights Yearbook*, 4: 231–54.

Shen, C., Kasra, M., Pan, W., Bassett, G. A., Malloch, Y. and O'Brien, J. F. (2019) 'Fake Images: The Effects of Source, Intermediary, and Digital Media Literacy on Contextual Assessment of Image Credibility Online'. *New Media & Society*, 21 (2): 438–63.

Taylor, P. M. (2003) *Munitions of the Mind: A History of Propaganda From the Ancient World to the Present era*. Manchester: Manchester University Press, 6.

Tibebu, T. (1996) 'Ethiopia the "Anolmaly" and "Paradox" of Africa'. *Journal of Black Studies*, 26 (4): 414.

UN Human Rights Committee (HRC) (2011) 'General Comment No. 34, Article 19, Freedoms of Opinion and Expression, CCPR/C/GC/34'. 12 September.

United Nations Office of the High Commissioner for Human Rights (2011) *Guiding Principles on Business and Human Rights*. Geneva: United Nations.

Wardle, C. and Derakhshan, H. (2017) *Information Disorder: Toward an Interdisciplinary Framework for Research and Policymaking*. Strasbourg: Council of Europe.

Wilmot, C., Tveteraas, E. and Drew, A. (2021) 'Dueling Information Campaigns: The War Over the Narrative in Tigray'. *The Media Manipulation Case Book*, September 14 (accessed 28 May 2022).

Woldekirkos, M. (2009) *Kedamawi Haile Selassie 1922–1927 E.C.* Addis Ababa University Press, 15, Translated from መርስዔ ኅዘን፡ ወ/ቂርቆስ፣ ቀዳማዊ ኃይለ ሥላሴ 1922 –1927 ዓ. ም. (አዲስ አበባ ዩኒቨርሲቲ ፕሬስ፣ 2009 ዓ.ም.) 15፡፡).

York, J. C. (2021) *Silicon Values: The Future of Free Speech Under Surveillance Capitalism*. London: Verso Publishing.

Zaugg, I. (2020) 'Digital Inequality and Language Diversity: An Ethiopic Case Study'. In M. Ragnedda and A. Gladkova (eds), *Digital Inequalities in the Global South*, Global Transformations in Media and Communication Research - A Palgrave and IAMCR Series, 247. Cham: Palgrave Macmillan.

Zelalem, Z. and Guest, P. (2021) 'Why Facebook Keeps Failing in Ethiopia'. *Rest of World*, 1 November (accessed 28 April 2022).

Chapter 6

(Re)writing history

Discursive practices of Gukurahundi disinformation on Twitter

Rutendo Chabikwa

'They will tell you, "It was not tribal, it was political". What's the difference?'
Zenzele Ndebele, Interview 2022

Introduction

In 1983, the then ZANU government under Robert Mugabe unleashed the North Korean trained Fifth Brigade in the Matabeleland and Midlands provinces of Zimbabwe, under the guise of suppressing a dissident movement (Ndlovu 2018; Alexander 1998). Tens of thousands of mostly Ndebele-speaking people disappeared or were tortured, raped and murdered. This genocide is commonly known as 'Gukurahundi', a word which has been used in other political contexts as well. 'Gukurahundi', as is used in this chapter, 'denotes the state-orchestrated violence that was unleashed upon Ndebele-speaking civilians in Matabeleland and Midlands provinces between 1983 and 1987' (Ndlovu 2018: 294). State-controlled media has effectively silenced any discussion of the genocide in the Zimbabwean media, but the advent of social media provided a relatively free online civic space where citizen discussion of Gukurahundi and demands for justice could not be completely supressed. This chapter analyses the coordinated disinformation campaign launched by state-aligned actors to attempt to maintain genocide denial online in order to protect the hegemonic narrative of Gukurahundi as a national security necessity that was not a genocide, but rather a civil war.

Digital ethnography and expert interviews are used to foreground citizen led counter-narratives of Gukurahundi and of the online disinformation campaign. I develop a three-part typology to highlight the discursive practices deployed by five key social media accounts central to the state-aligned disinformation network. The chapter asks:

1. What are the discursive practices used by Gukurahundi disinformation
   actors on Twitter?
2. How do these discursive practices uphold hegemonic power?

The flow of this chapter is as follows. First, I provide historic background on
colonial and post-independence disinformation practices before describing
Gukurahundi for the reader who is unfamiliar with Zimbabwe's history. I then
review the existing literature on disinformation and hegemonic narratives, digital
disinformation and the affordances of social media, and present Van Leeuwen's
typology of discursive practices. I move on to discuss my positionality and
epistemological approach before detailing the methodology employed which
combined digital ethnography, data scraping and in-depth interviews with
experts: individuals who encounter this disinformation almost daily either as
part of their work or because of their personal experiences. Afterwards, I briefly
touch on the process of establishing a coordinated disinformation network and
some difficulties I encountered in doing so. The next section presents my analysis
of the data which inductively resulted in three novel conceptions of online
discursive practices. I then discuss Gukurahundi as hegemonic discourse based
on these findings and how Twitter affordances enable this hegemonic narrative to
continue; thereby enabling my conclusion that these three discursive practices of
disinformation buttress hegemonic power by attempting to (re)write a defining
moment in Zimbabwean history.

It is important to note that, in this case, the hegemonic narrative is that
Gukurahundi was not a genocide, while the counter-hegemonic narratives are
the citizen perspectives that hold the state to account. I understand hegemonic
discourse to create a perception of reality and permission as to what can be
said and what cannot be said. Counter-hegemonic narratives cut through the
euphemistic hegemonic narrative and demand that the state acknowledges its role
in Gukurahundi and that some forms of justice and repair be served.

It is important to interrogate the digital echoes of this defining historical
moment, Gukurahundi, to trace the historical threads of the power dynamics
in national discourse. In so doing, we can show the power dynamics that are
still present in contemporary political discourse in Zimbabwe and how they
silence counter-hegemonic narratives and marginalized groups. These counter-
hegemonic narratives are the voices of citizens marginalized by powerful
interests – voices making rights-claims on the state: the right to political speech,
the right to hold perpetrators of human-rights abuses accountable and the right
to justice. These are fundamental human rights according to the Zimbabwe
constitution and international conventions. Any attempt to supress these rights-
claims (by disinformation or other means) is a violation of human rights. In this
chapter, I argue that accounts that intentionally spread disinformation related to
Gukurahundi are doing so in an attempt to rewrite history and push hegemonic
narratives that aim to absolve post-independent Zimbabwean leadership of
genocidal crimes. Gukurahundi disinformation thus legitimates the power of a
particular political elite and ethnic group in Zimbabwe. The identified accounts use

three main discursive practices: semantic rationalization, historical interception and misconstruction of textual authority.

Background

The liberation struggle for Zimbabwean independence was marked with tension between the two main nationalist parties, the Zimbabwe African People's Union (ZAPU) and the Zimbabwe African National Union (ZANU) and their armed wings: the Zimbabwe People's Revolutionary Army (ZIPRA) and the Zimbabwe African National Liberation Army (ZANLA) respectively (Alexander 2021). This tension also operated along ethnic lines, providing the foundation for Gukurahundi to be deployed against Ndebele-speaking people who were accused of harbouring dissidents. Although Gukurahundi was state-orchestrated, it is built upon ethnocentric constructions of nationhood and national building myths of the liberation struggle.

In 1983, the ZANU government under Robert Mugabe unleashed the North Korean-trained Fifth Brigade in Matabeleland and Midlands provinces under the guise of suppressing a dissident movement (Ndlovu 2018; Alexander 1998). In contemporary discourse, there is a solid academic consensus that Gukurahundi was indeed a genocide (W. Mpofu 2017; S. Mpofu 2015; Ndlovu 2018; Vambe 2012; Mathuthu 2021), including support from the International Association of Genocide Scholars (Auschwitz Institute for the Prevention of Genocide and Mass Atrocities 2011). The number of lives taken during this genocide is unclear, yet efforts have been made by different organizations including the Catholic Commission for Justice and Peace in Zimbabwe (CCJP) and The Legal Resources Foundation (LRF) in a 1997 report (Catholic Commission for Justice and Peace in Zimbabwe (CCJP) and The Legal Resources Foundation (LRF) 1997). The report used case studies of two accessible areas near Bulawayo: Tsholotsho Matabeleland North (including Nyamandlovu commercial farming area) and Matabeleland South. Matabeleland North had a massive Fifth Brigade onslaught in 1983 and Matabeleland South had a long and harsh food embargo and detentions in 1984 (Catholic Commission for Justice and Peace in Zimbabwe (CCJP) and The Legal Resources Foundation (LRF) 1997). The 1997 report also used CCJP archival material collected in the 1980s and some human rights reports. It is from this report that the figure of 20,000 killed, disappeared and assaulted is mostly extrapolated from in popular discourse. Many of these were civilians, including women and children. There are numerous popular anecdotes of sexual assault used as a weapon of war and other gruesome atrocities acted upon pregnant women.

While the Zimbabwean state has at different moments had differing responses to addressing the genocide, the common thread has been a suppression of memory, (re)membering, and (re)dress of the period (Alexander 2021; Ndlovu 2018). Prior to social media in the era of state-controlled newspapers, television and radio stations, the state's strategy was that the genocide should not be spoken of. However, social media has opened a new civic space in which alterative voices and viewpoints can exercise their agency. Beyond the hegemonic narrative that the state aims to sustain regarding the violence, Gukurahundi itself can also be understood as a state-deployed strategy to annihilate all those opposed to ZANU-PF hegemony (Ndlovu-Gatsheni 2012).

Under the former president Robert Mugabe, Gukurahundi was not acknowledged at all. The former president called it a 'moment of madness'. The current president, Emmerson Mnangagwa, who was minister of state in the prime minister's office during Gukurahundi and so was active during the genocide at a cabinet level, claimed that Gukurahundi was 'a closed chapter' (Ndlovu 2018: 295). The period itself has been shrouded in much silence (Alexander 2021). The current regime has inadequately addressed Gukurahundi and at various moments has made contradictory statements and actions regarding the issue. Early 2022, the Deputy Chief Secretary, Presidential Communications, Mr George Charamba made remarks that the construction of memorial plaque for victims of the Gukurahundi genocide was illegal (Crisis in Zimbabwe Coalition 2022). However, in March 2022, the president launched 'Gukurahundi hearings' with chiefs from Matabeleland (Netsianda 2022). In October 2022, the president also met with chiefs in Bulawayo to 'launch[ed] a Gukurahundi manual to guide and initiate the healing process' (Muromo 2022). Gukurahundi thus currently exists in the national discourse in this grey area between being completely silenced and only to be spoken about in state-controlled terms. Within the public sphere, Gukurahundi remains a contested and limited conversation.

There is much at stake in the debate about Gukurahundi in the Zimbabwean political scene. If the ruling party did not control the narrative, a lot about the historical nationalistic mythology would come into question. Such mythology includes the narratives about the leaders of the liberation struggles and the roles certain groups and individuals played, answers to which would delegitimize the current regime. Hegemonic historical narratives stand to be interrogated, bringing up questions of accountability, human rights, truth, reconciliation, justice and power. This chapter contributes to addressing some of these issues that are at stake by showing the digital echoes of this historical disinformation and beginning to interrogate one of the hegemonic narratives of Zimbabwean history.

Literature review

I will review literature that offers background on Gukurahundi and defines disinformation and disinformation practices; and I will also discuss Van Leeuwan's concept of legitimation practices as it is foundational to this research. These bodies of literature help build a lens through which to assess the Gukurahundi disinformation networks. In this chapter, I look at the discursive practices of disinformation networks on Twitter that are targeting the counter hegemonic narrative posts on Gukurahundi. I conceptualize these practices as strategies of maintaining hegemonic power through (re)instilling official narratives and upholding official silences surrounding the violence of Gukurahundi.

Gukurahundi is more than a historical event; it is also itself a strategy, an ideology and a form of discourse (Ndlovu-Gatsheni 2012). This is because it is part of how 'the Zimbabwe African National Union-Patriotic Front (ZANU-PF) sought to inscribe a nationalist monologic history in Zimbabwe in order prop up its claim to be the progenitor and guardian of the postcolonial nation' (Ndlovu-Gatsheni 2012, 1). Alexander (2021) highlights how the absence of truth and reconciliation processes and official recognition of the violence, together with the presence of irreconcilable narratives, has created a 'noisy silence'. 'Noisy silence' is 'a collective, imaginative response to a failure to grant recognition to a violent past' (Alexander 2021: 765). I hold that the internet is providing space for this noisy silence to occur, as people are creating and finding communities through the different affordances of various platforms and creating various collective and sometimes imaginative responses to this absence of recognition. This noisy silence is counter hegemonic. Those creating counter narratives which include memorialization and (re)membering in the public sphere are encountering seemingly organized attacks to counter the narratives they are creating.

Social media are becoming more and more ubiquitous and are playing a role in interjecting hegemonic narratives. Twitter has established itself as a space for much political interaction in many contexts (Velasquez and Rojas 2017), especially due to its ability to create asymmetrical relationships, 'since one does not need to reciprocate a tie in order to establish a public relationship. The relationship is one of following versus being followed, not of "friending"' (Postill and Pink 2012: 128). Additionally, social media have contributed to what has come to be termed a 'post-truth' era, which is a socio-political condition in which, 'appearances are given priority over objectivity, and so interpretations, emotional and subjective assessments and evaluations cloud the essence of things and so the truth' (Visvizi and Lytras 2019: 1). A post-truth era is also one in which disinformation spreads easily, and the ubiquitous nature of social media has made this easier. Such a condition comes at great cost and with great implications for democracy and for marginalized communities in different places.

As outlined in the introductory chapter to this book, I am here understanding disinformation to be, lies spread intentionally to manipulate belief and/or behaviour, with the effect of harming a social group (Wardle and Derakhshan 2017). In the realm of lies, I include intentionally misappropriated information. Harm includes the lack of acknowledgment of historical harms, a refusal to name a genocide and overall silencing of narratives. Gukurahundi disinformation harms people from Matabeleland and the Midlands and their descendants by denying them dignity and their right to social justice – by downplaying and ignoring their presence and realities in the national discourse and the harms that have come to them in the process of 'nation building'. This framing of disinformation through harm is an extension of Jones' (2019) framing of disinformation as a human rights issue. Jones (2019) argues that 'a failure to hold digital platforms to human rights standards is a failure to provide individuals with the safeguards against the power of authority that human rights law was created to provide' (Jones 2019: 4).

Online platforms have meant that more individuals and a diverse group of people get a say in the conversations between the citizens and the state, lowering the barriers to participation and removing institutional barriers (Nyabola 2018; Banda, Mudhai and Tettey 2009). Social media thus provides a space to perform counter publics, and in the case of Zimbabwe, the citizens form an 'unruly public' (Karekwaivanane 2019). One can consider citizen narratives of Gukurahundi on social media a manifestation of that unruly public, in how their efforts go against the hegemonic discourse.

Discourse is power, and as such, individuals need to be protected against the impacts of a hegemonic repressive discourse on social media. The power in discourse, and as such in discursive practices, lies in the way in which they construct, 'legitimation for social practices in public communication as well as in everyday interaction' (Van Leeuwen 2007: 91). This chapter holds that the Gukurahundi disinformation legitimates the power of a particular political elite and ethnic group in Zimbabwe. As Van Leeuwen (2007: 92) argues legitimation 'is always the legitimation of the practices of specific institutional orders'. (Van Leeuwen 2007: 92). Van Leeuwen (2007) identifies four categories of legitimation:

> 1) 'authorization', legitimation by reference to the authority of tradition, custom and law, and of persons in whom institutional authority is vested; 2) 'moral evaluation', legitimation by reference to discourses of value; 3) rationalization, legitimation by reference to the goals and uses of institutionalized social action, and to the social knowledges that endow them with cognitive validity; and 4) mythopoesis, legitimation conveyed through narratives whose outcomes reward legitimate actions and punish non-legitimate actions. (91)

Recent work has focused on the effects of disinformation on contemporary wars, genocides and unrest. For example, the Rohingya genocide in Myanmar was buttressed by disinformation that was spread on social media (Cosentino 2020; Miles 2018; Yue 2020). Such negative effects of digital disinformation have been considered as a reason to re-evaluate earlier techno-optimism that this technology would create a 'global village' (McLuhan 1964). While considering the effects of social media in contemporary global south communities, especially where atrocities have occurred is important, very few works consider the absence of redress of historical atrocities in the global South in the age of social media. Such a perspective provides a holistic consideration of social media and better unpacks the variety of disinformation practices.

With regards to considering discursive practices, similar work has been done concerning contemporary political elections (Recuero et al. 2021). Recuero and others (2021) studied former Brazilian president Bolsonaro's campaign as it relied heavily on social media and was connected to the spread of disinformation. Their work focused on Twitter and WhatsApp, where they conducted an analysis of the content at three levels: textual structure, legitimation strategies and social practices. The authors used Van Leeuwen's (2007) four categories of legitimation in analysing the legitimation strategies of the disinformation. This chapter draws heavily from this work, focusing only on discursive practices and adding a historical dimension and to uncover other discursive practices of disinformation and how they feed into the hegemonic narrative. I extend Van Leeuwen's (2007) categories in two ways. First, I am investigating disinformation as it relates to a historical moment that is contested in present day; and, second, I am centring the digital nature of these discursive practices. I arrive at three discursive practices, which emerged inductively from my empirical analysis, as opposed to looking to see what practices would fit Van Leeuwen's (2007) categories. The three discursive practices I identified are semantic rationalization, historical interception and the misconstruction of textual authority.

Positionality and epistemology

While Gukurahundi was a state-sanctioned genocide, a state ethnocentric discourse was deployed, pitting ordinary citizens from Matabeleland and Midlands – most of whom were Ndebele – against the majority/dominant 'Shona'[1] ethnicity. It is because of this narrative that my positionality is important to consider for this chapter. In Zimbabwean society, I am a Shona woman. I make no claim to be part of an ethnically marginalized community. It is thus important that I approach this topic with the utmost respect, capturing only the experiences of those affected.

A feminist research ethic not only recognizes power and its effects in the topic of research but also the presence of power relationships in the subjects of research (Ackerly and True 2010). The approach I am taking to this research is to thus understand the effects of this disinformation from the perspective of those directly affected by it. While through data scraping and analysing tweets, I can understand the practices of disinformation actors and untangle the ways in which narrative hegemonic power shows up, I cannot claim to understand the effects of such practices. As a feminist researcher, I have the 'ethical commitment to noticing the power of epistemology, particularly the power of privileged epistemologies' (Ackerly and True 2010: 25). Thus, in analysing the impact of this disinformation, I make the effort to privilege those directly affected by these practices through interviewing experts and content creators, who encounter this disinformation regularly. I considered these voices to be expert voices because they all provide ways of knowing that extend beyond, 'positivist oriented academia' (Heron and Reason 2008: 367). They all shared content that highlighted, what Heron and Reason argue is, the most fundamental way of knowing – experiential knowing. This is one's acquaintance with that which they encounter daily, or one's experiences in relation to the existence of other individuals (Heron and Reason 2008). Each of these creators either shared their personal experiences from their childhood during Gukurahundi, or the experiences of other individuals directly affected, through

---

1. I use the quotation marks because the very notion of Shona is itself contested and dynamic.

videos, photography or other media. In presenting their experiences and those of others, the experts also showed another form of knowing that made them experts, and that is presentational knowing – the ability to articulate experiential knowing (Heron and Reason 2008).

As a result of my positionality, I endeavoured to extend the epistemology around Gukurahundi through borrowing some aspects of co-operative inquiry, as it is 'not research on people or about people, but research with people' (Heron and Reason 2008: 366). Co-operative inquiry in full is a process of co-creating and co-reflecting between researchers and participants, working together to push and develop understanding on the issue. I focused heavily on the reflection aspect, by using the interviews and conversations as a space in which I could receive feedback on my analysis, be corrected, (re)directed and affirmed in the conclusions I am drawing.

Methods

Digital ethnography and expert interviews

My research began with a digital ethnography (Pink et al. 2016). This method was important to my research questions as it helped me identify accounts that spread disinformation as well accounts belonging to individuals creating the important counter hegemonic narrative that broke the official silence on Gukurahundi. In order to answer the first question 'What are the discursive practices used by Gukurahundi disinformation actors on Twitter?', I needed to not only identify the accounts, but also to see the disinformation in practice. During the digital ethnography, I also attended one Twitter space which was hosted by one of the accounts I visited. A Twitter Space is a live audio conversation that takes place on Twitter (Twitter Spaces 2021).

From this digital ethnography I identified three experts from Matabeleland to better understand the effects of these disinformation practices on their efforts to create counter hegemonic discourse on Twitter. As this research is grounded in feminist methodologies, it is important to note that expertise is not just defined and understood as professional expertise. I consider lived experiences as a legitimate way of knowing, and thus have included individuals with personal and direct Gukurahundi experiences. The first expert, Zenzele Ndebele, is a documentary film maker and journalist whose first documentary in 2005 was called Moment of Madness and was about Gukurahundi. The second expert, Mgcini Nyoni, defines himself as a story teller using the mediums of film, theatre and poetry, and while his work does not solely focus on Gukurahundi, it is a part of his personal family history as he lost his father to the atrocities when he was 'about 3 or so' (Nyoni 2022). As a result, the period sometimes seeps into his work, or he occasionally posts about it. The third expert, Samkeliso Tshuma, is an activist, human rights defender and the director of The Girls' Table – amplifying the voices of girls and young women on social and economic issues, political and cultural issues in

Zimbabwe through the use of media and ICT tools. She works together with two other human rights defenders learning about Gukurahundi victims, documenting their experiences and amplifying their voices on social media.

The interviews lasted between 45 minutes and an hour and were semi-structured. I conducted these interviews after I had scraped some data and done preliminary analysis. These interviews were essential in understanding whether what I was discovering in the data was also what the experts were experiencing. Additionally, the expert experiences were essential to answering the second question on how the discursive practices of disinformation actors uphold hegemonic discourse.

Data scraping from Twitter

During digital ethnography in which I identified the experts, I especially noticed how daily political issues were discussed within the framework of understanding Gukurahundi as a systemic issue. Some examples in which the topic is brought up include poor, inadequate and incorrect Ndebele translations on government or company communications. I looked at different comments, replies and retweets that some of the most influential voices were receiving. From there I chose five accounts that appeared more consistently. These five accounts have a total of approximately 35,375 followers among them, making them far reaching and relatively influential accounts. Data scraping was the corner stone to identifying the discursive practices of Gukurahundi disinformation. Data scraping also provided the advantage that I could access multiple tweets specific to the topic under investigation at once, as opposed to scrolling down a user's timeline and manually choosing the tweets.

The five accounts I identified do not necessarily garner much visible agreement to their sentiments, but they do receive some interaction. These five accounts receive retweets averaging about fifty retweets for most topics, which could be interpreted to signal agreement. The accounts also receive interaction through replies, an average of fifteen replies on some tweets. One post even had forty-six break out conversations in the replies, with every other reply starting a different thread of interaction. In the conversations I witnessed, there were few other accounts equally influential. I scraped data from these five accounts from January 2021 to February 2022. This timeline was chosen for two reasons.

The first is that the conversation of Gukurahundi shows up in daily interactions on social media, and while it occasionally is more pronounced around certain events, there really is no season or time that is dedicated to the discussion Gukurahundi. This is part of the official silence on the topic. It thus becomes important to seek to understand the quotidian nature of disinformation. The second reason is that within this time frame, in early January 2022 a memorial plaque erected to honour victims of the Gukurahundi genocide at Bhalagwe in Maphisa was bombed (Harris 2022). This allowed me to look at disinformation surrounding a time when Gukurahundi came up yet again in popular discourse. To add to the data I was getting from these accounts specifically, as well as to investigate the presence of a network, I analysed a discussion emanating from a post made by one of these accounts, which drew in more that forty accounts into a debate and spanned approximately five months.

Data analysis

From the five major Twitter accounts I scraped, I received a total of 1,362 tweets which include replies and retweets. For each account I arranged these tweets according to the retweet count, beginning with the most retweeted. This was so that I could find the sentiments that resonated the most. I then filtered for original tweets, not retweets to look at what was the user's 'original content'. This is important in understanding what ideas are created rather than regurgitated and how they fit into other existing ideas and discursive practices.

I conducted a qualitative thematic analysis of the tweets, looking to see similarities in the most common discursive practices that the tweets were using. From this analysis I inductively came to the three discursive practices that are the contribution of this chapter. Additionally, I also looked at the accounts mentioned in the tweets that were most retweeted to try and uncover the presence of any coordinated disinformation network.

Establishing a coordinated disinformation network

Methodologically, establishing the presence of a coordinated network is difficult and this poses challenges to the study of discursive practices of disinformation. The challenges in establishing a network are twofold. The first challenge is an ethical one to do with any researcher's safety. The largest and most influential of the accounts encountered that post Gukurahundi-related disinformation, are public accounts in which the individual does not hide their name or their affiliation with the ruling party and the current government. This poses a risk of insecurity for researchers engaging with an authoritarian regime. The other challenge in establishing whether there is a coordinated network is that the other accounts that the influential accounts were interacting with, especially with regards to Gukurahundi, were either new with few tweets and even fewer followers or were unidentified. It is therefore difficult to tell where within a potential network these accounts would fall.

There are however a few markers suggesting that these accounts are part of a disinformation network, understanding network to mean having a shared ideology with regular interactions supporting that ideology. To begin with, some of these accounts have the same profile picture of a slogan that supports the government's narrative of sanctions as the cause of Zimbabwe's economic downfall. This points to these accounts operating to propagate state-sanctioned narratives. Additionally, scraping data for the major accounts and mapping accounts that they have replied to within that period shows that these accounts have interacted on this issue and have mentioned each other. Furthermore, qualitatively looking at any replies, it was clear that the accounts shared the same sentiments around Gukurahundi and the discourse on sanctions in Zimbabwe. Interviewing experts on the issue further helped illuminate the presence of a network from their personal experiences. Both Nyoni and Ndebele state that based on direct encounters with certain individuals in different contexts that there are individuals paid to run such accounts. Nyoni stated that since he does not always post about Gukurahundi, he has noticed that when he does, there 'are tiny accounts that I am not following, and they are not following me, that seem to be created for that purpose, that only surface then. It is coordinated' (Nyoni 2022). He has even encountered, in person, individuals who agree on all political terms when they are offline but once they are online they are simply pushing the narratives supported by the government regarding sanctions and the presence of imperialist stooges in the political arena. So, while mapping the accounts has shown that they interact consistently, qualitative experiences of the experts also raise the concern of a coordinated disinformation campaign.

These identified accounts also have certain characteristics that make them worthy of investigation. Of the five accounts, three use their actual names and show their faces in some posts. The Gukurahundi discourse is not the only state aligned discourse they carry out. The accounts also engage in the debates on sanctions, some even declaring themselves to be active members of 'anti-sanctions' committees. The sanctions discourse in Zimbabwean politics consists of the current government blaming the economic decline on Western sanctions and not any domestic mismanagement of funds (Chingwere 2022). This further justifies the importance of considering Gukurahundi disinformation as hegemonic discourse that enacts power to silence an oppressed people. It is another tool in the arsenal of state disinformation practices. Beyond sanctions and Gukurahundi, another one of the state's disinformation practices is to do with creating a discourse around patriotism and labelling anyone who criticizes the state, mostly opposition leaders, a traitor. The accounts in this network also engage in some of these practices in their other posts.

Four of the five main accounts I analysed which used the real identity of individuals interacted with each other, especially within the context of a debate using the reply function. However, the other account which uses a pseudonym, appeared to use similar tactics, but without interacting with the other three accounts. While none of these accounts ever claimed to be speaking on behalf of the state, they would unashamedly tag the president, the ruling party and some ministers in some posts. This tagging functionality sends a message to the content creators and thought leaders from Matabeleland and the Midlands provinces. This communicates that the individuals are not afraid to engage with the state directly on the issue, implying some form of legitimacy to their contributions, painting themselves as state-aligned individuals. In the absence of rebuttal from official state accounts, such information can stand to be seen as supported by the state, especially coming from accounts that proclaim themselves to be card-carrying members of the ruling party.

Discursive practices of Gukurahundi disinformation on Twitter

From these tweets, I find that there are three main discursive practices used in an attempt to foment Gukurahundi disinformation: historical interception, semantic rationalization and recontextualized textual authority. I choose to focus on these three as they appear to work in a very particular way to prop up hegemonic discourse. There are of course other practices such as emotional gaslighting that have come up in the data, but I will not discuss those in the chapter. While this chapter builds upon the work of Van Leeuwen (2007), it extends the framework by looking at more contextual and specific ways in which discursive practices occur in disinformation networks. Additionally, it looks more specifically at discursive practices as they concern a historical subject. I will discuss these three discursive practices that have emerged from the data collected in turn.

Semantic rationalization

A discursive practice that is used by the Gukurahundi disinformation network is something I am calling semantic rationalization. Semantic rationalization is a method of definitional obfuscation intended to diminish the legitimacy of the rights-claim by questioning whether Gukurahundi meets the technical definition of genocide. This is when the false information is buttressed and supported by subtle shades of meaning and definitions. Such a tactic focuses on delegitimizing the moniker 'genocide' by selectively providing information with the aim of showing that Gukurahundi was *not* a genocide. An example is that one such tweet from the five main accounts claimed that the since the victims of the genocide have not filed 'a complaint' [*sic*] against it in the United Nations Human Rights Council (UNHRC), Gukurahundi could not be classified as a genocide. While the absence of recognition of Gukurahundi as a genocide by the United Nations is true, the disinformation stems from the implication that this is the only way in which genocide can be defined. Another example in which the semantic rationalization showed up within the network is in the responses to the previously mentioned tweet that started debate and discussion that lasted months, the atrocities are referred to as 'excesses' and not as atrocities, or even a genocide.

The Gukurahundi Memorial Centre, an independent online portal that curates information about Gukurahundi, argues that Gukurahundi was genocide under the United Nations Convention on the Prevention and Punishment of the Crime of Genocide, but there has not been any judicial process to determine that this is so (Makumbe 2021). The absence of this recognition, however, is not the only way in which a genocide can be determined as such. Scholars and experts have long declared that Gukurahundi is a genocide (Karimakwenda 2010; W. Mpofu 2017). In denying the term 'genocide' the disinformation network emphasizes the use of the word 'war' instead, a word that not only erases atrocities, but reconfigures the power and displaces responsibility in this historical event. Some accounts in the network claim that any information presented that identifies Gukurahundi as a genocide is, as one account put it, 'tailored to cause division, unrest and intervention'.

Another way in which semantic rationalization occurs within the network is through debate on the numbers of the people who were killed and/or disappeared during Gukurahundi. An example of such tweets are those in which the author responds numerous times that, '20 000 is an exaggeration for propaganda purposes' and 'GH [*sic*] victims numbers lower than 20,000. Why's there silence on Chimurenga[2] over 50,000 deaths?' This is the propaganda technique of whataboutism – a refusal to speak of the substantive issues by switching attention to a false equivalent. The most common number used by many sources, (Maedza 2019; Mathuthu 2021; S. Mpofu 2015; W. Mpofu 2017) is 20,000; this is a number that was potentially popularized by the extensive 1997 report by the Catholic Commission for Justice and Peace in Zimbabwe (CCJP) and The Legal Resources Foundation (LRF). Alexander (2021) notes that this report cites this from Joshua Nkomo's biography which highlighted this as a number of 'casualties' based on Catholic Church sources. While the official numbers continue to be a source of debate, the uncertainty in this single figure has been one of the main focuses of the semantic rationalization of the disinformation network, with some of the accounts studied referring to this figure as one that is only meant to elicit public sympathy. Ndebele (2022) highlighted that this rationalization around numbers is so common and is based on ignoring the granularities in the facts. This is semantic rationalization because, according to the disinformation accounts, the meaning of the term genocide is drawn from the numbers, and if one argues that the numbers are much less than 20,000 then logic would dictate that it was not a genocide. Such semantic rationalization further muddies the discourse.

I argue that such semantic rationalization, either through focusing on numbers or definitions of genocide, is disinformation as it is used with the intent to deceive and divert attention away from Gukurahundi, and thereby erasing the case for addressing it in contemporary political discourse. The deception lies in the implication that unless it can be declared a genocide by international judicial processes, then there is no need for redress, reparations, recognition and justice. The deception also lies in providing incomplete evidence, further contributing to a post-truth condition in which, 'appearances are given priority over objectivity, and so interpretations, emotional and subjective assessments and evaluations cloud the essence of things and so the truth' (Visvizi and Lytras 2019: 1). This contribution is important as it shows the importance of extending the understanding of disinformation to encompass various types of falsehoods. Semantic rationalization holds up hegemonic power by, essentially, belittling the historical atrocities and thereby making sure that they are not addressed with the reverence that they deserve. Semantic rationalization is genocide denial disinformation that falsely argues that what took place was not a genocide.

Historical interception

One of the major discursive practices that are used by the Gukurahundi disinformation network I studied is that of intercepting the historical narrative. I have chosen the word interception over interjection, because interception brings

---

2. The name given to the two liberation wars for Zimbabwean Independence.

to mind an interrupted and diverted flow, while interjection does not necessarily point to a diversion. Intercepting, in this case, is a form of disruption or challenge to overturn and redirect what is considered an attack on the hegemonic narrative. In this instance the five accounts use the strategy of casting doubt on the narrative by suggesting that there is some important information that those calling for accountability are missing, and they hold that when such information comes to light, it will be clear what Gukurahundi actually was. I call this practice an interception because its aim is to disrupt the flow of evidence-laden contributions from those holding a light to the genocide by providing seemingly historical perspectives.

One of the most common narratives used for historical interception is that of Gukurahundi simply being a continuation of precolonial relations. This interception holds that in precolonial times the Ndebele people's military prowess led to the repression of other ethnic groups. Some accounts in this network have held that the precolonial Ndebele King 'Lobengula[3] perpetrated genocide on local tribes for over 40 years'. Such a narrative ignores the fact that precolonial relations were always in a state of ebb and flow between different centres of power, and that modern configurations of ethnic groups are different to what they were at that time (Bayart 2009). More importantly, factually, the 'exaggerated estimates of the number, scope, and brutality of Ndebele raids on the Shona were later used to justify the conquest of the Ndebele by the British South Africa Company in 1893' (Beach 1974: 633). This nineteenth century colonial disinformation is integral to this discussion and has continued to shape debates about Shona–Ndebele relations in Zimbabwe. Such historical interceptions while serving contemporary hegemonic discourse intervention are rooted in colonialism. This historical interception intentionally misappropriates false historical information to reinforce dominant power interests, thereby fitting the understanding of disinformation used in this chapter.

Another example of such narrative interception is when one of the influential accounts posted that when people discussed Gukurahundi, they were not telling the entire story as 'There's many sides to GH [*sic*]' and accompanied this claim with an article from the state-owned *Sunday Mail* newspaper. This article was a feature which interviewed a man named Stephen Mugwagwa who served the Rhodesia African Rifles, a regiment of the Rhodesian Army whose ranks were recruited from the Black African population. This article begins by not discussing Gukurahundi, but when asked if he had any encounters with the enemy, Mugwagwa responds that the real war he witnessed was the 'dissident war', in reference to Gukurahundi. The article also posits that the word Gukurahundi was the nickname for a regiment trained in 1985 that comprised of unemployed youth and the term was used to refer to how the government eradicated youth unemployment by so doing (Mazara 2021). There are no questions about the word gukurahundi, a common Shona word, originally referring to rains before spring that wipe away chaff, and has been used to refer to other things. Although the article only had this story

---

3. Lobengula was the last king of the precolonial Ndebele kingdom.

from this one individual, the Twitter network took it upon themselves to use this article as the focus of the historical interception that there was more unknown about Gukurahundi, the genocide.

This discursive practice works as a form of disinformation, for two reasons. The first is that there is no external information that supports the special regiment story highlighted in the newspaper article, yet the Gukurahundi disinformation network took this as a historical fact. The tweet claiming that 'there are many sides' intercepts the history of Gukurahundi the genocide by recasting gukurahundi as a word used to name a regiment. Second, it is a selective utilization of the events that occurred during the genocide. Samkeliso Tshuma, in an interview, spoke of this disinformation practice. She highlighted that, 'on Twitter people like to say "but it was a civil war". Then the question becomes, ok if they were fighting [only] dissidents, why was there an attack on babies, why was there an attack on pregnant people?'. Tshuma's work on Gukurahundi mostly consists of sharing videos of victims of Gukurahundi retelling their experiences. She thus is acutely aware of the atrocities that occurred.

Following from the same article discussed earlier, in response to criticisms about how the article that an account claimed to show the 'many sides' of Gukurahundi does not address the genocide; the initial poster responded, 'When evidence of your ancestors' cruelty and barbarity is presented to you in abundance you cry spam?' There were also comments such as, 'There's a lot more to Gukurahundi than just the usual simplistic ZANU-bashing narrative. Govt responded to ZPRA insurgency'. This speaks to the power-relationship that underlie this whole story. History is written by the victor. At the point of independence ZANU wrote a foundational narrative about Zimbabwe in which it was the saviour, the freedom fighter and the protector of national unity and independence. The facts of the genocide are a threat to that narrative and therefore to its power and security. Not allowing Gukurahundi to be spoken of is a tactic of power maintenance. Speaking of Gukurahundi is to speak truth to power in a way that threatens that power. Framing speaking of the genocide as 'ZANU-bashing' reveals the feelings of existential threat experienced by state-aligned citizens at the mention of Gukurahundi. The state solution is silencing and genocide denial. It is interesting to note that in this camp, where the term 'genocide' is denied, it is usually by accounts that identify themselves and publicly state their unwavering support for the current regime.

Another way in which historical interception takes place is through making unsubstantiated claims with the aim of diverting the conversation surrounding the atrocities. Here unsubstantiated claims such as, '[T]he dissidents were more brutal than a trained Army' tweeted by one of the five accounts are a common take. Naturally, at the end of the day, this practice works through creating the idea of contested history. This serves the purpose of further fomenting hegemonic discourse on the Gukurahundi genocide by making it into a contested issue rather than an issue to be addressed, redressed and resolved. In so doing, this discursive practice constitutes disinformation because the creators of such content are knowingly tweeting disinformation to cause harm and redirect history.

The interview with Ndebele further revealed the uniformity in how such historical interception is applied with regards to the narrative concerning the presence of dissidents. Ndebele highlights that the term 'dissidents' has been used as part of the hegemonic discourse in other contexts outside of Gukurahundi. Ndebele noted that, 'the same lie has been used against Ndabaningi Sithole,[4] has been used against Tsvangirai,[5] it has been used against anyone else; if you are a threat to this government . . . no one ever bothers to find the facts' (Ndebele 2022). This observation highlights a continuity in the disinformation that not only bolsters Gukurahundi as a discourse but continues to uphold the state's hegemonic discourse in which the state can decide who is patriotic and who isn't, who is a friend and who is an enemy and what is legitimate and illegitimate history. Thus, this discursive practice upholds hegemonic power by creating discourse that is in line with the state's perception of itself. Historical interception does not deny that a genocide took place but instead tries to disrupt online truth claims using rhetorical devices to sow doubt and distrust in the public mind.

Misconstruction of textual authority

The last discursive practice that emerged out of the data is one I am naming misconstruction of textual authority. I am taking misconstruction to refer to a false and inaccurate interpretation of evidence. This differs from Van Leeuwen's (2007) 'expert authority'. According to Van Leeuwen (2007), 'expert authority' is a discursive practice in which 'legitimacy is provided by expertise rather than status' (94). In multimedia contexts, such as social media, 'the credentials may be visual, signified by laboratory paraphernalia, books, or other professional attributes' (Van Leeuwen 2007: 95). Misconstruction of textual authority goes further in two ways. The first is that the textual authority does not come from the expertise of the account that posts it, as Van Leeuwen's categorization would suggest. Rather, it is taken from other sources, sometimes unidentified, that an account would be claiming to be expert. The second extension is that the text is not taken to mean what it was initially meant to represent. Rather it is recontextualized and posted to show agreement and support of a statement made by the account, which may not have been the initial intention of the text.

One such example is that such expert authority is borrowed to further bolster the historical interception. One of the five main accounts in this network posted screenshots of academic texts, describing precolonial relations among different ethnicities in the regions, and used this as evidence to claim that 'Seeds of GKH

4. Ndabaningi Sithole was a writer, politician and church pastor who founded the Zimbabwe African National Union (ZANU). He was forcibly removed from ZANU under Robert Mugabe and went on to form ZANU Ndonga.

5. Morgan Tsvangirai was a politician, president of the Movement for Democratic Change (MDC) and later the MDC – Tsvangirai. The MDC was a prominent opposition party in Zimbabwe's history.

[*sic*] violence were sown by Ndebeles'. A deeper dive into these images shows that three for the four images that are attached to the tweet are from a 2015 doctoral thesis that was submitted at the Durban University of Technology. The pages that the account chose to post are from a chapter that 'examines the relevant literature on the nature of relations between the Shona and Ndebele groups during the pre-colonial and colonial epochs' (Muchemwa 2015: 53). The author of the tweet uses pictures form this chapter to claim that '[T]here were harmonious tribal[6] relations' in Zimbabwe until the arrival of the Ndebele. This is an intentional misrepresentation of this literature review which was initially written in an attempt to 'transcend[ing] the existing debates and controversy, especially the over-emphasis on who did what, when, why and how which has not helped much in understanding the real meaning behind the polarisation of relations' (Muchemwa 2015: 53).

This practice of selectively choosing aspects of texts and recontextualizing them helps cement the disinformation by acting as though it were substantiated in academic research and knowledge. Another way in which this discursive practice works is through the use of the tropes of fact-checking, or fact-finding, although they are disinformation practices. One such example is a tweet in which one of the five main accounts I analysed made the claim that Gukurahundi was a war as was 'confirmed by six independent reports including one from the CIA'. The author then went on to post an image of a document he claimed to be a sanitized copy of some CIA document on Gukurahundi. The image contained elements present in other similar documents that exist and have been sanitized for release. These elements include a twenty-four-digit file number, a release date and markings in the margin. At first glance, the image does look like other CIA sanitized files online. A reverse image search to try and ascertain the origins of the image was unsuccessful. Searching the file number and text on the image also brought up no results. The document also contains red text boxes drawing attention to some aspects of the document and red arrows pointing to added red text, not original to this document, commenting on the various parts highlighted by the aforementioned red boxes. The red elements on the image highlight the practice of using tropes of fact-checking and fact-finding. One of the statements that are highlighted in red boxes reads, 'We believe 1,500 to 2,000 civilians died as a result of Army excesses'. A red arrow leads away from the box to red text that reads, '5 [*sic*] Brigade was not all Shona. There is a You Tube Video of an interview with a Ndebele 5th Brigade member'. This 'fact-checking' attempt neither provides the facts nor responds to what is on the document. This practice is effective because without reverse image searching or paying attention to font differences within this 'official' document, this looks like a fact-checked document but provides no context or links to external sources.

The author of the tweet does not share a link or any other image that points to the rest of the 'claims' made in the document, and so one is left only with the narrative

---

6. The use of the word tribal here is as used in the text. It is a Eurocentric term.

and the context that the author of the tweet provides. In an interview, Ndebele (2022) noted that he had repeatedly seen this practice of relying upon untraceable internal documents, purporting to reveal accurate facts. Disinformation actors used it because of an absence of information to rebut the facts that he provides as a journalist and documentary filmmaker who is building the counter-hegemonic narrative regarding Gukurahundi. It is difficult to verifiably refute the authenticity of a supposedly 'secret' document. However, this document is marked 'approved for release' yet the text strings that it contains appear nowhere on the web, in Google Scholar or other catalogues searched by the author, and the claims made in the document are not corroborated by the historical records. The only intelligence assessment of the period that I found online was on ZANU-ZAPU rivalry, which was approved for release ten days before the aforementioned image was allegedly released. All this suggests that the image is a fabrication produced merely to further a campaign of disinformation.

Knowing how this disinformation network used misconstructed textual authority, Ndebele says, 'it has taught me that I don't post something that I am not 100% sure it happened. I have facts backed by either a newspaper article, a scholarly book that has been written, or an account of someone who was there, because I know they are waiting for me to post something that is not correct, then use that to try and deal with my credibility' (Ndebele 2022). Tshuma also mentioned that in her experience, such posts only ever occurred whenever Gukurahundi was mentioned in the abstract, that is – in the absence of videos of victims telling their story. She said that, 'What I have noticed is that when it is the victim speaking for themselves [on video], they can't dispute that because it is in their face, but where I find that there is most trolling or there is some backlash, is that when I mention that Gukurahundi happened or that I spoke to a victim and there is no video' (Tshuma 2022). In my own data collection, I found this to be commonly true for this practice specifically, that misconstructed textual authority was easily presented when there was no other primary evidence in the discussion, thereby making the text provided the only authority. Misconstructed textual authority holds up hegemonic power by providing false or incomplete information that supports a narrative that downplays or ignores Gukurahundi. Misconstruction of textual authority can also be read as a specific form of historical interception that deploys falsified evidence sources to lend authority to disinformation.

Gukurahundi as hegemonic discourse

Having understood the discursive practices of disinformation, it is also important to understand how they bolster hegemonic discourse. Here, I move on from discussing the three discursive practices of disinformation that emerged from the data to consider how they help sustain the hegemonic discourse of ZANU-PF paternalism. I present additional data that illustrates how disinformation actors defend vested interest and how they are challenged by the agency of digital citizens offering counter narratives. In order to holistically answer how discursive practices of disinformation hold up hegemonic discourse, it is important to understand that Gukurahundi is not only genocidal violence but also the ideology that constitutes part of hegemonic discourse in Zimbabwe (Ndlovu-Gatsheni 2012). I am using discourse to include language 'as a form of social practice' (Fairclough 1993: 63). Such an understanding points to a relationship between social practice and social structure in which, 'the latter is both a condition for, and an effect of, the former' (Fairclough 1993: 64). Thus, this chapter, by analysing the discursive practices associated with the disinformation on Gukurahundi, understands that such disinformation reproduces certain sociopolitical structures and aims to highlight the power relations entailed within the Gukurahundi discourse.

In an interview with storyteller and creative Mgcini Nyoni, he highlighted that one of the ways in which the subject of Gukurahundi is always brought up on Twitter is when the question of language is brought up. The use of Shona language in Matabeleland is directly linked to Gukurahundi as 'the first phase of Gukurahundi, was the genocide, and people would be forced to sing Shona Songs' (Nyoni 2022). Gukurahundi can thus be understood as an ideology of sociocultural control, in addition to the atrocities. Thus, the disinformation supporting the hegemonic discourse emerges out of various topics, showing the efforts of creating a homogenizing discourse.

With regards to the disinformation that buttresses the hegemonic discourse on Twitter today, the experts noted that these discursive practices are not new; they are simply adapted for social media. In an interview, Ndebele stated, 'From the onset, the Gukurahundi genocide was a huge [dis]information[7] campaign, which up to today people have not come to grips with because they used ZBC (Zimbabwe Broadcasting Cooperation), they used *The Chronicle*[8] . . . so that [dis] information that happened in the 80s continues up to now' (Ndebele 2022). This observation helps recognize the adaptability of disinformation in social media platforms and the nature of this disinformation as being in line with the need to maintain and safeguard a hegemonic discourse that denies that Gukurahundi was a genocide. These same practices have transferred online; however, the affordances of the social media, when compared to state-controlled media, provide new action possibilities to other citizens.

While the actual Gukurahundi atrocities were driven by disinformation that claimed the over presence of 'dissidents', contemporary disinformation practices work to foment that discourse in national memory. Ndebele argued that while such disinformation does not affect the work he does directly, it is effective in muddying national discourse and leaving the general population unsure of what exactly happened. As result, Gukurahundi then becomes an issue that is considered an aspect of politicking, without real engagement. Effectively, such

---

7. From an expert definition, due to the intentionality of the false information, this can be seen to refer to disinformation.

8. The Chronicle is a state-owned daily newspaper published in Bulawayo and mostly reports on news in the Matabeleland region and in the southern part of the country.

disinformation makes sure that Gukurahundi is never fully addressed and is only considered a 'sensitive' topic, such that, as Ndebele argues, even the opposition party does not engage with Gukurahundi although they have representation in parliament. Ultimately, the result of such discursive practices of disinformation are that they threaten open democratic political discourse (Jones 2019) and represent an obstacle to the attainment of truth and reconciliation. Nyoni attested to this in an interview when he noted that 'unfortunately things like Gukurahundi have a strong bearing on our identity as a nation' (2022). Gukurahundi disinformation is rife on Twitter, as seen by engagement on the issue even on quotidian topics, such as language used in advertising by corporations.

Twitter affordances and disinformation discursive practices

Outside these themes from the tweets that come out of this analysis, it is also important to note that there are other communication practices, specific to digital communications, that bolster this network of disinformation actors. To fully extend the understanding of digital discursive practices of disinformation, I will address to what extent these disinformation practices are specifically enabled by digital affordances of Twitter. I am understanding affordances as 'a concept that captures the relationship between the materiality of media and human agency' (Bucher and Helmonds 2017: 239). I consider affordances to also encapsulate decisions to use certain material features of Twitter, made by the users to achieve a certain goal, intentionally or unintentionally. This is 'relational affordance' which is, 'the interplay between mobile social media, users and their varied contexts' (Willems 2020: 2).

One of those decisions relating to affordances that the five disinformation actors make to achieve their goal was making sure that they could attack the counter-hegemonic narrative creators, without bringing them in to the conversation through direct tagging. When the disinformation actors are addressing something said by either a content creator holding truth to power, or by a political actor expressing counter hegemonic sentiments, the disinformation actors do not tag them directly or respond. Rather, they either turn their name into a hashtag or just write it without tagging them. An example is that one of the five disinformation accounts wrote of Ndebele, the expert I interviewed, 'that #Zenzele [Ndebele] and co gravestones, provocative mischief'. This tweet is in reference to the aforementioned memorial plaque to remember Gukurahundi victims at Bhalagwe that was destroyed. The result of this is that only their followers will directly engage with this unless the target of the disinformation seeks out the tweet, something that is highly unlikely as they are on opposite sides of this discourse divide. This could contribute to creating an echo chamber within the disinformation circles as Ndebele himself did not receive a notification of the tweet and therefore did not engage.

Beyond Twitter's most well-known text interface, its voice interface called Twitter Spaces also provides disinformation actors with another material feature they can employ to spread disinformation. It is also important to highlight that Twitter's Space functionality shows an interesting juxtaposition in written discursive practices versus verbal/auditory ones. Twitter Spaces allow users to start and host a broadcast that can be recorded and allow others to speak and engage via audio. In speaking to the three experts, they mentioned that some of the notable figures in the disinformation network host Twitter Spaces where they will spew the same disinformation, but the interviewees were never 'given the mic' even after requesting to speak. This shows intent in spreading disinformation and cementing the hegemonic narrative on Gukurahundi. One of the five major accounts I analysed has 10,000 followers and was mentioned in the interviews as one of the main players in the Gukurahundi disinformation network. However, in scraping data from this account, for the thirteen months in consideration, there were only thirty-five tweets; but the account makes use of Twitter Spaces, something I know as I have sat in on one Space and saw about three others in progress that I decided not to join. This is also bolstered by how some of these few tweets that came up in the data are responses to a Twitter Space the account was hosting and deploying the semantic rationalization tactic.

The distinct affordances of Twitter Spaces (no textual record) make it more difficult, not only to analyse and understand the network but also to evaluate the spread and resonance of disinformation over time. This is because we cannot conclude that simply because a Space was attended by tens of thousands of people that it was influential.[9] Additionally, the effect of such practices such as hash tagging one's name instead of tagging them directly is difficult to measure. Although these make it difficult to quantitatively ascertain the reach of disinformation, they show the multiple ways in which bad actors can buttress their networks and continue to spread disinformation outside the written tweet and by coming up with other hashtags that are not necessarily related to Gukurahundi. These affordances, combined with the discursive practices identified in this chapter, highlight the quest to retain power through upholding the hegemonic discourse. However, the quest for justice continues to motivate the narrative contestation within the same space.

Conclusion

This chapter set out to identify and examine the discursive practices used in Gukurahundi disinformation on Twitter and how they maintain hegemonic power. Using data from a digital ethnography of Zimbabwean Twitter and interviews with experts impacted by the genocide and whose activism includes countering online genocide disinformation, a typology of three kinds of discursive practices was developed. The analysis showed that state-aligned actors used a range of discursive practices to intentionally disseminate lies online as strategies

---

9. I attended one such space during my digital ethnography.

of power maintenance. We also saw how affected citizens have made creative use of the affordances provided by online spaces and social media to make public rights-claims, produce counter-narratives that expose the truth and mobilize calls for political accountability and justice. The new practices of digital citizenship are creating forms of counter power, enabling citizens to speak truth to power.

This chapter has highlighted three major discursive practices that contribute to the construction of a post-truth condition surrounding Gukurahundi in Zimbabwe: semantic rationalization, historical interception and misconstruction of textual authority. Although Gukurahundi is a historical event, it is still important to the nation building and myth-making of the current state. So, although social media are more recent, the case of Gukurahundi in Zimbabwe highlights that when it comes to harms of disinformation, we also need to consider historical cases. Understanding the discursive practices of such disinformation actors also uncovers how contemporary political hegemonic discourse is buttressed to the detriment of marginalized individuals.

Finally, I believe that it is important that I highlight that though there are efforts to maintain hegemonic discourse around Gukurahundi, various experts and citizens exercise their agency and counter this discourse in the same space. Individuals have more agency within this communication structure to counter the power that disinformation actors have, and the three highlighted here are only a few of many, using various discursive practices used to shine a light on the truth.

Bibliography

Ackerly, Brooke and True, Jacqui (2010) *Doing Feminist Research in Political and Social Science*. Basingstoke: Palgrave Macmillan.

Alexander, Jocelyn (1998) 'Dissident Perspectives on Zimbabwe's Post-Independence War'. *Africa: Journal of the International African Institute*, 68 (2): 151–82. https://doi.org/10.2307/1161277.

Alexander, Jocelyn (2021) 'The Noisy Silence of Gukurahundi: Truth, Recognition and Belonging'. *Journal of Southern African Studies*, 47 (5): 763–85. https://doi.org/10.1080/03057070.2021.1954356.

Auschwitz Institute for the Prevention of Genocide and Mass Atrocities (2011) 'Zimbabwe: New Calls for Prosecution of Killings'. *Auschwitz Institute for the Prevention of Genocide and Mass Atrocities* (blog), 21 July. http://www.auschwitzinstitute.org/blog/genprev-in-the-news-21-july-2011/.

Banda, Fackson, Mudhai, Okoth Fred and Tettey, Wisdom J. (2009) 'Introduction: New Media and Democracy in Africa - A Critical Interjection'. In Okoth Fred Mudhai, Wisdom J. Tettey and Fackson Banda (eds), *African Media and the Digital Public Sphere*, 2009th ed., 1–20. New York: Palgrave Macmillan.

Bayart, Jean-François (2009) *The State in Africa : The Politics of the Elly*. 2nd ed. London; New York: Polity Press. http://hdl.handle.net/2027/mdp.39015080896650

Beach, D. N. (1974) 'Ndebele Raiders and Shona Power'. *The Journal of African History*, 15 (4): 633–51.

Bucher, Taina and Helmonds, Anne (2017) 'The Affordances of Social Media Plaforms'. In Jean Burgess, Alice E. Marwick and Thomas Poell (eds), *The SAGE Handbook of Social Media*, 233–53. London: SAGE Publications. http://ebookcentral.proquest.com/lib/oxford/detail.action?docID=5151795.

Catholic Commission for Justice and Peace in Zimbabwe (CCJP), and The Legal Resources Foundation (LRF) (1997) *Breaking the Silence, Building True Peace: A Report on the Disturbances in Matabeleland and the Midlands, 1980 to 1988.* 1st ed. Harare: CCJPZ and LRF.

Chingwere, Mukudzei (2022) '"Zim Rising above Illegal Sanctions"'. *The Herald*, 25 October, sec. National. https://www.herald.co.zw/zim-rising-above-illegal-sanctions/.

Cosentino, Gabriele (2020) *Social Media and the Post-Truth World Order: The Global Dynamics of Disinformation.* 1st ed. Palgrave Pivot Cham. https://link.springer.com/book/10.1007/978–3–030–43005–4.

Crisis in Zimbabwe Coalition (2022) 'State Confirms Intention to Silence Victims and Sweep Gukurahundi under the Carpet'. *The Zimbabwean*, 19 January. https://www.thezimbabwean.co/2022/01/state-confirms-intention-to-silence-victims-and-sweep-gukurahundi-under-the-carpet/.

Fairclough, Norman (1993) *Discourse and Social Change.* Cambridge: Polity Press.

Harris, Lulu Brenda (2022) 'Third Gukurahundi Plaque Bombed'. *CITE* (blog), 6 January. https://cite.org.zw/third-gukurahundi-plaque-bombed/.

Heron, John and Reason, Peter (2008) 'Extending Epistemology Within a Co-Operative Inquiry'. In Peter Reason and Hilary Bradbury (eds), *The SAGE Handbook of Action Research*, 366–80. London: SAGE Publications Ltd. https://doi.org/10.4135/9781848607934.

Jones, Kate (2019) 'Online Disinformation and Political Discourse: Applying a Human Rights Framework'. Research Paper. Chatham House, The Royal Institute of International Affairs. https://www.chathamhouse.org/2019/11/online-disinformation-and-political-discourse-applying-human-rights-framework.

Karekwaivanane, George Hamandishe (2019) '"Tapanduka Zvamuchese": Facebook, "Unruly Publics", and Zimbabwean Politics'. *Journal of Eastern African Studies*, 13 (1): 54–71. https://doi.org/10.1080/17531055.2018.1547257.

Karimakwenda, Tererai (2010) 'Zimbabwe: Gukurahundi Finally Classified as Genocide by Leading Experts'. *SW Radio Africa*, 17 September, sec. News. https://allafrica.com/stories/201009170018.html.

Maedza, Pedzisai (2019) '"Gukurahundi - a Moment of Madness": Memory Rhetorics and Remembering in the Postcolony'. *African Identities*, 17 (3–4): 175–90. https://doi.org/10.1080/14725843.2019.1657000.

Makumbe, Ruwadzano (2021) 'Lack of Justice and Accountability for 1980s Zimbabwe Massacres'. *Human Rights Pulse* (blog), 10 August. https://www.humanrightspulse.com/mastercontentblog/lack-of-justice-and-accountability-for-1980s-zimbabwe-massacres.

Mathuthu, Mthulisi (2021) 'Subversive Verses: How Ndebele Musicians Counter-Framed the State Propaganda on The Gukurahundi Genocide'. *Journal of Literary Studies*, 37 (3): 83–99. https://doi.org/10.1080/02564718.2021.1959763.

Mazara, Garikai (2021) 'Tale of the "Tamed Terrorist"'. *The Sunday Mail*, 4 April sec. Opinion & Analysis. https://www.sundaymail.co.zw/tale-of-the-tamed-terrorist.

McLuhan, Marshall (1964) *Understanding Media: The Extensions of Man.* 1st ed. Cambridge, MA: McGraw-Hill.

Miles, Tom (2018) 'U.N. Investigators Cite Facebook Role in Myanmar Crisis'. *Reuters*, 12 March, sec. Technology News. https://www.reuters.com/article/us-myanmar-rohingya-facebook-idUKKCN1GO2PN.

Mpofu, Shepherd (2015) 'When the Subaltern Speaks: Citizen Journalism and Genocide "Victims" Voices Online'. *African Journalism Studies*, 36 (4): 82–101. https://doi.org/10.1080/23743670.2015.1119491.

Mpofu, William (2017) 'Zimbabwe's Gukurahundi Genocide Beyond the Forgetfulness and Silences of Coloniality'. In Mammo Muchie, Nicasius Achu Check and Samuel Oloruntoba (eds), *Regenerating Africa: Bringing African Solutions to African Problems*, 114–37. Pretoria: Africa Institute of South Africa.

Muchemwa, Cyprian (2015) 'Building Friendships Between Shona and Ndebele Ethnic Groups in Zimbabwe'. Doctoral Thesis, Durban: Durban University of Technology.

Muromo, Lorraine (2022) 'Analysts Call for Independent Gukurahundi Commission'. *Southern Eye*, 25 October, sec. Local News. https://www.newsday.co.zw/southerneye/local-news/article/200002523/analysts-call-for-independent-gukurahundi-commission.

Ndebele, Zenzele (2022) Interview with Zenzele Ndebele, Online.

Ndlovu, Mphathisi (2018) 'Speaking for the Dead: Testimonies, Witnesses and the Representations of Gukurahundi Atrocities in New Media'. *Journal of African Cultural Studies*, 30 (3): 293–306. https://doi.org/10.1080/13696815.2017.1359084.

Ndlovu-Gatsheni, Sabelo J. (2012) 'Rethinking Chimurenga and Gukurahundi in Zimbabwe: A Critique of Partisan National History'. *African Studies Review*, 55 (3): 1–26. https://doi.org/10.1017/S0002020600007186.

Netsianda, Mashudu (2022) 'President to Launch Gukurahundi Hearings'. *The Chronicle*, 10 March. https://www.chronicle.co.zw/president-to-launch-gukurahundi-hearings/.

Nyabola, Nanjala (2018) *Digital Democracy, Analogue Politics: How the Internet Era Is Transforming Politics in Kenya*. London: Zed Books Ltd.

Nyoni, Mgcini (2022) Interview with Mgcini Nyoni, Zoom.

Pink, Sarah, Sinanan, Jolynna, Hjorth, Larissa and Horst, Heather (2016) 'Tactile Digital Ethnography: Researching Mobile Media Through the Hand'. *Mobile Media & Communication*, 4 (2): 237–51. https://doi.org/10.1177/2050157915619958.

Postill, John and Pink, Sarah (2012) 'Social Media Ethnography: The Digital Researcher in a Messy Web'. *Media International Australia*, 145 (1): 123–34. https://doi.org/10.1177/1329878X1214500114.

Recuero, Raquel, Soares, Felipe and Vinhas, Otávio (2021) 'Discursive Strategies for Disinformation on WhatsApp and Twitter during the 2018 Brazilian Presidential Election'. *First Monday*, 26 (1). https://doi.org/10.5210/fm.v26i1.10551.

Tshuma, Samkeliso (2022) Interview with Samkeliso, Online.

Twitter Spaces (2021) 'Spaces Is Here, Let's Chat'. 3 May. https://blog.twitter.com/en_us/topics/product/2021/spaces-is-here.

Vambe, Maurice T. (2012) 'Zimbabwe Genocide: Voices and Perceptions from Ordinary People in Matabeleland and the Midlands Provinces, 30 Years On'. *African Identities*, 10 (3): 281–300. https://doi.org/10.1080/14725843.2012.715456.

Van Leeuwen, Theo (2007) 'Legitimation in Discourse and Communication'. *Discourse & Communication*, 1 (1): 91–112. https://doi.org/10.1177/1750481307071986.

Velasquez, Alcides and Rojas, Hernando (2017) 'Political Expression on Social Media: The Role of Communication Competence and Expected Outcomes'. *Social Media + Society*, 3 (1): 2056305117696521. https://doi.org/10.1177/2056305117696521.

Visvizi, Anna and Lytras, Miltiadis D. (2019) 'Politics and ICT: Issues, Challenges, Developments'. In Anna Visvizi and Miltiadis D. Lytras (eds), *Politics and Technology in the Post-Truth Era*, 1–8. Bingley: Emerald Group Publishing.

Wardle, Claire and Derakhshan, Hossein (2017) *Information Disorder: Toward an Interdisciplinary Framework for Research and Policy Making*. Strasbourg: Council of Europe.

Willems, Wendy (2020) 'Beyond Platform-Centrism and Digital Universalism: The Relational Affordances of Mobile Social Media Publics'. *Information, Communication & Society*: 1–17. https://doi.org/10.1080/1369118X.2020.1718177.

Yue, Neriah (2020) 'The 'Weaponization' of Facebook in Myanmar: A Case for Corporate Criminal Liability Notes'. *Hastings Law Journal*, 71 (3): 813–44.

Chapter 7

Are claims of Russian disinformation in Africa founded?

Elections in Zimbabwe, South Africa and the Democratic Republic of the Congo

Seyoung Jeon

After the 2016 US presidential election drew attention to the subject of Russian disinformation globally, similar concerns were raised for African countries. Facebook revealed in 2019 that networks of inauthentic Russia-linked accounts were targeting users across the continent (Alba and Frenkel 2019), and Russian propaganda or disinformation has been observed in nearly half of all African countries (Akinlolu and Ogunnubi 2021; Zwicewicz 2019; Rozhdestvensky et al. 2019). Concerns over Russian intervention permeated domestic political discussions as well. When the results of the 2018 presidential election in Zimbabwe were announced, the main opposition candidate Nelson Chamisa accused Russia of helping the incumbent ZANU-PF party manipulate the polls (Meyer et al. 2018). In South Africa, the *Daily Maverick* newspaper published documents allegedly detailing a Russia-linked organization's plans to create and disseminate disinformation about the EFF and DA online during the 2019 South African general election (Haffajee and Dossier Centre 2019). The threat of Russian intervention was also a key talking point for presidential candidate Martin Fayulu during the 2018 general election in the Democratic Republic of the Congo (Shekhovtsov 2020).

There is a widespread narrative that Russia is launching disinformation campaigns to interfere in African elections, but this claim has not been sufficiently assessed to date. While authors have examined Russian influence campaigns in African countries (Grossman et al. 2019) and Russian disinformation on social media targeting the United States (Linvill and Warren 2020), there has yet to be an empirical assessment of the veracity of the claims made regarding the extent and influence of Russian disinformation in African elections. This chapter asks: what was the scale and content of Russia-linked disinformation on Twitter around recent elections in Zimbabwe, South Africa and the DRC? I analyse a dataset containing more than 15 million tweets and conduct twelve key informant interviews to understand the level of Russian disinformation targeting the 2018 presidential election in Zimbabwe, the 2018 general election in the DRC and the 2017 ANC leadership conference (ANC54)[1] and 2019 general election in South Africa. The empirical results of this investigation refute the narrative that Russia is using disinformation on Twitter to interfere in African elections.

Many governments are known to conduct influence campaigns using digital disinformation to affect politics in other countries. Twitter has disclosed that state-backed accounts in China and Saudi Arabia sought to amplify pro-government messaging globally (Twitter 2019, 2020), while competing inauthentic French and Russian campaigns targeted Mali in 2020 (Gleicher 2020). However, the decision to investigate Russia-linked disinformation was partly due to the availability of data. At the time of this study, Twitter was employing a team to identify and suspend suspected inauthentic state-linked accounts and making this data available to researchers ('Update on Twitter's review of the 2016 US election' 2018). In this context, 'inauthentic' accounts refer to Twitter profiles that use a fake identity to engage in behaviour that manipulates other users' experience on the platform, such as creating multiple fake accounts that interact with each other to artificially inflate engagement (Twitter 2022). Between 2018 and 2022, Twitter released the most consistent data about inauthentic Russian networks. Analysis of Russia-linked disinformation in three African countries is possible, which is not the case for most other potential candidates. All of the datasets analysed in this chapter come from Twitter.

This chapter contributes to a growing body of literature on the characteristics of disinformation targeting African audiences that will be reviewed in the next section. By examining the scale and content of Russia-linked information operations in three countries on Twitter, I demonstrate that online disinformation exists but must be interpreted in comparative and local political contexts to understand how these campaigns are conducted in different countries. The empirical results from the case studies reveal stark differences in the content of disinformation campaigns targeting Zimbabwe, South Africa and the DRC, and this chapter argues in favour of a more contextualized local investigation of disinformation to capture the diversity of power relations it reflects.

This chapter proceeds in five parts. First, it establishes a definition for disinformation and provides context on Russia's disinformation ecosystem. Second, it reviews the literature on Russian disinformation targeting African countries and the patterns that emerge from such campaigns in Europe and the United States. The third section discusses the methodology while the fourth presents the three case studies of Zimbabwe, South Africa and the DRC. This chapter concludes by arguing there was an inconsequential level of Russian disinformation on Twitter targeting recent elections in these three countries.

---

1. The 2017 ANC leadership conference is referred to as ANC54 because it was the fifty-fourth national conference.

Definitions

As discussed in the introductory chapter, *disinformation* is generally defined as the organized and deliberate manipulation of the information environment using false or misleading information to cause harm or serve another's political interests (Reddi et al. 2021; Wardle and Derakhshan 2017). Disinformation and misinformation are often used interchangeably but should be distinguished by several features. *Disinformation* is the organized production and deliberate spreading of false or misleading information that seeks to cause harm or serve another's political interest, whereas *misinformation* is unintentionally inaccurate information (Wardle and Derakhshan 2017; Ong and Cabanes 2018).

This chapter uses the term *information operations* to describe more generally state-linked efforts to intentionally alter the information environment to manipulate public perceptions (Starbird et al. 2019). This can include disinformation, but also other types of political propaganda that do not necessarily include information that is factually false (Moy and Gradon 2020). Social media sites like Facebook and Twitter use *information operations* to describe deliberate and systematic attempts to influence public opinion using inauthentic accounts and/or inaccurate information (Jack 2017: 6). The term *fake news* is avoided for reasons noted by Wardle and Derakhshan (2017), namely that it is inadequate to describe the complex phenomena of information pollution and has been weaponized by some politicians to describe news coverage they dislike.

Russia's disinformation ecosystem

The Internet Research Agency (IRA), Evgeny Prigozhin and the Russian foreign military intelligence agency (GRU) are three actors that appear consistently throughout discussions of Russia-linked disinformation both in African countries and elsewhere. The IRA is a Russian organization alleged by the US Justice Department in a 2018 indictment to have engaged in operations to interfere with elections and political processes in the United States (US District Court for the District of Columbia 2018). Although the IRA is officially a private company registered in Saint Petersburg, Russian businessman Evgeny Prigozhin, who is believed to be its de facto leader and financier, retains close ties to Russian President Vladimir Putin and the organization has produced pro-Kremlin content, including criticisms of opposition activist Alexei Navalny, for a domestic Russian audience (Zhegulev 2016; Benyumov et al. 2018). Finally, GRU operatives have also been indicted by the US Justice Department in connection to disinformation operations (US Department of Justice 2018).

The term *Russia-linked* is used at times throughout this chapter to emphasize ambiguity in the origin of disinformation campaigns. Twitter identified the IRA, other Prigozhin affiliates (e.g. employees of his other businesses) and the GRU as being the main groups associated with Russian information operations on its platform (Twitter 2021). The division between public and private interests in contemporary Russian politics is nebulous, and it is immensely difficult to assess the extent to which some activities can be linked directly to the Russian state as opposed to private actors or interests. In the dataset provided, Twitter did not identify which group they believe each tweet originated from, only disclosing that the IRA, Prigozhin affiliates and the GRU were all suspected to have engaged in information operations on their platform (Twitter 2021). Accordingly, the term Russia-linked is preferred over Russian at times to highlight uncertainties regarding the precise role of the Russian state in these activities.

Literature review

This section proceeds in three parts. It begins with a review of contextual literature to establish what is already known about Russian disinformation around African elections. It then discusses some of the patterns observed from research on Russia-linked information operations in other countries, primarily in the United States and Europe, to place disinformation within information operations more broadly. The final section focuses on conceptualizing Russian disinformation both in a historical context and regarding the power dynamics that shape it.

Russian information operations and African elections

Much literature on Russian information operations in African elections consists of journalistic accounts or policy briefs. Mapping existing findings on these activities suggests that the content spread on Twitter and Facebook by these inauthentic accounts is more often hyper-partisan rather than factually inaccurate (Grossman et al. 2019; Linvill and Warren 2020).

One of the most comprehensive reviews of Russia-linked information operations in Africa was published in a 2019 white paper by Grossman et al. (2019). The authors used data shared by Facebook to map the activities of inauthentic Russian accounts in six African countries including Mozambique, the Central African Republic (CAR) and the DRC. They found that posts generally sought to promote Russia-aligned actors and politicians or presented positive coverage of Russia's activities on the continent. While much of the content was partisan, there were few cases of factually inaccurate information mentioned in the report.

The Dossier Centre is another major source of information about Russian interests and involvement around African politics. This is an investigative unit created and funded by former oil tycoon Mikhail Khodorkovsky, who was imprisoned in Russia in 2003 after financing opposition groups and has lived in exile in London since 2013 (Sandford 2013). The organization gathers data through anonymous digital dropboxes and aims to expose illicit activities carried out by Putin's administration, frequently partnering with journalists or researchers to publicize these details. Their documents have informed several investigations. Anton Shekhovtsov reported on the Association for Free Research and International Cooperation (AFRIC), a Prigozhin-linked think tank that participated in biased election observation missions in Africa between 2018 and 2019 (Shekhovtsov 2020). Journalist Ferial Haffajee from the South African newspaper *The Daily Maverick* used Dossier Centre documents to detail AFRIC's plans to interfere in South Africa's 2019 election, which recommended running negative messages about the Economic Freedom Fighters (EFF) and Democratic Alliance (DA) (Haffajee 2019).

There are three characteristics of existing literature on Russian disinformation in Africa that limit efforts to understand the scale and scope of Russia-linked involvement in democratic processes. First, much reporting focuses on the IRA's intended activities instead of what was attempted or accomplished in reality (Haffajee 2019; Shekhovtsov 2020). This is partly due to the prominence of the Dossier Centre's documents in these investigations, which claim to communicate Prigozhin's but do not detail the extent to which they are implemented. The assumption that Russia engaged in the full extent of its stated ambitions regarding election interference contributes to inflated expectations. This chapter measures evidence of actual disinformation rather than reviewing plans.

Second, descriptive reports of Russia-linked disinformation around African elections tend to rely on samples of IRA activity pre-selected by social media companies. Twitter and Facebook share the profiles of some users identified as being part of inauthentic networks or brief summaries of posts from inauthentic Russian accounts, but it is difficult to determine how representative those samples are of IRA activity online (Alba and Frenkel 2019). Furthermore, the reports often exclude details like the volume of posts or the variety of political messaging. By using the entire dataset of Russian information operations released by Twitter, this chapter presents a more comprehensive image of the volume and trends in disinformation targeting Zimbabwe, South Africa and the DRC.

Finally, journalistic works tend to construct the unit of analysis as 'Africa' rather than interrogating involvement in specific countries. This lens reinforces a particular construction of Africa that has been criticized in more recent scholarship (Ferguson 2006) and also carries a serious empirical flaw in its tendency to overlook the possibility that information operations might be carried out differently across countries. Accordingly, there is a need to examine how disinformation campaigns manifest in countries with distinct social, political and economic contexts. This study aims to address a gap in current literature by examining Russian disinformation in three African countries while taking into account historic and political specificity.

Characteristics of Russian information operations

There is minimal scholarship addressing recent Russian disinformation around elections in Zimbabwe, South Africa or the DRC, but some patterns of IRA activity emerge from research on information operations more broadly elsewhere. These studies most often focus on the United States (Linvill and Warren 2020; Badawy et al. 2018; Starbird et al. 2019), but they serve as a useful frame of reference to help assess the nature and content of online activity targeting the three case studies.

The first characteristic observed of Russian information operations in these studies is that rather than promoting the interests of one side as might be expected, these accounts tend to promote content on both sides of major sociopolitical issues to deepen existing cleavages (Badawy et al. 2018; Broniatowski et al. 2018; Starbird et al. 2019). Despite widespread allegations that the IRA intervened on behalf of the Republican Party in the 2016 US election, Badawy et al. (2018) identified a near equal number of conservative and liberal Russian troll accounts tweeting about the event. Linvill and Warren (2020) also find that the IRA did not intervene primarily on behalf of one party in their analysis of more than 9 million tweets targeting the United States. There was not a huge disparity between the number of tweets posted by left and right-wing troll accounts, and the inauthentic users prioritized promoting content that was intentionally divisive, like attacking moderate politicians, rather than broadcasting traditional ideological narratives such as raising or lowering taxes (Linvill and Warren 2020). Academic studies about Russian information operations targeting non-US countries are much scarcer, but Morgan's research on the 2018 French presidential elections found evidence of Russian influence on both sides of divisive issues like migration (Morgan 2018).

A second pattern is the creation of disinformation or conspiracy news stories to pollute the information environment. This is not completely distinct from the previous strategy because these stories can seek to exacerbate social cleavages. However, this phenomenon should be examined as a separate category because such polarization can be achieved without the production of fabricated news. Linvill and Warren's (2020) study of the United States revealed that IRA-linked users shared content about fictitious crisis events like an outbreak of Ebola in Atlanta, Georgia. Stelzenmüller (2017) found that in the lead-up to the 2016 German federal elections, inauthentic Russian accounts fabricated stories of crimes committed by migrants. Hindman and Barash's (2018) report on IRA-linked accounts active around the 2016 US election found that falsified or conspiracy news was only a small fraction of the content they posted, which mainly consisted of unremarkable pro-Trump and pro-Republican messages. Although the proportion of disinformation appears to be lower than other types of content propagated by inauthentic Russia-linked accounts, this behaviour retains a prominent position in discussions of IRA activity.

These two characteristics cannot claim to describe all elements of Russia-linked information operations, but they provide insight into some of its recurring features. The case studies in this chapter both challenge and reinforce these patterns to demonstrate how greatly information operations vary by country.

Conceptualizing Russian disinformation

Social media is a relatively new phenomenon, but the concept of state-sponsored disinformation pre-dates the digital era. The Soviet-era practice of *dezinformatsiya* involved operations that aimed to 'pollute' the opinion-making process (echoing the disinformation practices used to disrupt online discourse in the previous chapter by Rutendo Chabikwa) in the West and drive wedges in the Western alliance (Holland 2006). Most scholars appear to characterize Russia-linked information operations on social media as a close continuation of former Soviet active measures rather than as a distinctly new form of political interference (Abrams 2016; Starbird, Arif and Wilson 2019; White 2016). Interviewing former Soviet-era intelligence officers, Rid says the objectives of dezinformatsiya included discrediting certain politicians, supporting anti-establishment tendencies and manipulating people into acting in ways that supported Soviet policy objectives (Rid 2020). These aims are echoed in contemporary disinformation targeting elections. Starbird et al. (2019) and Abrams (2016) both emphasize the ambition to influence outcomes in a favourable way, referring to the IRA's content in support of Trump in 2016 and anti-EU parties in France and Greece. Additionally, some argue that Russian information operations primarily seek to worsen political polarization. Hanson et al. (2019) claim that most efforts are intended to disrupt societies or undermine faith in important institutions rather than directly impacting voting outcomes. This is supported by Starbird, Arif and Wilson (2019) and Linvill and Warren (2020) who argue that IRA accounts inserted themselves into both sides of highly polarized conversations and sought to use inauthentic networks to worsen existing sociopolitical divisions.

Swaying election results and increasing political polarization are not two mutually exclusive objectives and most authors propose multiple reasons motivating disinformation. However, they help identify existing patterns in Russia-linked information operations against which the findings from this chapter can be assessed. The question of what *motivates* disinformation, however, opens a discussion about the power relations at play in disinformation campaigns and online information environments more broadly.

Historically, the process of Russian dezinformatsiya was to get a fabricated news story published by a non-Communist news outlet and then watch if the story was picked up more widely and received major news coverage in target countries (Holland 2006; Rid 2020). This strategy today has been named 'trading up the chain', which involves planting a misleading or false story with a small news outlet that will be covered by larger news organizations if the story can perform well enough (Marwick and Lewis 2017). In the case of the 2016 US election, Lukito et al. (2020) argue that journalistic 'uptake' of Russian disinformation by US news outlets amplified its message. Disinformation that is shared widely within its target audience can acquire agenda-setting or opinion power. Agenda-setting power is the ability for news media to influence the salience of a topic in people's minds (McCombs and Shaw 1972). Helberger (2020) defines 'opinion power' as the ability of the media to influence processes of individual and public opinion formation.

Many of the potential objectives of disinformation campaigns, like altering voting behaviours or deepening political divisions, are ones that require the initial message to be amplified by other accounts. Rather than audiences being passive recipients of disinformation, they are key participants within successful campaigns, retweeting or reposting narratives. Howard (2020) characterizes these operations as lie machines, where producers create the false information, which is then distributed by inauthentic accounts that aim to have the content circulated by ordinary citizens. When the target audience shares this content at sufficient scale, they lead messages to go viral nationally or globally. Tandoc, Lim and Ling (2018) argue that disinformation is co-constructed by the audience because its 'fakeness' depends on whether it was perceived as real in the first place. Asmolov (2018) also observes participatory features of disinformation, such as its ability to provoke emotions such as outrage and the way people engage with disinformation that approaches their social circles in a form of 'peer-to-peer propaganda'. Wardle and Derakhshan (2017) characterize widespread amplification as the ultimate goal of those who seek to manipulate beliefs, but this process is one that requires an audience's participation.

Methodology

This research comprises of a mixed-methods study of how coordinated Russian information operations on Twitter appeared around three general elections: Zimbabwe and the DRC in 2018 and South Africa in 2019. It draws from a dataset of more than 15 million tweets from accounts affiliated with the IRA, Prigozhin and the GRU targeting countries both in Africa and elsewhere. This data was obtained through Twitter's Transparency Centre, which made tweets and media from suspected state-linked information operations publicly available starting in October 2018. Date and keyword filters are applied to identify the most relevant tweets for each country and election. Hundreds of tweets were then reviewed individually to assess if they contained relevant content. These quantitative findings were then supplemented by twelve key informant interviews conducted with journalists and scholars of disinformation and African and Russian politics to aid in the content analysis.

This research focuses on Russian disinformation on Twitter because the platform's data sharing practices allow for the most comprehensive look into Russian influence campaigns and therefore the greatest scope to empirically provide insight into answering the question. Facebook only provides a few samples of the content from deleted accounts suspected of spreading disinformation and WhatsApp's end-to-end encryption precludes large-scale content collection. Accordingly, this chapter cannot claim to be comprehensive in its account of Russian disinformation in African countries. There are certainly methodological issues that arise with research using Twitter data, including but not limited to the fact that users are not necessarily representative of the wider population (e.g. the views of urban middle-class citizens can be overrepresented) and that users engage in behaviours not captured through data collection methods, such as 'subtweeting' without directly linking to the original tweet (Tufeckci 2014). Despite these shortcomings, Twitter is still a politically relevant platform that provides the most comprehensive access to data.

Twitter investigation

The dataset obtained from Twitter contained all content and metadata from accounts discovered to be engaging in information operations. These accounts were deactivated by Twitter for attempting to 'manipulate Twitter to influence elections and other civic conversations' (Twitter, n.d), but the exact mechanisms through which such behaviour is detected remain undisclosed.

Date and keyword filters helped identify tweets relevant to elections in Zimbabwe, South Africa and the DRC. Most excluded tweets were apolitical, such as advertisements for sunglasses or clearly targeted at a foreign audience.[2] Tweets that could be considered disinformation were flagged for further analysis to assess the narratives they produced and the ways in which they were deployed around the election. Inductive coding was performed following a review of the contents of each tweet, with categories and tags varying by country.

To keep the investigation focused on elections, a date filter selected tweets in the period of one year before to one month after the election being analysed. While this thirteen-month period was a starting point, the range was altered for South Africa and the DRC based on specific circumstances to more fully explore the nature and content of Russian influence campaigns.

Due to the size of the dataset, only tweets containing specific keywords relevant to elections or politics were retained.[3] The keyword bank for each country followed a similar format, including twelve to fifteen terms for major parties, candidates, places, important national figures and other political hashtags. For the DRC, the search was also conducted in French. An example of the search parameters for Zimbabwe's 2018 election is shown as follows.

DATES	July 2017 to August 2018
KEYWORDS	ZimDecides, ZimVotes, ZimElections, ElectionZW, kwekwe, Harare, ThisFlag, Chamisa, Mnangagwa, edpfee, ZANU, MDC, Mugabe, varakashi, nerrorist[a]

[a]This is a play on Nelson Chamisa's nickname during his involvement in student politics. He called himself Nero after the Roman Emperor, so his online supporters were dubbed 'nerrorists' by the ruling party.

Key informant interviews

I interviewed twelve journalists and academics specializing in disinformation and African and Russian politics to help interpret the results of country-specific content analysis. This content is cited as supporting evidence for claims when the empirical findings supported interviewees' interpretations but was not used as the sole basis for advancing specific arguments.

Methodological limitations

There are several challenges with data collection and interpretation limiting the extent to which this research can provide an accurate and comprehensive account

---

2. E.g., tweets raising concerns about the number of Malian migrants in France were likely targeted at a French audience.

3. More precisely, it was conducted as a case-insensitive string search. E.g., 'ZANU' would also return rows with 'ZANU-PF' and 'zanu'.

of Russia-linked disinformation around elections in Africa. First, it trusts that social media companies have correctly identified inauthentic Russian accounts, as the exact methods of detection are protected as trade secrets. Second, as boyd and Crawford (2012) caution, large internet datasets are often imperfect due to gaps and errors. Third, a keyword search cannot capture the full extent of political discussion. Political conversations on Twitter do not necessarily include a political keyword in each exchange because participants understand the previous context of discussion. Misspellings are missed in the search, as is political content that was solely shared through non-text-based media like videos.

The focus on Twitter also has implications for what can be confidently argued about Russian disinformation around African elections and many of these limitations are inherent to the study of online information operations. However, many researchers treat Twitter and Facebook's identification of inauthentic accounts as being sufficiently accurate to base their research on (Grossman et al. 2019; Linvill and Warren 2020). Despite its shortcomings, this research design provides some insight into how Russia engages with these countries on Twitter while not aiming to be representative of its interactions across multiple social media platforms or the entire continent.

Ethical considerations

This research was approved by the Research Ethics Committee of the Department for Political and International Studies at the University of Cambridge. Several steps have been taken to address potential user privacy considerations as. First, all Twitter users mentioned in this chapter have been assigned pseudonyms when it is necessary to discuss the handles of these accounts. Second, these inauthentic accounts and their tweets were removed by Twitter from the platform, so it is not possible to identify which real accounts and users interacted with their content.

Regarding the key informant interviews, all participants have published on their topics of expertise, and in compliance with ethical guidelines, they were given the option to be anonymized. Any attribution in this work has occurred with participants' consent.

Case studies

Zimbabwe

2018 election

There were loud claims from opposition groups that Russian disinformation was a factor in Zimbabwe's 2018 Presidential election. The 2018 election was notable for being the first since Zimbabwe's 1980 independence in which Robert Mugabe was not running as a presidential candidate, having stepped aside following a military 'coup' in November 2017. Both major parties – the incumbent ZANU-PF and opposition Movement for Democratic Change (MDC) – were experiencing serious internal discord.

ZANU-PF was split into rival factions. 'Lacoste', led by the interim president Emmerson Mnangagwa, retained strong links to the military and key ministries. Mnangagwa was previously Robert Mugabe's 'right-hand man', but his participation in the 2017 coup effectively ended that relationship (Karekwaivanane interview 2021). Meanwhile, Generation 40 (G40) can be characterized as the pro-Mugabe faction, including his wife Grace Mugabe and several prominent Ministers within its ranks.[4]

Following the death of veteran opposition leader Morgan Tsvangirai, the opposition MDC split into two factions due to a power struggle between his deputies Nelson Chamisa and Thokozani Khupe. Chamisa eventually led the main MDC Alliance, which will be referred to as the MDC throughout this chapter, and Khupe a splinter group called the MDC-T (Ndakaripa 2020).[5] Mnangagwa (ZANU-PF) and Chamisa (MDC) emerged as the main presidential contenders. The contest was predicted to be very close; a pre-election survey found Mnangagwa had only a three-point lead over Chamisa (Afrobarometer 2018). On the eve of the election, Robert Mugabe publicly condemned Mnangagwa's ZANU-PF by declaring he would vote for Chamisa's MDC.

Although the election was held on July 30, the results of the presidential contest were delayed to 3 August, raising concerns that the Zimbabwe Electoral Commission (ZEC) was intervening to ensure Mnangagwa won in the first round (Beardsworth et al. 2019). Mnangagwa was awarded 50.8 per cent of the vote to Chamisa's 44 per cent, just passing the threshold required to avoid a run-off election (Banerjee 2018). However, the MDC accused the ZEC of manipulating the vote count in favour of Mnangagwa and Chamisa declared victory on 1 August, before the official results announcement. When MDC supporters staged demonstrations in Harare on 1 August, the Zimbabwe Defence Forces (ZDF) shot and killed six protesters (Mhaka 2018). The election's legitimacy was disputed again on 10 August, when Chamisa filed a petition to the Constitutional Court challenging the results (Dzirutwe 2018a). However, the results were unanimously upheld on August 24. Chamisa himself accused Russians of having manipulated the polls, but the ZANU-PF continues to deny any such involvement (Meyer et al. 2018).

Social media in the 2018 election

Research on the use of social media in the 2018 election reveals that supporters of both the ZANU-PF government and the MDC opposition attempted to spread

---

4. The 40 in G40 refers to a younger group of ZANU-PF politicians.

5. The T in MDC-T stands for 'Tsvangirai', as he led this faction after the party split in 2005.

disinformation. Pro-government 'Varakashi'[6] and pro-opposition 'Nerrorists' groups emerged online during the campaign period and conducted Twitter battles, but the content noted by Munoriwarya and Chambwera (2020) was mostly hyper-partisan rather than factually false. Other authors have observed cases of disinformation that emerged during this period, such as falsified news stories detailing plans by the ZEC to rig the election, incorrect polling results and reports that the European Union election observation mission had condemned the ZEC's conduct (Mare and Matsilele 2020).

Examining Twitter data for Zimbabwe

The data collection process for Zimbabwe was adjusted slightly from the standard date and keyword parameters to more fully capture the scope of Russia-linked disinformation. The initial search returned 292 'politically relevant' tweets between June 2017 and August 2018, but most activity was traced to three users. All tweets associated with those three accounts were pulled from the original dataset of more than 15 million tweets and reviewed individually, resulting in an additional 354 tweets for the Zimbabwe dataset. Many were missed in the initial search because they contained misspelled keywords or conveyed their message through image rather than text. With the new additions, the total Zimbabwe dataset contained 646 tweets.

The tweets were assigned content codes to help identify those explicitly mentioning the 2018 election and separate them from other politically significant topics like Robert Mugabe's resignation or land reform. Tweets that displayed partisanship or other markers of political identity (e.g. sharing articles praising certain policies) were labelled accordingly.

Findings from Twitter investigation

User accounts, political identities, activity over time and engagement were the lenses used to structure the examination of the Twitter dataset. Three observations emerge: the messaging is deeply one-sided, activity is concentrated around the election and accounts are responsive to ongoing events.

Messaging is one-sided

The overwhelming majority of the tweets in the Zimbabwe dataset (566 out of 646) were explicitly pro-ZANU-PF or anti-opposition MDC. Seven were anti-Mugabe tweets, and the remaining seventy-three appeared to be more neutral comments on economic issues and current events. There was no positive content about opposition parties or politicians in the entire dataset, which contradicted the pattern of Russian activity observed in other countries like the United States and France (Badawy et al. 2018; Morgan 2018). From this dataset, only 4 per cent,

---

6. Varakashi is derived from a Shona term meaning 'destroyers' or 'thrashers'.

or twenty-seven tweets, were clear cases of disinformation, such as spreading false polling numbers or claiming the political opposition orchestrated an assassination attempt against Mnangagwa in June 2018.[7] The remaining 547 tweets were hyper-partisan but did not meet the definition of disinformation. The majority of tweets in the Zimbabwe dataset were hyper-partisan and propagandistic but did not spread factually false information.

Of the eighteen accounts in the dataset, much of the pro-Mnangagwa activity could be traced to three highly active users. 'EMarshall', 'DavidKangwa' and 'Tavonga21' who together accounted for 89 per cent of the 646 tweets in the original Zimbabwe dataset, increasing to 95 per cent after the review of users' tweet histories in the expanded dataset. They attempted to present themselves as local users by displaying full names and tweeting exclusively about Zimbabwe but were as verified as Russian-linked accounts by Twitter. Activity is concentrated around the election.

The number of tweets spiked in the month preceding the election, as shown in Figure 7.1, and there is little political Russia-linked activity occurring in the background throughout 2017 and early 2018. Many of the tweets between June and August 2018 were posted by the three accounts mentioned previously. Separating tweets by subject reveals that the increase in activity around June/July 2018 contains messaging relevant to the election (zimelection), while the November 2017 tweets following the coup are entirely about Robert Mugabe (RM).

Accounts are responsive to events
Since intense election-related activity starts after interim president Mnangagwa announces a July election on 30 May 2018, this study zooms in on the period from June to August 2018 in Figure 7.2. When analysed by event, the pattern of activity indicates that Russian accounts were highly responsive to developments on the ground rather than simply posting canned content. Immediately after the 23 June bombing at a ZANU-PF rally in Bulawayo, the proportion of tweets mentioning the attack clearly outweighed other election-related content. Most of these tweets expressed sympathy for the bystanders and security personnel who were injured in the attack, but others are cases of disinformation as they alleged Chamisa and the MDC had attempted to assassinate Mnangagwa at the rally despite a clear lack of evidence. Tweets discussing the legitimacy of the election results were concentrated in August (results) and were generally hyper-partisan in favour of ZANU-PF rather than factually false.[8] Disinformation tweets about US sanctions

---

7. E.g., 'It's so nice to see that majority of Zimbabweans weren't fooled by Chamisa's web of lies. All polls show that ~70 per cent of Zimbabwe supports @edmnangagwa.' (21 June 2018); 'ED's enemies have proven themselves to be not only weak, but also very stupid. They have shown their true face with this assassination attempt. Now only blind and dumb ppl will vote for MDC. Smart and peaceful ppl will vote for ED!' (26 June 2018).

8. E.g., 'This powerful couple will lead us to the brighter future for sure. I'm so glad our nation made the right choice.' (02 August 2018); 'Don't be fooled by fake news and social

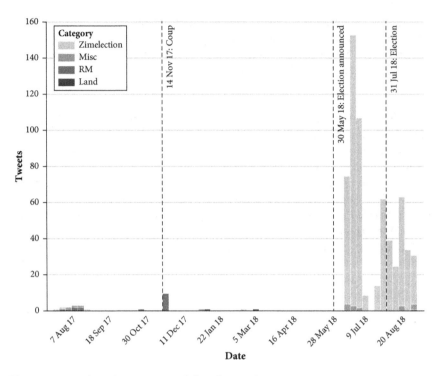

Figure 7.1 Number of tweets per week by subject, July 2017–August 2018.

targeting Zimbabwe are represented in yellow in Figure 7.2, but these did not present any noticeable trends.

Discussion of Zimbabwe findings

The investigation into Russian activity in Zimbabwe unearths evidence of one-sided support on Twitter for Mnangagwa and the ZANU-PF in the 2018 election but only twenty-seven tweets that could clearly be considered disinformation. The results from the Zimbabwe dataset confirm some existing research about patterns in Russia-linked disinformation while challenging others. Rather than promoting content on both sides of major sociopolitical divisions, all relevant messages in this dataset took a pro-government position, either by promoting Mnangagwa's candidacy or criticizing Chamisa's. The campaign also did not appear to exploit divisions within the traditional ZANU-PF bloc, as there was no mention of Grace Mugabe or other G40 members. The absence of tweets mentioning any major candidates or parties throughout most of 2017 also reveals the IRA did not

media supporting #MDCAlliance. Everything is a lie don't waste your time. We have elected our President free and fair.' (16 August 2018).

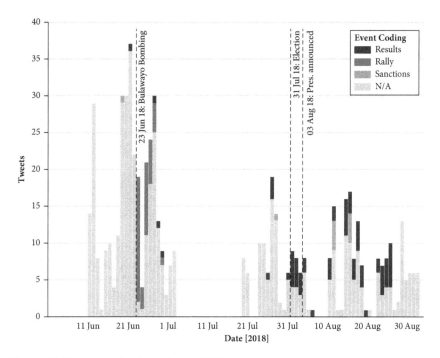

Figure 7.2 Tweets per day, June–August 2018.

promote polarization outside of election cycles, unlike the continuous background 'noise' directed at the United States (Linvill and Warren 2020).

A small portion of tweets in this dataset could be considered disinformation according to the definition set out at the beginning of the chapter. Most tweets shared hyper-partisan opinions rather than overtly false or misleading information,[9] which is compatible with the characterization of Russian information operations on Facebook in other African countries that other researchers have identified (Hindman and Barash 2018; Grossman interview 2021).

There were two interesting cases of disinformation regarding the Bulawayo bombing and the renewal of US sanctions against Zimbabwe. On 23 June 2018, a grenade exploded at Mnangagwa's campaign rally in Bulawayo, killing two and injuring dozens of attendees including Vice President Kembo Mohadi. A few tweets in the dataset suggested the Chamisa-led MDC had attempted to assassinate Mnangagwa.[10] However, this was not a conspiracy theory that was popular within

9. E.g., 'Would you trust your 6yearold [*sic*] son to drive a car? That's how I feel about @nelsonchamisa running for president.' (21 June 2018).

10. E.g., '@nelsonchamisa always threatened to resort to extreme measures in case he was going to lose, guess he is losing . . . No surprises here.' (23 June 2018); 'Thank God out president is safe after all what happened to him!!! Chasima [*sic*] has to explain what he meant by "response is coming, it will be red"?!' (25 June 2018).

Zimbabwe (Mano interview 2021). Mnangagwa himself announced soon after the event that he suspected members of the G40 linked to Grace Mugabe were behind the attack (Dzirutwe 2018b). This position was widely publicized by major Zimbabwean newspapers like *The Herald* (Mugabe 2018) and *The Zimbabwe Independent* (Gagare 2018) and also received coverage in international media (Cotterill 2018). The theory that this was orchestrated within the ZANU-PF is further supported by the security layout of the event, as bypassing three high-level perimeters would have required inside knowledge (Karekwaivanane interview 2021). The inauthentic accounts attempted to create or amplify a conspiracy that had little credibility even among ZANU-PF supporters.

A second set of tweets that classify as disinformation discussed US sanctions on Zimbabwe, with ten tweets blaming Chamisa for their renewal. This claim lacks credibility; most US sanctions on Zimbabwe were introduced during Robert Mugabe's reign over election rigging and human rights abuses (Mavhunga 2021). The sanctions renewed in August 2018 cited irregularities with the July election and violence against protesters as reasons for their continued application (Mhlanga-Nyahuye and Duzor 2018). This narrative was one that had more traction in the political mainstream than the bombing conspiracy theory. *The Herald*, the most widely read newspaper in Zimbabwe, has published editorials tying Chamisa to the renewal of sanctions and accusing him of 'treachery' (Wafawarova 2021). In this case, it appears the inauthentic accounts tried to amplify an existing narrative rather than creating one from scratch, reflecting the historical techniques of disinformation in the Soviet Union described by Rid (2020).

Overall, disinformation formed only a small portion of the Russia-linked tweets targeting Zimbabwe, and none of them received much engagement from authentic users. They failed to popularize the Bulawayo conspiracy and only posted a few tweets about Chamisa and US sanctions. Unlike the falsified anti-migrant 'news' stories that were seen in Russian disinformation campaigns on German social media (Stelzenmüller 2017), 547 out of 646 tweets in this dataset promoted narratives that are hyper-partisan but not clearly disinformation. The one-sided promotion of political content around the 2018 presidential election in Zimbabwe diverges from patterns established elsewhere. Accordingly, we cannot assume that analysis and findings about the role of disinformation in Russian information operations in the United States or Europe are directly applicable to other countries like Zimbabwe.

South Africa

Electoral politics, 2017–19

There were allegations of Russian election interference in South Africa in 2019. Haffajee, working with the Dossier Centre, published documents containing an alleged Russia-linked organization's plans to create and disseminate disinformation about the EFF and DA online during the 2019 South African general election

(Haffajee and Dossier Centre, 2019). The close ties between Jacob Zuma and members of the Russian elite had also been a subject of public discussion and concern for some years preceding the election (Toyana 2018; Plaut 2017; 'Jacob Zuma's Mysterious Mission to Russia' 2014).

In South African politics, the period from 2017 to 2019 marked a transition of power away from incumbent ANC leader Jacob Zuma, an event that potentially expanded openings for political contestation. Zuma's second and final term as president of South Africa was marked by serious public discontent and disunity within the ANC. Several waves of large-scale protest occurred in 2017 and thousands of protesters took to the streets across South Africa in April 2017 to call for Zuma's resignation, a stance publicly endorsed by some senior members of the ANC (Roelf and Stoddard 2017). Following these protests, Cyril Ramaphosa and Jacob Zuma's ex-wife Nkosazana Dlamini-Zuma announced their candidacies for the ANC presidency, which would be determined at the national conference in December 2017. In the months preceding the ANC leadership conference (ANC54), the party was divided between Ramaphosa's anti-Zuma faction and Dlamini-Zuma's pro-Zuma loyalists (Winning and Macharia 2017). The race was projected to be close and Ramaphosa narrowly won the ANC presidency. After his victory, Ramaphosa's faction pressured President Zuma to step down before the end of his full term in mid-2019 (Onishi 2018). Jacob Zuma announced his resignation on 14 February 2018.

Disinformation on Twitter in South Africa

Potential Russian interference aside, South Africa's social media ecosystem has already experienced domestic disinformation campaigns. In 2017, a propaganda war between pro- and anti-Zuma factions occurred on Twitter (Wasserman 2020). The wealthy Gupta family, which had close ties to Jacob Zuma, hired UK public relations firm Bell Pottinger to influence public opinion and the company created a Twitter network of more than 100 fake accounts to push pro-Zuma or pro-Gupta content (Findlay 2016). The campaign was prolific, consisting of at least 185,000 tweets. While much of the content here was again hyper-partisan rather than factually incorrect,[11] there was a notable element of disinformation. One of the three major hashtag campaigns fabricated by these inauthentic accounts was #Jonasisaliar, which sought to destroy then-Deputy Finance Minister Mcebisi Jonas' credibility.[12] Jonas was a key whistleblower in the state capture inquiry which revealed the Gupta family's influence over President Zuma (Pilling 2017). Inauthentic accounts also amplified existing disinformation narratives, for

---

11. E.g., 'It's a sign blacks must know Their place. And whites don't need law to teach us. #HandsOffBrianMolefe.' 'Thuli's shady conduct in state capture probe'.

12. E.g., 'Jonas fooled the whole nation & drama queen wasted millions in this #statecapture investigation.'

example, by retweeting false allegations about an alleged coup being orchestrated against Zuma by several of his ministers (Findlay 2016).

Approach to examining the Twitter data

Due to its significance in political discourse and the presence of substantial home-grown disinformation, Twitter is an especially interesting platform to investigate Russian influence campaigns. The South Africa dataset contained 170 tweets from December 2016 to June 2019, which were derived from a two-step data collection process. The initial search for tweets around the 2019 election retrieved only eighteen results, so the search date was extended back to December 2016, one year before the ANC54 conference. 152 tweets were added to the dataset. Instead of discarding activity around the 2019 election, these tweets were retained to conduct a more thorough examination, as the lack of activity is itself worth interrogating in the context of greater Russia-linked activity around the ANC54 conference in 2017.

Twitter findings

User accounts, political identities, activity over time and engagement were the lenses used to examine the dataset. Two observations emerge: only a small portion of the tweets can be considered disinformation and these tweets were distributed across many accounts but almost all contained race-themed disinformation.

Few disinformation tweets

Much like the Zimbabwe dataset, most tweets targeting South Africa were hyper-partisan rather than factually false.[13] Only eighteen out of the 170 tweets could clearly be classified as disinformation and among them, seventeen explicitly mentioned race, all referring to the white replacement conspiracy theory. Examples of disinformation included the false allegations that millions of white people in South Africa were living in squatter camps and the government was attempting to carry out a 'white genocide'.[14]

Tweets are widely distributed across accounts

A striking feature of the Zimbabwe dataset was that three accounts posted the majority of tweets. This pattern is not reflected in South Africa, where seventy-nine accounts participated, but most only contributed one tweet. 'DominantUS' and 'PeytonCash' were the most prolific users, posting fifteen and eleven times respectively, but both tweeted about several countries and the South Africa content

---

13. E.g., 'Out of all super villains Zuma has by far most evil laugh #SONA2017' (11 February 2017); '#OffendEveryoneIn4Words Zuma mustn't step down' (11 April 2017).

14. E.g., 'South African Government refuses to help millions of Whites living in 'squatter camps' (08 August 2017); ' The world's media continues to ignore Genocide in South Africa. The horror is real.' (06 February 2018).

only accounted for a small fraction of their overall activity. There appeared to be no accounts dedicated to tweeting solely at South Africa.

Discussion of South Africa findings

There was a very low volume of Russia-linked disinformation detected in South Africa and the patterns of activity suggest there was no coordinated attempt to influence the information environment around elections. No accounts were intensely tweeting about South Africa and tweets were usually partisan or propagandistic, demanding Zuma's resignation or praising land expropriation, rather than factually false. Unlike in Zimbabwe, the disinformation tweets for South Africa focused almost entirely on race instead of referencing specific candidates.

Despite concerns over Russia-linked interference, domestic actors played a much more significant role in disinformation targeting South Africa. It was a major component of the Bell Pottinger operation that aimed to shift public opinion in favour of Jacob Zuma or the Guptas (Findlay 2016; Cave 2017). From a total of 170 tweets targeting South Africa among which only eighteen could be clearly classified as disinformation is an insignificant volume of disinformation originating from Russia-linked networks. This cannot be reasonably interpreted as an attempt to seriously pollute the information environment or sway opinion. The low volume of tweets spread over three years indicates they did not seriously aspire to acquire agenda-setting or opinion power. Rather, the power interests in evidence appear to be domestic ones, given the much greater volume and indications of intentionality around the disinformation campaign orchestrated by Bell Pottinger.

Democratic Republic of the Congo

Electoral politics, 2016–19

Russian interference was a key talking point for presidential candidate Martin Fayulu during and after the 2018 general election in the DRC (Meyer, Arkhipov, Rahagalala 2018; Shekhovtsov 2020). Fayulu claimed that Russia was involved in the DRC for its mineral wealth and that then-President Joseph Kabila was desperate for external intervention (Meyer, Arkhipov, Rahagalala 2018), presumably because he would not be able to contest the presidency again.

In 2016 Kabila was nearing the end of his second consecutive term, which is the maximum permitted by the DRC's constitution. There were widespread concerns that he was seeking to extend his presidency (Litanga interview 2021). The Independent National Electoral Commission (CENI) petitioned the DRC's Constitutional Court to postpone the November 2016 general election, claiming more time was needed to prepare election materials like ballot boxes and updating the voter register (Mbaku 2016). In addition to postponing the election, the court ruled that the incumbent president could stay in office until elections were held (Clowes 2016), effectively extending Kabila's term.

These delays sparked serious political unrest in the DRC and dozens of people were arrested or killed in anti-Kabila protests throughout 2017 and 2018 (*BBC News* 2018). The National Episcopal Conference of the Congo (CENCO) was an important organizing force behind many marches (Litanga 2018). Two years after the end of his constitutionally permitted term, Kabila stepped down and elections were held in December 2018.

There were three main candidates in the 2018 election. Emmanuel Shadary was Kabila's handpicked successor leading the incumbent Common Front for Congo (FCC). The two main opposition candidates were Felix Tshisekedi and Martin Fayulu. Tshisekedi was the leader of the Union for Democracy and Social Progress (UDPS), the DRC's largest opposition party. Fayulu represented the Lamuka alliance, which was a movement that united prominent opposition figures like Jean-Pierre Bemba and Vital Kamerhe.

Multiple observers including the National Episcopal Conference of the Congo (CENCO) and the Congo Research Group have alleged that the 2018 election was rigged in favour of Tshisekedi, but these organizations did not specifically accuse Russia of intervention (Keane 2019; Stearns 2019). Polling conducted by the Congo Research Group in late 2018 showed Fayulu to be the clear frontrunner, winning 47 per cent of the vote compared to Tshisekedi's 24 per cent (Stearns 2019). CENCO fielded almost 40,000 observers on election day and recorded that 62.8 per cent of votes cast were in favour of Fayulu, and *a Financial Times* investigation of a dataset with the 'authentic' vote counts confirmed these partial results (Wilson, Blood and Pilling 2019). However, CENI announced that Tshisekedi was the winner, having earned 38.5 per cent of the vote, with Fayulu at 34.7 per cent. The official results announcement was widely disputed, and many observers speculated that Tshisekedi's unexpected win was orchestrated through a backroom deal between Tshisekedi and the FCC coalition to help Kabila retain some political power (Englebert 2019).

Findings from Twitter investigation

As a case study, the DRC cannot be analysed as comprehensively as Zimbabwe and South Africa because there was much less data available for analysis. The search returned only 115 tweets from Russia-linked networks, forty-one of which were written in French and seventy-four in English. The especially low number of French-language tweets is notable because English is not widely spoken in the DRC, even among the political class (Curtis and Litanga interviews 2021). This points to two possibilities: there was a lack of knowledge on the Russian side that English was not often used in the DRC, or the tweets mentioning DRC politics were actually intended for a different audience. Irrespective of language choices, the tweets did not contain factually false information and thus there was no evidence of a coordinated Russian disinformation campaign on Twitter in the DRC.

The low volume of tweets can be asserted with a high degree of confidence because multiple precautions were taken to minimize the risk of missing content. First, the search was conducted over a three-year period from January 2016 to

January 2019. Although the general election occurred in December 2018, this had been postponed several times since 2016 by former president Joseph Kabila. If there was substantial Russia-linked content targeting DRC elections, expanding the search to include 2016 should have returned activity that occurred around the original election day or on subsequent dates in 2017.

Second, the search for tweets targeting the DRC in the Twitter dataset was very thorough, with fifteen terms included in the keyword bank.[15] In addition to the standard election-related phrases, the search included ones relevant to the security situation in the DRC (MONUSCO, Kivu), other political actors (Bemba, CENCO) and a Lingala term used by the anti-Kabila movement (Telema). These supplementary terms returned few new results, indicating a general lack of Russia-linked disinformation on Twitter around DRC politics.

While it is important to avoid over-interpreting the contents of such a small dataset, there are a few observations about the broad characteristics of the DRC tweets that can be compared to previous cases. First, the dataset contained hyper-partisan content but nothing that could clearly be classified as disinformation. Second, there was no clear spike in activity around any event and most tweets received no authentic engagement. Third, the account 'SansTravailFixe' was responsible for more than half the tweets in the dataset, but unlike the three highly active users in Zimbabwe, DRC-related content only accounted for a small fraction of SansTravailFixe's tweet history. Finally, the absence of a clear message is one similarity the tweets shared with the DRC Facebook pages in Grossman et al.'s (2019) paper, as the tweets were generally anti-Kabila but did not publish positive content about any opposition figures.

It is not possible to conclusively ascribe specific motivations for the creation of some DRC-related content by inauthentic Russian networks. Diversifying content could have been an attempt by developers to evade bot detection measures on Twitter or a strategy to build up authentic followers for these accounts that would engage in coordinated disinformation campaigns targeted elsewhere (Cresci 2020). However, this is very much speculative.

While there was no evidence of Russian disinformation targeting the DRC, this is a case of domestic power interests posing a more substantial threat to political processes. CENI and Kabila likely altered the results of the 2018 election to manufacture a Tshisekedi victory, in addition to supporting measures that would suppress voter turnout for the opposition (Congo Research Group 2019). These offline methods of influencing election outcomes appear to have been effective.

Conclusion

Serious allegations concerning Russian intervention have been raised around recent elections in Zimbabwe, South Africa and the DRC. In Zimbabwe and the

---

15. Kabila, Kinshasa, Congo, Tshisekedi, RDC, Fayulu, Shadary, Lamuka, UDPS, Bemba, CENCO, Goma, MONUSCO, Kivu, Telema.

DRC, the main opposition presidential candidate accused Russia of helping to manipulate the polls (Meyer, Arkhipov and Rahagalala 2018; Shekhovtsov 2018). In South Africa, concerns over Russian interference were raised when a newspaper published documents that appeared to detail Prigozhin's plans for a disinformation campaign during the 2019 general election (Haffajee and Dossier Centre 2019). This chapter aimed to evaluate these claims of Russia-linked intervention by conducting a mixed-methods analysis of large datasets of supposed coordinated campaigns from inauthentic Russian accounts on Twitter.

In response to the research question: 'what was the scale and content of Russia-linked disinformation on Twitter around recent elections in Zimbabwe, South Africa, and the DRC?', the evidence indicates there was little to no Russian disinformation targeting these three countries. The highest level of disinformation was detected in Zimbabwe, yet this only consisted of twenty-seven tweets. None of them received much authentic engagement. South Africa had eighteen disinformation tweets and the DRC zero. This lack of amplification indicates the disinformation pushed by Russia-linked accounts, when it existed, failed to acquire substantial opinion or agenda-setting power.

These findings indicate the importance of critically analysing claims about foreign disinformation in elections. Despite strong claims of interference in the DRC after the 2018 presidential election, no evidence of Russian disinformation was found. In Zimbabwe and South Africa, low volumes of Russian disinformation were identified but it is clear that they had little if any influence on the election.

The high degree of heterogeneity between the three African case studies, and their divergence from analysis drawn from studying Russian disinformation targeting the United States, provide a warning about the pitfalls of generalizing findings from one country to another. Examining Russian disinformation in 'Africa', to the exclusion of specific countries, can overlook more localized dynamics. Inauthentic Russian accounts tweeting fringe conspiracy theories designed to exacerbate racial tensions in South Africa affirm the 'both sides' polemic observed by scholars of Russian disinformation in other countries. However, this was not the case in Zimbabwe, where disinformation was heavily skewed to support Mnangagwa over Chamisa. More granular investigations of Russian disinformation reveal nuances that may be overlooked at a higher level. Situated analysis that draws on an understanding of the historical and political context produced distinct findings in each location studied in this chapter, showing claims of Russian intervention must be assessed on a country-by-country basis.

This research also helps contextualize the relative significance of different electoral threats. Among the three case studies examined, the DRC and Zimbabwean elections carried allegations of significant offline irregularities. Concerns over Russian interference were repeatedly raised by the opposition before the 2018 DRC election, but the actual manipulation of results was likely coordinated by CENI and Kabila's faction (Congo Research Group 2018). In Zimbabwe, Mnangagwa's narrow victory in the first round was trailed by concerns over widespread voter suppression and suspicions that the results had been inflated in sparsely populated rural areas (European Union Election Observation Mission 2018; interview with scholar of Zimbabwean politics, *name withheld*). Despite the elevated concern over Russian interference online, the more meaningful threats to election integrity in these countries were home-grown and offline.

This research has broader implications for the study of social media influence campaigns and efforts to secure the integrity of democratic processes. First, the case studies contribute additional reference points to track evolution or variation in the disinformation strategies employed by Russia-linked groups. This is potentially useful for social media platforms to detect and attribute coordinated inauthentic behaviour. Second, it helps observers, policymakers and election commissions in these countries assess the actual threat posed by Russian disinformation compared to other forms of intervention and allocate resources accordingly. In Zimbabwe, South Africa and the DRC, despite serious domestic concern over Russian interference, in reality the level of disinformation was insignificant.

Bibliography

Abrams, S. (2016) 'Beyond Propaganda: Soviet Active Measures in Putin's Russia'. *Connections*, 15 (1): 5–31.

Akinlolu, A. and Ogunnubi, O. (2021) 'Russo-African Relations and Electoral Democracy: Assessing the Implications of Russia's Renewed Interest for Africa'. *African Security Review*, 30: 1–17. https://doi.org/10.1080/10246029.2021.1956982.

Alba, D. and Frenkel, S. (2019) 'Russia Tests New Disinformation Tactics in Africa to Expand Influence'. *The New York Times*, 30 October. https://www.nytimes.com/2019/10/30/technology/russia-facebook-disinformation-africa.html (accessed 3 November 2022).

Asmolov, G. (2018) 'The Disconnective Power of Disinformation Campaigns'. *Journal of International Affairs*, 71 (1.5): 69–76.

Badawy, A., Ferrara, E. and Lerman, K. (2018) 'Analyzing the Digital Traces of Political Manipulation: The 2016 Russian Interference Twitter Campaign'. *2018 IEEE/ACM International Conference on Advances in Social Networks Analysis and Mining (ASONAM)*, 258–65. https://doi.org/10.1109/ASONAM.2018.8508646.

Banerjee, V. (2018) 'Even After Mugabe, Zimbabwe's Elections do not Appear Free or Fair'. *Washington Post*, 22 August. https://www.washingtonpost.com/news/monkey-cage/wp/2018/08/23/post-mugabe-zimbabwes-elections-still-look-irregular-much-as-rhodesias-once-did/ (accessed 20 May 2021).

BBC News (2018) 'DR Congo: Several Deaths in Anti-Kabila Protests'. 21 January. https://www.bbc.com/news/world-africa-42766151 (accessed 8 June 2021).

Beardsworth, N., Cheeseman, N. and Tinhu, S. (2019) 'Zimbabwe: The Coup That Never was, and the Election That Could Have Been'. *African Affairs*, 118 (472): 580–96. https://doi.org/10.1093/afraf/adz009.

Benyumov, K., Bekbulatova, T., Golunov, I. and Dmitriev, D. (2018) 'Translators, Psychologists, and Inventors: Who are the Russians Indicted for Interfering in the 2016 U.S. Presidential Election?'. *Meduza*, 19 February. https://meduza.io/en/feature/2018/02/19/translators-psychologists-and-inventors (accessed 3 July 2021).

boyd, danah and Crawford, K. (2012) 'CRITICAL QUESTIONS FOR BIG DATA: Provocations for a Cultural, Technological, and Scholarly Phenomenon'. *Information, Communication & Society*, 15 (5): 662–79. https://doi.org/10.1080/1369118X.2012.678878.

Broniatowski, D. A., Jamison, A. M., Qi, S., AlKulaib, L., Chen, T., Benton, A., Quinn, S. C., Dredze, M. (2018) 'Weaponized Health Communication: Twitter Bots and Russian Trolls Amplify the Vaccine Debate'. *American Journal of Public Health*, 108 (10): 1378–84. https://doi.org/10.2105/AJPH.2018.304567.

Cave, A. (2017) 'Deal That Undid Bell Pottinger: Inside Story of the South Africa Scandal'. *The Guardian*, 5 September. https://www.theguardian.com/media/2017/sep/05/bell -pottingersouth-africa-pr-firm (accessed 13 November 2022).

Clowes, W. (2016) 'DR Congo: Can Anyone Stop Joseph Kabila?'. *African Arguments*, 21 July. https://africanarguments.org/2016/07/dr-congo-can-anyone-stop-joseph-kabila/ (accessed 8 June 2021).

Congo Research Group (2018) *Elections 2018: An Anxious Electorate Demands Change. 6.* New York, NY: Congo Research Group.

Congo Research Group (2019) *Tshisekedi's First 100 Days in Office. 9.* Congo Research Group. https://www.congoresearchgroup.org/wp-content/uploads/2019/06/English -100-days-Tshisekedi-04–05–19.pdf (accessed 6 August 2022).

Cotterill, J. (2018) 'Zimbabwe President Accuses 'normal Enemies' of Bomb Blast'. *Financial Times*, 24 June. https://www.ft.com/content/699a0190-7795-11e8-bc55 -50daf11b720d (accessed 1 July 2021).

Cresci, S. (2020) 'A Decade of Social Bot Detection'. *Communications of the ACM*, 63: 72–83. https://doi.org/10.1145/3409116.

Dzirutwe, M. (2018a) 'Zimbabwe's Chamisa Challenges Election Result; Inauguration Halted'. *Reuters*. https://www.reuters.com/article/us-zimbabwe-elections-court -idUSKBN1KV1PI (accessed 20 May 2021).

Dzirutwe, M. (2018b) 'Zimbabwe's Mnangagwa Says Grenade Caused Blast at Rally Last Week'. *VOA*. https://www.voazimbabwe.com/a/zimbabwe-attack-was-a-grenade -terrorism-act/4460803.html (accessed 21 June 2021).

Englebert, P. (2019) 'Congo's 2018 Elections: An Analysis of Implausible Results'. *African Arguments*, 10 January. https://africanarguments.org/2019/01/drc-election-results -analysis-implausible/ (accessed 8 June 2021).

European Union Election Observation Mission (2018) *Final Report: Republic of Zimbabwe, Harmonised Elections 2018.* European Union Election Observation Mission. https://eeas.europa.eu/sites/default/files/eu_eom_zimbabwe_2018_-_final _report.pdf (accessed 19 June 2021).

Ferguson, J. (2006) *Global Shadows: Africa in the Neoliberal World Order.* Duke University Press. https://doi.org/10.2307/j.ctv11g97mg.

Findings from a pre-election survey in Zimbabwe: June/July 2018 (2018) *Afrobarometer.* https://afrobarometer.org/media-briefings/findings-pre-election-survey-zimbabwe -junejuly-2018 (accessed 20 May 2021).

Findlay, K. (2016) 'Running Interference: The Fake 'white Monopoly Capital' Propaganda Community on Twitter'. *Superlinear*, 18 November. https://www.superlinear.co.za/ running-interference-the-fake-white-monopoly-capital-propaganda-community-on -twitter/ (accessed 1 June 2021).

Gagare, O. (2018) 'Bulawayo Bomb Blast Escalates Mnangagwa, Chiwenga Tensions'. *The Zimbabwe Independent*, 29 June. https://www.theindependent.co.zw/2018/06/29/ bulawayo-bomb-blast-escalates-mnangagwa-chiwenga-tensions/ (accessed 1 July 2021).

Gleicher, N. (2020) 'Removing Coordinated Inauthentic Behavior From France and Russia'. *Meta*, 15 December. https://about.fb.com/news/2020/12/removing-coordinated -inauthentic-behavior-france-russia/ (accessed 15 July 2022).

Grossman, S., Bush, D. and DiResta, R. (2019) *Evidence of Russia-Linked Influence Operations in Africa*. Palo Alto, CA: Stanford Internet Observatory.

Haffajee, F. and Dossier Centre (2019) 'Did Putin's 'Chef' Attempt to Interfere in South African Election?'. *Daily Maverick*, 7 May. https://www.dailymaverick.co.za/article /2019–05–07-exclusive-did-putins-chef-attempt-to-interfere-in-south-african-election/ (accessed 8 May 2021).

Hanson, F., O'Connor, S., Walker, M. and Courtois, L. (2019) *Hacking Democracies*. Australian Strategic Policy Institute. https://www.aspi.org.au/report/hacking -democracies (accessed 5 April 2021).

Helberger, N. (2020) 'The Political Power of Platforms: How Current Attempts to Regulate Misinformation Amplify Opinion Power'. *Digital Journalism*, 8 (6): 842–54. https://doi .org/10.1080/21670811.2020.1773888.

Hindman, M. and Barash, V. (2018) *Disinformation, 'Fake News, and Influence Campaigns on Twitter*. Washington, DC: Knight Foundation, 62.

Holland, M. (2006) 'The Propagation and Power of Communist Security Services Dezinformatsiya'. *International Journal of Intelligence and CounterIntelligence*, 19 (1): 1–31. https://doi.org/10.1080/08850600500332342.

Howard, P.N. (2020) *Lie Machines: How to Save Democracy From Troll Armies, Deceitful Robots, Junk News Operations, and Political Operatives*. New Haven; London: Yale University Press.

Jack, C. (2017) *Lexicon of Lies: Terms for Problematic Information*. New York, NY: Data & Society Research Institute, 22.

Keane, F. (2019) 'DR Congo Presidential Election: Outcry as Tshisekedi Named Winner'. *BBC News*, 10 January. https://www.bbc.com/news/world-africa-46819303 (accessed 1 November 2022).

Linvill, D. L. and Warren, P. L. (2020) 'Troll Factories: Manufacturing Specialized Disinformation on Twitter'. *Political Communication*, 37 (4): 447–67. https://doi.org/10 .1080/10584609.2020.1718257.

Litanga, P. (2018) 'Democratic Republic of Congo: A Country on the Brink'. *Al Jazeera*, 22 February. https://www.aljazeera.com/opinions/2018/2/22/democratic-republic-of -congo-a-country-on-the-brink (accessed 8 June 2021).

Lukito, J., Suk, J., Zhang, Y., Doroshenko, L., Kim, S. J., Su, M-H., Xia, Y., Freelon, D. and Wells, C. (2020) 'The Wolves in Sheep's Clothing: How Russia's Internet Research Agency Tweets Appeared in U.S. News as Vox Populi'. *The International Journal of Press/Politics*, 25 (2): 196–216. https://doi.org/10.1177 /1940161219895215.

Mare, A. and Matsilele, T. (2020) 'Hybrid Media System and the July 2018 Elections in "Post-Mugabe" Zimbabwe'. In *Social Media and Elections in Africa, Volume 1: Theoretical Perspectives and Election Campaigns*. Springer International Publishing. https://doi.org/10.1007/978–3–030–30553–6.

Marwick, A. and Lewis, R. (2017) *Media Manipulation and Disinformation Online*. New York, NY: Data & Society Research Institute.

Mavhunga, C. (2021) 'Zimbabwe's President Calls for Unity on 41st Independence Day'. *Voice of America*, 21 April. https://www.voanews.com/africa/zimbabwes-president -calls-unity-41st-independence-day (accessed 25 May 2021).

Mbaku, J. M. (2016) 'The Postponed DRC Elections: What Does the DRC's Situation Look Like now?'. *Brookings*, 22 November. https://www.brookings.edu/blog/africa-in-focus/2016/11/22/the-postponed-drc-elections-what-does-the-drcs-situation-look-like-now/ (accessed 8 June 2021).

McCombs, M. and Shaw, D. L. (1972) 'The Agenda-Setting Function of Mass Media'. *Public Opinion Quarterly*, 12 (2): 176–87.

Meyer, H., Arkhipov, I. and Rahagalala, A. (2018) 'Putin's Notorious "Chef" Is Now Meddling Across Africa'. *Bloomberg.com*, 20 November. https://www.bloomberg.com/news/features/2018–11–20/putin-chef-yevgeny-prigozhin-is-now-meddling-in-africa (accessed 24 May 2021).

Mhaka, T. (2018) 'How did Mnangagwa win Zimbabwe's Landmark July 30 Election?'. *Al Jazeera*, 6 August. https://www.aljazeera.com/opinions/2018/8/6/how-did-mnangagwa-win-zimbabwes-landmark-july-30-election (accessed 20 May 2021).

Mhlanga-Nyahuye, M. and Duzor, M. (2018) 'US: Reforms First, Then Removal of Zimbabwe Sanctions'. *VOA*, 14 September. https://www.voanews.com/africa/us-reforms-first-then-removal-zimbabwe-sanctions (accessed 25 May 2021).

Morgan, S. (2018) 'Fake News, Disinformation, Manipulation and Online Tactics to Undermine Democracy'. *Journal of Cyber Policy*, 3 (1): 39–43. https://doi.org/10.1080/23738871.2018.1462395.

Moy, W.R. and Gradon, K. (2020) 'COVID-19 Effects and Russian Disinformation Campaigns'. *Homeland Security Affairs*, 16: 27.

Mugabe, T. (2018) 'Those Behind Byo Bombing Now Known'. *The Herald*, 10 August. https://www.herald.co.zw/those-behind-byo-bombing-now-known/ (accessed 22 June 2021).

Munoriyarwa, A. and Chambwera, C. (2020) 'Tweeting the July 2018 Elections in Zimbabwe'. In *Social Media and Elections in Africa, Volume 1: Theoretical Perspectives and Election Campaigns*. Springer International Publishing. https://doi.org/10.1007/978–3–030–30553–6.

Ndakaripa, M. (2020) 'Zimbabwe's 2018 Elections: Funding, Public Resources and Vote Buying'. *Review of African Political Economy*, 47 (164): 301–12. https://doi.org/10.1080/03056244.2020.1735327.

News24 (2014) 'Jacob Zuma's Mysterious Mission to Russia'. 21 August. https://www.news24.com/News24/Jacob-Zumas-mysterious-mission-to-Russia-20140831 (accessed 2 July 2021).

Ong, J. C. and Cabanes, J. V. A. (2018) *Architects of Networked Disinformation: Behind the Scenes of Troll Accounts and Fake News Production in the Philippines*. University of Massachusetts Amherst. https://doi.org/10.7275/2CQ4-5396.

Onishi, N. (2018) 'Jacob Zuma Resigns as South Africa's President'. *The New York Times*, 14 February. https://www.nytimes.com/2018/02/14/world/africa/jacob-zuma-resigns-south-africa.html (accessed 31 May 2021).

Pilling, D. (2017) 'How Corruption Became 'state Capture' in South Africa'. *Financial Times*, 5 October. https://www.ft.com/content/36895cd6-a907-11e7-93c5-648314d2c72c.

Plaut, M. (2017) 'The Zuma – Putin Connection'. *Martin Plaut*, 22 October. https://martinplaut.com/2017/10/22/the-zuma-putin-connection/ (accessed 2 July 2021).

Reddi, M., Kuo, R. and Kreiss, D. (2021) 'Identity Propaganda: Racial Narratives and Disinformation'. *New Media & Society*, 14614448211029292. https://doi.org/10.1177/14614448211029293.

Rid, T. (2020) *Active Measures: The Secret History of Disinformation and Political Warfare*. London: Profile Books.

Roelf, W. and Stoddard, E. (2017) 'South Africa Anti-Zuma Protests Harden ANC Succession Divides'. *Reuters*, 27 September. https://www.reuters.com/article/us-safrica -protests-idUSKCN1C20WV (accessed 31 May 2021).

Rozhdestvensky, I., Rubin, M. and Badanin, R. (2019) 'How Russia Interfered in Electionsin Twenty African Countries'. *Проект[Proekt]*, 11 April. https://www.proekt .media/investigation/russia-african-elections/ (accessed 18 May 2021).

Sandford, D. (2013) 'Analysis: Mikhail Khodorkovsky in Exile'. *BBC News*, 22 December. https://www.bbc.com/news/world-europe-25488303 (accessed 18 July 2022).

Shekhovtsov, A. (2018) 'The Globalisation of Pro-Kremlin Networks of Politically BiasedElection Observation: The Cases of Cambodia and Zimbabwe'. Berlin: EPDE. https://www.epde.org/en/news/details/the-globalisation-of-pro-kremlin-networks-of- politically-biased-election-observation-the-cases-of-cambodia-and-zimbabwe-1686.html.

Shekhovtsov, A. (2020) *Fake Election Observation as Russia's Tool of Election Interference*. Berlin: European Platform for Democratic Elections.

Starbird, K., Arif, A. and Wilson, T. (2019) 'Disinformation as Collaborative Work: Surfacing the Participatory Nature of Strategic Information Operations'. *Proceedings of the ACM on Human-Computer Interaction*, 3 (CSCW). https://doi.org/10.1145/3359229.

Stearns, J. (2019) 'Who Really won the Congolese Elections?'. *Congo Research Group | Groupe d'Etude Sur le Congo*, 16 January. http://congoresearchgroup.org/congolese -election-leaks/ (accessed 8 June 2021).

Stelzenmüller, C. (2017) 'The Impact of Russian Interference on Germany's 2017 Elections'. *Brookings*. https://www.brookings.edu/testimonies/the-impact-ofrussian -interference-on-germanys-2017-elections/.

Tandoc, E. C., Lim, Z. W. and Ling, R. (2018) 'Defining "Fake News": A Typology of Scholarly Definitions'. *Digital Journalism*, 6 (2): 137–53. https://doi.org/10.1080 /21670811.2017.1360143.

'The Impact of Russian Interference on Germany's 2017 Elections' (2017). *Brookings*.

The United States of America v. Internet Research Agency LLC (2018) https://www.justice .gov/file/1035477/download (accessed 18 July 2022).

Toyana, M. (2018) 'South Africa's Zuma Fired me for Blocking Russian Nuclear Power Deal: Nene'. *Reuters*, 3 October. https://www.reuters.com/article/us-safrica-politics -finmin-idUSKCN1MD0TJ (accessed 2 July 2021).

Tufekci, Z. (2014) 'Big Questions for Social Media Big Data: Representativeness, Validity and Other Methodological Pitfalls'. In *Eighth International AAAI Conference on Weblogs and Social Media*, 10.

Twitter (2019) 'New Disclosures to our Archive of State-backed Information Operations'. 20 December. https://blog.twitter.com/en_us/topics/company/2019/new-disclosures-to -our-archive-of-state-backed-information-operations (accessed 15 July 2022).

Twitter (2020) 'Disclosing Networks of State-linked Information Operations we've Removed'. 12 June. https://blog.twitter.com/en_us/topics/company/2020/information -operations-june-2020 (accessed 15 July 2022).

Twitter (2021) 'Disclosing Networks of State-linked Information Operations'. February. https://blog.twitter.com/en_us/topics/company/2021/disclosing-networks-of-state -linked-information-operations- (accessed 24 March 2023).

Twitter (2022) 'Platform Manipulation and Spam Policy, Twitter Help'. https://help.twitter .com/en/rules-and-policies/platform-manipulation (accessed 4 November 2022).

Twitter (no date) 'Information Operations, Twitter Transparency Center'. https://transparency.twitter.com/en/reports/information-operations.html (accessed 23 July 2022).

'Update on Twitter's Review of the 2016 US Election' (2018) *Twitter Public Policy*, 19 January. https://blog.twitter.com/en_us/topics/company/2018/2016-election-update (accessed 3 November 2022).

US Department of Justice (2018) *U.S. Charges Russian GRU Officers With International Hacking and Related Influence and Disinformation Operations, The United States Department of Justice*. https://www.justice.gov/opa/pr/us-charges-russian-gru-officers -international-hacking-and-related-influence-and (accessed 18 July 2022).

Wafawarova, R. (2021) 'Unforgivable Treachery'. *The Herald*, 25 May. https://www.herald .co.zw/unforgivable-treachery/ (accessed 25 May 2021).

Wardle, C. and Derakhshan, H. (2017) *Wardle and Derakhshan 2017 Information Disorder .pdf*. DGI(2017)09. Council of Europe.

Wasserman, H. (2020) 'Fake News From Africa: Panics, Politics and Paradigms'. *Journalism*, 21 (1): 3–16. https://doi.org/10.1177/1464884917746861.

White, J. (2016) *Dismiss, Distort, Distract, and Dismay: Continuity and Change in Russian Disinformation. 13*. Institute for European Studies, 4.

Wilson, T., Blood, D. and Pilling, D. (2019) 'Congo Voting Data Reveal Huge Fraud in Poll to Replace Kabila'. *Financial Times*, 15 January. https://www.ft.com/content/2b97f6e6 -189d-11e9-b93e-f4351a53f1c3 (accessed 8 June 2021).

Winning, A. and Macharia, J. (2017) 'South Africa's Ramaphosa Wins Election as ANC President'. *Reuters*, 19 December. https://www.reuters.com/article/us-safrica-politics -idUSKBN1EC05I (accessed 31 May 2021).

Zhegulev, I. (2016) 'Evgeny Prigozhin's Right to be Forgotten What Does Vladimir Putin's Favorite Chef Want to Hide From the Internet?'. *Meduza*, 13 June. https://meduza.io/en /feature/2016/06/13/evgeny-prigozhin-s-right-to-be-forgotten (accessed 4 July 2021).

Zwicewicz, J. (2019) *Russia in Africa: Manipulation and Expanding Influence*. North York, ON: Canadian Forces College.

Chapter 8

Digital disinformation in Cameroon's 2018 presidential election

Simone Toussi

The October 2018 presidential elections in Cameroon were marked by several waves of disinformation, before, during and after the vote, causing confusion, heightening tensions and fuelling the post-election crisis. Disinformation is defined here as false information intentionally disseminated for political ends. If we cannot assert that the intentional spread of election disinformation, primarily on social networks, potentially confused voters, we can at least say that it elevated political tensions and significantly fed the dynamics of the post-electoral narrative. This chapter examines the unprecedented levels of public concern raised about the influence of digital disinformation on the election process and on informed political participation in Cameroon's first social media election. The chapter addresses a series of linked questions about the deployment of election disinformation: What motivated the deployment of disinformation during the 2018 elections in Cameroon? What types of disinformation were deployed as part of what strategies, and how did the deployment of disinformation during the election both reflect and impact existing dynamics of power in Cameroon's political process?

Starting from the hypothesis that disinformation, as a discourse, 'aims to act on others [and appears as] a voluntarist act of influence . . . the purpose of which lies in seeking support of the recipient' (Seignour 2011), we see disinformation during elections as the manifestation of power dynamics. In order to verify this premise, the study conducts content analysis on examples of online disinformation before, during and after the 2018 presidential elections. Considering this, the chosen corpus reflects 'disinformational' occurrences from or towards the protagonists of the election, namely the government (outgoing power), the opposition, activists or journalists and the voters. This qualitative approach will be carried out in two main stages. First, a descriptive stage presenting ten empirical examples of disinformation during the election period. Second, an analytical stage that will identify the underlying strategies for the deployment of disinformation through an analytical frame of content, actors and interactions to deduce the intended effect or purpose sought through each tactic used by disinformation perpetrators.

These unfold the chapter into four sections. The first section provides contextual background for the reader who is unfamiliar with Cameroon by providing an overview of its political, digital and media landscape. The second section outlines the theoretical framework used to analyse election disinformation which is produced by reviewing previous studies on Cameroon, disinformation and political power. The third section presents the data: empirical examples of disinformation that occurred from the pre-electoral period in October 2017 through to the post-election crisis in early 2022. It focuses on the disinformation content, types, actors and channels used. The fourth section conducts a content analysis of the disinformation using the analytical framework in order to identify the drivers, strategies and effects of election disinformation on the democratic process and power relations immanent to the 2018 election.

Contextual background – the realities underpinning the birth of disinformation

Cameroon is a Central African country located between Nigeria, Chad, the Central African Republic, the Republic of Congo, Gabon, Equatorial Guinea and the Gulf of Guinea, with approximately 28 million inhabitants. It has cultural diversity characterized by 240 ethnic groups, divided into three major groups (Bantu, Semi-Bantu and Sudanese) and 240 national languages (The Presidency 2021) (Figure 8.1). English and French are two official languages inherited from Franco-British colonization, a bilingualism controversial to the minority Anglophone part – barely 20 percent of the total population – which complains of being marginalized by the central government since the 1972 constitutional referendum.

A political history rooted in colonization and marred with crisis

The German Empire claimed Kamerun as a colony in 1884. Then, after the defeat of Germany in the First World War, the territory was divided into the French colony of Cameroun and the British colony of Cameroon. The southern French part became the independent Republic of Cameroon in 1960, and the British colony split in two in 1961, with the mainly Muslim North joining Nigeria and the mainly Christian South joining the Republic of Cameroon to form the Federal Republic of Cameroon. These arbitrary divisions of territory to serve colonial interests violated the local ethic, religious and cultural polities of indigenous people, creating artificial divisions and tensions that continue to scar contemporary power relations in Cameroon.

The first President of independent Cameroon was Ahmadou Ahidjo, who had been Prime Minister since 1958 under French rule. After his resignation in 1982, he was replaced by Paul Biya who celebrated forty uninterrupted years in power in November 2022. There are 316 political parties in Cameroon (MINAT 2021). The Cameroon People's Democratic Movement (CPDM) is the ruling party since Cameroon's independence in 1960, and the country's had a single president, Paul Biya, since 1982 (Kouam 2022), who is often accused of manipulating opinion through disinformation campaigns paid to foreign companies (Gillis 2020). All of

Figure 8.1 Map of Cameroon. *Source*: Wikimedia Commons.

President Biya's electoral mandates have been marred by controversial elections, arrests of opposition parties' members, journalists and activists. Cameroon is ranked 143 out of 167 countries on the democracy index (Economist Intelligence Unit 2021). According to Freedom House (2022) President Biya 'has maintained power by rigging elections, using state resources for political patronage, and limiting the activities of opposition parties. Press freedom and nongovernmental organizations (NGOs) are restricted, and due process protections are poorly upheld'.

Beyond the ethnic conflicts that have animated the political climate since the colonial era, Cameroon has recently experienced bloody conflicts linked both to the Islamic sect of Boko Haram and to the 'Anglophone crisis' (International Crisis Group 2017). These two conflicts are outlined in the following sections.

Boko Haram was passively present in the far north of Cameroon since 2009. The Islamic group carried out different forms of trafficking and gradually infiltrated the population while carrying out deadly attacks in areas bordering Nigeria. The Nigerian government and media accused the Cameroonian government of serving as a base for the sect and of supporting it. By 2014, Boko Haram gradually increased its military offences within Cameroon, was declared a terrorist organization by international bodies and caused the Cameroonian government to declare war. Over 400 Boko Haram attacks and incursions were registered between March 2014 and March 2016, together with about fifty suicide bombings killing ninety-two members of the military and more than 1,350 civilians, with over 120 injured. Clashes between the army and Boko Haram escalated, making Cameroon the second-largest target of the Islamist group after Nigeria. This protracted and deadly crisis resulted in thousands of deaths and tens of thousands of internally displaced refugees and an influx of 65,000 Nigerian refugees to Cameroon (International Crisis Group 2017).

The term 'Anglophone crisis', refers to 'the conflict between separatists who call for a complete independence of the two anglophone regions of Cameroon and the government military forces fighting to maintain the unity and peace of the country' (Ngange and Mokondo 2019). The Anglophone Crisis was triggered by resentment of what some claim is discrimination against those in the region and efforts to undermine local autonomy and institutions. Protest about this claimed Anglophone marginalization in 2016 led to clashes with the military and to an escalation of violence (International Crisis Group 2017). At least 3,000 people have lost their lives due to the crisis and more than 700,000 others had to flee their homes and relocate mainly in the urban centres of Douala, Yaoundé or neighbouring regions (France 24 2020).

> From 2016, the crisis escalated and increasingly became an armed conflict opposing the army to anglophone separatists. In this context, several citizen journalists engaged in producing and disseminating news about the conflict on various social media platforms. While some of them are in support of the current form of the state, others strongly stand for the secessionist cause. A third category prefers a return to the federation of 1961. (Nounkeu 2020: 25)

A symbolic declaration of Anglophone independence for the Federal Republic of Ambazonia on 1 October 2017 by Sisiku Julius Ayuk Tabe triggered heavy suppression by the Cameroonian army, resulting in deaths, injuries, riots, barricades, demonstrations, lockdowns and thousands of internally displaced people. In the two predominantly Anglophone regions of Cameroon, the South West and the North West, separatists have violently opposed the army since 2017 and both sides are regularly accused of abuses against civilians by non-governmental organizations (NGOs) (Sombaye Eyango 2018: 23). The crisis continued after the 2018 presidential election and despite the holding of the 'Grand National Dialogue' where the parties were supposed to find a solution to it, it punctuated the 2020 parliamentary elections and is still continuing at the time of writing (Sa'ah 2022).

Increasing adoption of ICTs with divisive legislation

Cameroon has been connected to the internet since 1997 and witnessed a significant connectivity boost in 2016 through increased investments in telecommunication and information and communication technologies (ICT) infrastructure. This included the extension of the national optical fibre backbone to about 12,000 km, connecting 209 of the country's 360 sub-divisions, as well as linking Cameroon to neighbouring countries. These improvements were made possible through the launch in May 2016 of the National ICT Strategic Plan 2020, which recognized the digital economy as a key driver for development (Toussi 2019). Today, Cameroon has over fifty active internet service providers (ISPs), as well as a plurality of mobile phone operators. This rise of ISPs contributes to the widening and democratization of mobile and internet usage in the country. At the beginning of 2023 Cameroon had 24 million mobile phone users out of a total population of 28 million, of whom 13 million were internet users and 4 million social media users (Dataportal 2023).

The Constitution guarantees access to information and freedom of expression in its preamble, specifying that 'freedom of communication, freedom of expression, freedom of the press, freedom of association and the right to strike are guaranteed under the conditions set by law'. However, some provisions contained in the 2010 laws on Cybersecurity and Cybercrime, the law governing Electronic Communications and the Penal Code are considered as traps against dissent and critical voices. Under article 113 of the 2016 Penal Code, 'Is punishable by imprisonment of three months to three years and a fine of one hundred thousand to two million CFA – African Financial Community – francs (USD 157 to 3,155), anyone who issues or propagates false news, when such news is likely to harm public authorities or national cohesion'. Article 85 of the 2010 Law on Electronic Communications punishes with imprisonment of six months to one year and a fine of 1,000,000 to 10,000,000 CFA francs (USD 1,578 to 15,775) 'whoever knowingly, transmits or puts into circulation on the radio electric channel, false or misleading distress signals or calls'. Articles 75 to 78 of the 2010 Law on Cybersecurity and Cybercrime essentially punish cyber harassment even by minors, hate speech of a tribal nature and the spread of false news. These laws have been criticized for their loopholes, lack of precision and clarity in provisions against 'false news' that may constitute a threat to freedom of expression, access to information, democratic participation and the right to privacy on the national territory. These concerns are especially worrying as Cameroon does not have an Access to Information Act so far (LEXOTA 2022).

Media pluralism and government censorship

Until 1990 the Cameroonian media landscape was dominated by state-controlled media such as Cameroon Radio Television and the Cameroon Tribune. Print media was liberalized in 1990 by the Law on Social Communication (year) and opened up not only to the private press but to new forms of expression. The Law on Audiovisual Communication (year) under Article 9(2) further requires publishers of audiovisual services to provide pluralistic and balanced information.

The liberalization of traditional media and the advent of social media in the absence of appropriate regulation in Cameroon quickly led to the proliferation of less trustworthy media outlets. Journalists are not required to register or have operating license, as the law on social communication recognizes as a journalist any person who, based on their intellectual faculties, training and talents, is suitable for the research and processing of information intended for social communication (Article 46(1)). The country reportedly has more than 600 newspapers, 150 radio stations and 100 TV channels in 2021 (Ngono 2021), thirty years after the liberalization of print and audiovisual media. Extensive internet penetration and mobile phone use have also increased online news services – thirty-nine online media outlets (Ngono 2021) – and blogs, with users increasingly manipulating news, thus compromising the quality of media content.

Faced with the challenge of regulating and organizing the digitalized media landscape, the government tends to resort instead to authoritarianism, often characterized by intimidation, arrests, prosecution of journalists or shutdowns of websites, social media, messaging applications and the whole internet (CIPESA 2022). Cameroon is currently ranked 118 out of 180 in the World Press Freedom Index (Reporters without Borders 2022) and considered 'one of the continent's most dangerous countries for journalists, who operate in a hostile and precarious environment'.

Disinformation

This section explores some scholarly definitions of disinformation and their reflections through existing studies on digital disinformation in Cameroon.

Theoretical approach of disinformation

As discussed in the introduction to this book, disinformation is commonly defined as false information, which is intended to mislead, especially propaganda issued by a government organization to a rival power or the media (Mississippi State University Library). Wardle and Derakhshan (2017) consider disinformation as part of a wider 'information disorder', which also includes misinformation and mal-information, and they distinguish disinformation as 'false', 'imposter', 'manipulated or fabricated' content that is 'knowingly shared to cause harm'. In the same vein, the European Commission (2018) has defined disinformation as 'all forms of false, inaccurate, or misleading information designed, presented and promoted to intentionally cause public harm or for profit'. What these definitions have in common is that they outline the fact that disinformation is generally intentional and intended to be misleading, in the form of false, manipulated or fabricated information. The definition from Benkler, Faris and Roberts (2018) keeps the same premise as the previously cited definitions, but is a bit narrower as it defines disinformation as 'manipulating and misleading people intentionally to achieve political ends'. This view is echoed by Philip Howard (2020), who also equates disinformation with political interests, a definition that is more consistent with this chapter, which focuses on disinformation during election periods, a time when high political interests are at stake in Cameroon.

Disinformation in Cameroon before 2017

Disinformation in politics was present in Cameroon before the arrival of the internet and social media, noticeable especially through the beginning of the post-colonial era and the 2004 presidential election, as Gillis (2020) underlined.

Takougang stressed disinformation as a commonly used pretext by state officials to justify media censorship in the early years of Ahidjo, the first president after the 1960 independence. While no evident case of disinformation was cited, it was stated that unsupervised freedom of expression would 'spread disinformation and threaten the unified public opinion necessary for national construction' (Takougang 1993: 279).

As to Nfi (2017: 4), disinformation arose in the late 1960s as a British foreign influence strategy to seek Southern Cameroons' independence from Nigeria. The false information was the argument for the impossibility of '*economic viability*' of this region, thus covering up its oil wealth to maintain it under British influence.

A recent investigation (Gillis 2020) stresses how the Paul Biya regime hired American public relations firms to disseminate disinformation through local traditional media during the 2004 presidential election. A prominent headline generated to obscure election rigging was 'Voting impresses American observers', published by the *Cameroon Tribune*, referring to a testimony 'the election was fair' from the alleged observers from the Association of Former Members of American Congress including Greg Laughlin. That statement was considered to be a lie by the opposition who argued that the election lacked transparency, and that the claim that the election was 'impressive' and 'fair' was an example of disinformation.

To date, there is very little published research on disinformation in Cameroon. Most of the reports are media articles, government communications and civil society studies. One exception is Sombaye Eyango's (2018) study of the use of social media in this Anglophone crisis. Eyango documents the use of disinformation by Anglophone separatists and the use of social media for online mobilization on social media platform such as Facebook, at the height of the Anglophone crisis and mainly between 2016 and 2017. The author highlights the role of the Cameroonian diaspora mainly in the United States, United Kingdom and Nigeria. Eyango (2018: 52) argues that disinformation in the form of manipulated videos was shared 'in order to encourage population on the field to join armed groups and fight for the independence of the Anglophone region'.

According to Koumnde Mbaga (2021: 21), disinformation appears as the main communication strategy that both camps in the Anglophone crisis – separatists and the Cameroonian government – used to frame each other in the worst possible image. Disinformation mainly happened through exaggeration of the supposed crimes in the conflict, leading to radicalization and decreasing the possibility of dialogue, with separatists calling for revenge and international support, while the government was calling for dialogue, stepping up the suppression in the meantime.

Other studies address disinformation in a general perspective, mostly seen as a growing issue especially fuelled by the rising and unregulated use of social networks (Ngapout 2021). The government, especially the Ministry of Posts and Telecommunication, also shares this view when it tags social media as 'real tools of disinformation, intimidation, call to hatred, to murders, to violence'. From the minister's perspective, online disinformation in Cameroon 'generally emanates from individuals, whose goal is to harm the reputation of individuals or institutions of the Republic' (Libom Li Likeng 2020).

Election disinformation (2017–18)

This section describes disinformation in Cameroon during the election period. It first considers various perceptions of online disinformation in Cameroon during that period, then describes specific occurrences of disinformation that were directly or indirectly linked to the election process.

Perceptions of online disinformation in Cameroon

The 2018 presidential election was Cameroon's first social media election. In the 2004 and 2011 elections digital disinformation was not a significant factor in Cameroon. Internet penetration in 2004 stood at just 0.98 per cent and mobile penetration at 9 per cent. By the 2011 elections those figures had risen to 5 per cent and 50 per cent respectively (World Bank 2020); however social media remained in its infancy in the country. Although the main presidential candidates had Facebook and Twitter profiles in 2011, these platforms were still used by less than 2 per cent of the population, so online civic space had a negligible effect on political participation or election engagement (Tande 2011). By 2018 this had changed.

The 2018 poll marked a turning point in Cameroon's electoral history, with more debate, more online participation and more disinformation and hate speech, especially on digital platforms. It was also described as the 'first social media election' because of the increased use of social media by aspiring candidates on the one hand and the heavy use by potential voters on the other hand (Africanews 2018). By 2018, Cameroon's internet penetration stood at 25 per cent, while mobile penetration was 90 per cent and social media use at 11 per cent (Datareportal 2018). Gillis (2020) argues that Biya regime's disinformation campaigns on social media during the 2018 presidential elections were a game changing strategy that helped recuperate his tarnished reputation following the Anglophone and Boko Haram crises. Gillis points to contracts signed by the president with American public relations firms Mercury Public Affairs, Glover Park Group and Clout Public Affairs between 2017 and 2020. This coincided with the appearance of some 'remarkably one-sided' social media accounts like @CameroonTruth and @AgenceCamPresse created between July and August 2018. The accounts were influential in online debates in the run-up to the presidential election and in the controversy of the fake election observers who falsely claimed to be Transparency International staff on a national television channel (discussed in what follows).

Emphasizing the role of social media in perpetuating disinformation, Nounkeu (2020: 20) demonstrates how self-proclaimed 'citizen journalists' or bloggers spread disinformation on Facebook about the Anglophone crisis from 15 August to 15 September 2018, a period close to the presidential election. Ngange and Mokondo (2019: 64) also point out the role of social media in helping the 'spread of falsehood by activists in order to reinforce resistance on Anglophone Cameroonians against the government', and explain how the government used that disinformation as a pretext to justify the ninety-three-day complete internet shutdown in the two Anglophone Regions of Cameroon from 17 January to 20 April 2017 (Ngange and Mokondo 2019: 56), depriving all citizens of their digital rights.

According to recent studies by civil society organizations, various security and social crises have favoured the spread of disinformation. As discussed earlier the overlapping Boko Haram and Anglophone crises provide the context of instability and contested truth-claims for disinformation in Cameroon. A report by the NGO ADISI Cameroun – Association for Integrated Development and Interactive Solidarity – (2022) discusses a third overlapping 'post-election' crisis that further crystallizes the proliferation of disinformation and hate speech. The Boko Haram crisis from 2014 was overlaid with the Anglophone crisis, especially from its violent phase since December 2016, and now the Cameroonian 'post-election crisis' from 2018. The term post-election crisis refers to a period of protests, claims of electoral fraud and violent government suppression that followed the 2018 election and extended into 2020. This post-election period was characterized by claims that the president had stolen the election from the opposition, street protests of citizens were met with armed response from the government and the arrest and detention of protestors – including opposition presidential candidates.

Analysis on disinformation in Cameroon, by digital policy experts CIPESA (2022), concluded that the country's disinformation is fuelled by three factors: the existing security situations linked to the Anglophone crisis, the terrorist threat of Boko Haram and the instability and political controversies due to forty years of a quasi-autocratic regime. These political controversies, they argue, surf on the ethnic differences created by colonial partition to fuel online disinformation and hate speech. In addition, the adoption of social media has enabled new forms of expression or civil participation without an adequate legal framework and hence the flourishing of hate speech, online violence and disinformation (ADISI-Cameroun 2022). These abuses in both the press and all other forms of online expression have led to increased government control over online expression and harsh suppression of critical media. In Cameroon, the ability to disseminate disinformation has benefited from a fast-growing but under-regulated media landscape. Citizens have come to rely on the internet and social media as primary sources of information, which are not necessarily the most reliable sources. Some actors suggest the adoption of access to information legislation and fact checking as solutions to increase the reliability of information shared on the internet (Data Cameroon 2022).

Cases of disinformation during the election
This section presents and describes a range of disinformation cases that were evidenced in Cameroon before, during and after the 2018 elections, cases which will then be analysed in subsequent sections. The cases were derived from an extensive literature search of academic, grey literature reports and media sources. There is very little peer-reviewed academic literature on the use of disinformation around the 2018 election in Cameroon (see, however, Ngange and Mokondo (2019) and Nounkeu (2020) on disinformation in the Anglophone Crisis). This made necessary recourse to civil society reports (e.g., CIPESSA 2022) and a reliance on media commentary. It is hoped that bringing this data together for the

first time in this publication a platform is provided upon which other researchers can build. From these sources examples of disinformation were selected that fell within the twelve months before and twelve months after the 2018 presidential election. This timeframe allowed the inclusion of pre-election disinformation as well as disinformation contributing to the post-election crisis. Of the wider sample of disinformation, the following examples were purposefully selected for their relevance to the election and to illustrate the range of types, tactics and techniques of disinformation deployed.

Case one: Internet restriction

In October 2018 citizens experienced disruption to their internet service. In the run-up to the election there was widely disseminated information about an internet shutdown being prepared by the government. However, such claims were denied by the then Minister of Post and Telecommunications, Minette Libom Li Likeng (Digital Business Africa 2018). Despite repeated denials, internet users witnessed a bandwidth throttling on messaging applications, especially Facebook Messenger and WhatsApp. The government publicly denied that this ever happened, but the internet suppression denial was later proven to be untruthful with evidence from the independent international internet monitoring agency NetBlocks (NetBlocks 2018). This untruth disseminated intentionally during the election period by the government meets the definition of disinformation used in this chapter.

Case two: Army torture and killing

In the midst of the election campaign in July 2018, a horrific video was widely shared on social media showing Cameroonian soldiers torturing and killing two civilian women and two children. The authenticity of the video was denied by the government of Cameroon and it was tagged as 'false news' by Issa Tchiroma Bakary, then Minister of Communication. A subsequent BBC News (2018) investigation of the incident found that the video was authentic and that it accurately depicted rights violations perpetrated by the Cameroon army. As such, the untrue statements of denial disseminated by the Government of Cameroon qualify as disinformation.

Case three: Fake election observer

On 7 October 2018, two individuals posing as independent elections observers working for Transparency International were interviewed live on the national television and state-controlled station Cameroon Radio Television (CRTV), with a stream on their web page. The widely circulated video showed the 'Transparency International' election observer explain that they were deployed to ensure 'the smooth running of the election'. The first person stated, 'I'm here as an independent observer, and from what I see, everything is going well', while the second said 'From what I saw yesterday during the counting, it was a real lesson in democracy, it was very instructive, very informative'. Their statements were widely spread by the local mainstream media and online, to reassure national and international observers that the election was free and fair despite being highly criticized locally

(TV5 Monde 2018). However, these two actors turned out to be imposters, after a press release from Transparency International denounced their trickery explaining that the individuals did not work for them. The untrue statements disseminated by the imposters via mainstream and online media channels meet the definition of being election disinformation.

Post-election disinformation (2019–22)

The fake observer scandal, coupled with allegations of widespread electoral fraud during the voting process and ballot counting, led to an unprecedented post-election crisis in Cameroon. This crisis was fuelled by online disinformation and hate speech from the day after the election until the parliamentary elections that took place in February 2020 and beyond. Disinformation in this period took the form of fake allegations, out-of-context news and fabricated content, presented in the six cases that constitute this sub-section (CIPESA 2022).

Case four: False victory claim

On 8 October 2018, in the aftermath of the presidential election, the Cameroon Renaissance Movement (CRM) candidate Maurice Kamto claimed victory before the official election results were announced. He gave no figures to back up his assertions, nor did he specify the reports upon which he relied to declare his victory over Paul Biya. Yet, he said, 'I have received a clear mandate from the people that I intend to defend to the end [. . .] I invite the outgoing President of the Republic to organize the conditions for a peaceful transmission' (Jeune Afrique 2018). This has led to several online movements, social media campaigns, widely circulated petitions and offline demonstrations in different cities in Cameroon with the slogan 'No to the Electoral Hold-up' (Jeune Afrique 2019). Following these demonstrations, which were violently repressed with gunfire and arrests, Kamto was accused of propaganda and manipulation of national opinion and the international community by the local partisan press (Le Bled Parle 2018), of making unfounded claims by the Ministry of Communication, then arrested and detained with some of his party members. Given the highly contested nature of the election process and the widespread claims of electoral fraud it is difficult to say with absolute certainty exactly who secured the most votes. If the government failed to secure sufficient votes but untruthfully declared itself the winner, then that claim meets the definition of disinformation. On the other hand, if the opposition candidate was not in possession of evidence that he had won but publicly claimed to have won then that claim meets the definition of disinformation.

Case five: Journalist disinformation

On 7 November 2018, journalist Mimi Mefo was arrested for 'spreading of fake news and cybercrime' and was released after one day of detention. She had relayed the words of a source claiming that the American missionary Charles Wesco, who died on 30 October during a clash between English-speaking separatists and Cameroonian security forces in the North West, was killed by regular army bullets (Federation of African Journalists 2018). After one day in detention, she was released under pressure from the journalists' union and international organizations (BBC News 2021). According to lawyer Me Alice Nkom, 'None of the offenses with which she was accused could be legally established, even if it was in front of a competent court, which was already not the case.' Given the frequency with which journalists and activists are arrested for spreading disinformation without any credible evidence it is suspected that the government's motive is not to prosecute but to send a warning and create a 'chilling effect' causing journalists to self-censor.

Similarly, web journalist and whistleblower Paul Chouta was detained following a complaint by Calixte Beyala accusing him of defamation and dissemination of false news. However, this detention was deemed 'abusive and disproportionate' because the detainee was denied access to a lawyer and exceeded the maximum prison sentence for the charges against him: he spent more than two years in prison from May 2019. In fact, he incurred six months in prison according to the Penal Code and up to two years according to the law on cybercrime in force in Cameroon (Reporters Without Borders 2021). Denouncing the trickery behind his detention, the opinion noted that there is 'an absurd discrepancy between the facts of which he is accused and the treatment he has received over the past two years', and the fact that he is detained for more than two years justifies 'the desire to remove a disturbing journalist' (Reporters Without Borders 2021). The arrest and imprisonment of Emmanuel Mbombog Mbog Matip, director of the private newspaper *CliMat Social* in August 2020 for 'spreading fake news', was also interpreted as a way to 'silence political dissent' (Committee to Protect Journalists 2020). The absence of evidence to demonstrate the genuineness of the 'disinformation' charges against these journalists makes the complainants' statements untruthful, which meets the definition of disinformation used in this chapter.

Case six: Mass identity theft

In May 2019, the Cameroonian Minister of Employment and Vocational Training, Issa Tchiroma Bakary, was a victim of identity theft and the dissemination of disinformation in his name on social networks. The fake accounts were allegedly 'disseminating false information on the socio-political situation in Cameroon and on certain high personalities who have marked national political life'. While denying being the author of these allegations, the Minister warned that the disinformation aimed to undermine his honour and to tarnish the image of Cameroon (Adjouda 2019). Similarly, in February 2021, a member of the Cameroonian Party for National Reconciliation (PCRN), Nourane Fotsing, filed a complaint for aggravated identity theft and fraud. As a parliamentarian and business leader, her identity was being used to falsely advertise her products, receive orders and then money through phone numbers on mobile money (Actu Cameroun 2021). These two persons represent two of the antagonistic political parties in the post-presidential and parliamentary elections (RDPC and PCRN). That whole period was marked by identity theft through massive fake social network accounts targeting public figures in Cameroon and displaying intentionally misleading information to the followers, potentially voters, that expect accountability from political leaders. According to the Minister of Post and Telecommunications, Cameroon recorded 3,016 cases of identity theft between October 2018, the month of the Presidential election, and April 2020, right after the parliamentary election (Cameroun Web 2020).

Case seven: Falsified threats
In January 2020, a Facebook video claiming threats on a government authority in an Anglophone region was disseminated claiming that the people of Lebialem, a town in southwest Cameroon, had threatened the administrative authority and government representative to leave the town. After investigation it became clear that the video was a montage of content from other locations created to mislead and polarize voters along ethnic lines, on the eve of the 2020 legislative elections (Data Cameroon 2020). The video was viewed 16,000 times and achieved 1,000 shares in the first three hours.

Case eight: Falsified resignation and rumour of death
An article published on 28 February 2020 on the website camerounweb.com announced the upcoming resignation of Paul Biya, president of the Republic of Cameroon. According to the article, the information came from the German newspaper *Die Zeit Online* and was accompanied by a screenshot of an article on *Die Zeit*'s website entitled '*Präsident Paul Biya tritt zurück*', which translates as 'President Paul Biya resigns' (Data Cameroon 2020). The *Die Zeit* article was re-published on the Facebook page 'Martin Tajo Official' (40,298 fans and followed by 79,286 people) and was shared more than 1,800 times in various groups and Facebook pages. Later on 25 March 2020, the rumour began to circulate on Facebook first, and on all social media announcing the death of Paul Biya, before being formally denied by the Minister of Communication René Emmanuel Sadi on 26 March 2020 by a press release. Following that, the opposition leader Maurice Kamto gave Paul Biya seven days to assume his presidential function which, according to him, was obtained via an electoral heist (Cameroun Web 2020). The disinformation was flagged as false when it became clear that the president was alive and well.

Case nine: False claim that Doctors without Borders supplied ammunition
In January 2020, the Cameroonian government accused the humanitarian NGO Doctors without Borders of helping separatists in the Anglophone regions, an allegation which was denied by the organization, especially since the government could not provide the factual evidence. In fact, the Cameroonian government has systematically accused the NGO of illegal support to separatists in Anglophone regions, affected by bloody fighting between the military and independence rebels since 2017, accusations that were always denied by the NGO. In January 2020, the Minister of Territorial Administration, Paul Atanga Nji, accused them of transporting 'ammunitions, binoculars, and Android mobile phones' along with their humanitarian goods supply to the crisis victims in the South West region.

That fact was denied by the Field Communications Officer of Doctors Without Borders who said that they provide medical assistance in Buea, Kumba, Mamfe, Bakassi and Bamenda to ensure the safety of their patients. She added that they have 'a zero-tolerance policy to having arms and ammunition in any of the health facilities they support, vehicles transporting their teams and patients, in any of the places where they operate in the world' (Data Cameroon 2020). Despite this, the government suspended their activities in the region from December 2020 to date. Human rights advocates interpreted this as a manipulation by the government to get rid of humanitarian NGOs that report truthfully on human rights violations in crisis zones (Ben Ahmed 2021). The absence of any presented evidence from the government and no attempt to arrest or prosecute the alleged arms smugglers of Doctors Without Borders suggests that this was another episode of political disinformation.

Case ten: DeepFake video of French ambassador

In June 2020, a video of the French ambassador making revolting and hateful remarks appeared on social media. The video, which circulated on Facebook and WhatsApp, featured the French ambassador saying, 'The French Republic is the controlling power which colonised Cameroon . . . My ancestors conquered this land by force and cunning and international law.' After investigation it became clear that the video was a 'deepfake', a form of artificial intelligence that manipulates video to make it possible to substitute fake images and words into a video (France 24 2021). In the period following the February 2020 parliamentary elections social media was awash with manipulated videos and posts that intensified disruption and popular discontent during the post-election crisis, targeting the state governance, foreign relations and multiple crisis management.

Power struggle and disinformation

The previous section documented nine cases of disinformation that occurred before, during or after Cameroon's 2018 presidential election. This section analyses those instances of disinformation to identify their underlying motivations, strategies and impacts. It analyses the use of disinformation first as a way to take power, then as a strategy to close civic space and finally as a power maintenance strategy.

Disinformation to take power

Opposition groups in Cameroon have used disinformation to contest power and as part of a strategy to seize power from the incumbent. It is a strategy that has been used by both the power in place and the opposition. Indeed, both sides have deployed instances of disinformation whether before, during or after the elections, to win the ballot or to withdraw power at the end of the ballot.

Immediately after the election date, the opposition party used a false victory claim (Case 4) in an attempt to unsettle the incumbent party and challenge their legitimacy while the counting of the votes was still on-going. If the gesture was justified by arguments of fraud observed during the election, a declaration of victory can be understood as part of a strategy to sow doubt among voters and encourage large numbers of people to reject the results announced later. This act contributed to the post-election crisis in which anti-government demonstrations were violently suppressed resulting in arrests and detentions, including of the main presidential opponent. Moreover, other disinformation tactics were deployed to discredit the incumbent government and its elected officials by fraudulently using their social media identities for unethical causes (Case 6). Other disinformation tactics aimed to challenge those in power by criticizing their inefficiency or inactivity in the face of multiple overlapping crises (Case 8), or denouncing negative foreign interference from France (Case 10).

Disinformation to close civic space

In some instances, disinformation about journalists and the supposed 'fight against disinformation' has become a pretext for the Cameroonian government to shrink civic space and repress opposition. By means of internet shutdowns, arrests and detentions of journalists and opposition, the government is able to intimidate critics, create a 'chilling effect', promote self-censorship and supress anti-government criticism.

Cracking down on civil society has been described as a prominent tactic of African governments' strategy to shrink civic space (Smidt 2018; Roberts and Mohamed Ali 2021). During election periods, the Cameroonian government used both mainstream and online media to denounce humanitarian organizations including Doctors Without Borders in the crisis regions (Case 9). Despite the organization's denial of 'carrying ammunition and telephones', the government's sanctions were unquestionable and disproportionate because no thorough investigation was carried out, which human rights advocates saw as a blatant use of disinformation to manipulate public opinion to justify expelling them. What may confirm the strategy of state manipulation through these accusations is the widespread approach that has followed, according to human rights organizations. This threat was extended in 2021 by a generalized restriction against international NGOs that were allegedly in an irregular situation in Cameroon (MINAT 2021). This blanket approach was viewed by human rights organizations as a threat to local organizations, through which most international humanitarian organizations operate in Cameroon (RFI 2021).

Furthermore, arrests and detention of journalists under pretext of disinformation constitute violation of the freedom of expression in breach of international law – the International Covenant on Civil and Political Rights (United Nations 1966: Article 19(3)). The arbitrary arrests of journalists and the long detentions without evidence or legal basis (Case 5) exposed a strategy of the government to warn all critical voices of the type of treatment to be expected in case of government criticism. In the end, the evidence was not clearly established against Mimi Mefo or Paul Chouta, which classifies their arrests and detention as an abuse and intimidation strategy by the government. The network limitation during the election (Case 1), denied by the government, echoed the long internet shutdown of ninety-three days earlier in the country in the crisis regions, and even if it was not total, still betrayed a government propensity to limit the freedom of speech and access to information in sensitive times. Government internet shutdown denial comes as a state disinformation tactic to limit public access to multiple sources of information – online media in particular – thus compelling exposure to potentially partisan and manipulative state-owned media.

Disinformation as power maintenance

Perhaps the clearest evidence that emerges from this analysis is the deployment of disinformation as a strategy of power maintenance. Powerholders with the ability to dominate electoral counts and the ability to arrest journalists and opposition candidates without evidence are able to deploy disinformation to cover their tracks and to manipulate public awareness.

Disinformation as power maintenance consists in denying the real abuses of the government or its agencies. When government abuses of power are denounced and even documented by other stakeholders, disinformation is deployed to maintain an always polished image of the government in place. This strategy of digital disinformation in power maintenance has increased since the government employed three commercial public relations consultancies from the United States. The use of disinformation as a tactic in power maintenance appears clearly in the Cameroonian state's denial of wrong-doing in detention of journalists (case 5) and in the army's denial of the torture and killings of civilians (Case 2). Disinformation is also used to present citizens as threatening government officials, as if to justify its own power and abuses or quite simply to sow doubt in public opinion (Case 7). And ultimately, the government uses disinformation as an all-purpose reason to limit access to the internet network, limit the actions of civil society, limit expression for journalists and critics on social media, muzzle the opposition and critics of governance in general (Cases 1–10).

This strategy is, on the one hand, aided by the absence of a national policy or regulation on access to information that would compel the government to make truthful information available to the public. On the other hand, it is reinforced by the existing law provisions on online expression, included in the Electronic Transactions Law, the Cybersecurity and Cybercrime Law and the Penal Code that lack clarity and can be used vaguely against innocent people.

Conclusion and recommendations

The quest to obtain and retain power is central to understanding the use of disinformation around elections. This chapter has brought together for the first time evidence of a wide range of types of disinformation deployed before, during and after Cameroon's 2018 presidential elections. It essentially focused on the strategies and motivations behind the types of disinformation during the election and how their deployment both reflect and impact existing dynamics of power in Cameroon's political process.

Incumbent and opposition parties, professional advisors, journalists and media channels were all actors in the deployment of disinformation to serve powerful election interests. Disinformation took the form of untrue statements, social media posts, falsified pictures, videos and deepfakes. In analysing these deployments of election disinformation, three main strategies emerged: the use of disinformation to contest and take power; the use of disinformation to close civic space; and the disinformation to retain power. Of these three, the use of disinformation in power retention was most evident in Cameroon.

Reducing the power of political opponents lies at the centre of all the disinformation dynamics that animated the 2018 presidential election. The strategies seek to make the democratic process less open and amount to intentional misleading of public opinion. Importantly the chapter located the disinformation and the election within the wider context of overlapping crises. The triple crises of Boko Haram, the Anglophone and post-election crisis provide the context of insecurity in which the government seeks to justify its exercise of repressive power. From a socio-security perspective disinformation hyperbolizes the misdeeds of the crisis or diminishes them depending on the protagonists and their intentions in an electoral context. In any case, altering the truth and the facts through disinformation leads to a radicalization of stakeholders, creates a polarization within the groups, thus reducing any possibility of ending the crisis, finding peace and reconciliation.

The advent and rapid adoption of ICTs in Cameroon has been a double-edged sword. Social media has provided citizens with a platform for raising issues long ignored by state-controlled media but a lack of adequate regulation and protection of digital rights leaves citizens vulnerable to arrest for exercising their right to expression in online civic spaces. The occurrence of digital disinformation, whether politically motivated or not, is therefore structured by these contextual facts, especially in the political heat of an election period.

As the chapter illustrated, disinformation predates the digital period and is as old as Cameroon itself. The literature illustrated how disinformation existed in traditional press and TV media in Cameroon. However, the deployment of disinformation in the 2018 presidential election was greatly amplified by three factors: the popular uptake of mobile, internet and social media, the inadequacies of the legal and regulatory environment to govern that uptake and the incendiary context of the Boko Haram, Anglophone and post-elections crises.

The parameters of this study were limited and further research is necessary into the deployment of digital disinformation in Cameroon's political processes. This study does not consider every instance of disinformation in the period; instead, the study focused on those that had an explicit or implicit link with the election and illustrated different types of disinformation. From the analysis three strategies emerged to explain the rationale of deployment of election disinformation: gain power, close the civic space for opposition and retain power.

Given that analysis the following five recommendations arise for the government, academia, civil society human rights defenders and the media. The government should expedite legislation to protect free expression online, as well as laws relating to freedom of information and freedom of the press/media. Several of Cameroon's existing laws are inadequate for the digital era. This would facilitate the process of fact-checking, enshrine speech limitations in clear and precise legal frameworks and limit abuses of power over civic space. New laws should use the framework of international human rights law to which Cameroon is a signatory, taking into account the principles of necessity, legitimacy and proportionality that guarantee protection of rights to privacy and speech as protected in Cameroon's constitution.

There is a compelling need for researchers to continue to document disinformation and other restrictions on digital rights before, during and after elections in Cameroon in order to better equip democratic actors to exercise, defend and expand democratic freedoms and rights. The media has the responsibility to respect its code of ethics and deontology, holding power to account and always fact-checking information before publication, whether online or offline. To defend and expand democratic and digital rights it is necessary for civil society organizations to form effective alliances with key stakeholders and deploy tactics to produce trustworthy information and carry out practical actions to secure political integrity in Cameroonian polity.

Bibliography

Actu Cameroun (2021) 'Usurpation d'identité: Nourane Foster porte plainte'. March. https://bit.ly/3pDPjFV.

ADISI-Cameroun (2022) *General Report*. Forum International de Yaoundé sur la désinformation.

Adjouda, Eric (2019) 'Victime d'une usurpation d'identité sur Twitter, le Ministre Tchiroma hausse le ton'. https://bit.ly/3Xi4ioe

Africanews (2018) 'Cameroon's First "Social Media Election"'. https://shorturl.at/auwD0 (Last update on December 2019).

BBC (2018) 'Cameroon drops fake news charges against Mimi Mefo'. November. https://www.bbc.com/news/world-africa-46194532.

BBC News (2018) 'Anatomy of a Killing'. October. https://bit.ly/2IgnrAJ.

Ben Ahmed, L. (2021) 'Cameroun: Le gouvernement "rappelle à l'ordre" les ONG'. https://bit.ly/3ehMg3R.

Benkler Y., Faris R. and Roberts, H. (2018) *Network Propaganda: Manipulation, Disinformation, and Radicalization in American Politics*. New York: Oxford University Press.

Bradshaw, S., Bailey, H. and Howard P. N. (2021) *Industrialized Disinformation: 2020 Global Inventory of Organized Social Media Manipulation*. Oxford: Programme on Democracy & Technology. demtech.oii.ox.ac.uk.

Cameroun Web (2020a) 'Usurpation d'identité des personnalités: Samuel Mvondo Ayolo sort son artillerie'. 22 May. https://bit.ly/3V1ra9Y.

Cameroun Web (2020b) 'Voici la chronologie de la vraie fausse mort de Paul Biya'. 25 May. https://bit.ly/3AJUkT7.

CIPESA (2022) *Disinformation Pathways and Effects: Case Study from Five African Countries*. Report.

Data Cameroon (2020) *Fact-Checking: Doctors Without Borders Deny Ever Transporting Arms*. https://bit.ly/3EmqaYJ.

Data Cameroon (2022) *Médias: 'Le fact-checking est une réponse a la crise de l'information'*. https://bit.ly/3fRbG8X.

Digital Business Africa (2018) 'Cameroun:Le Minpostel et l'UPF Cameroun forment les journalistes sur les techniques de FactChecking sur le web et sur les réseaux sociaux'. https://shorturl.at/lFLNS.

Economist Intelligence Unit (2021) *Democracy Index 2021: The China Challenge, 2021 Rankings*. https://shorturl.at/lmru2.

European Commission (2018) *A Multi-dimensional Approach to Disinformation: Report of the Independent High Level Group on Fake News and Online Disinformation*. https://shorturl.at/fpUY1.

France 24 (2020) 'Un village du Cameroun anglophone cible d'une attaque armée, 14 enfants tués'. February 2020. https://urlr.me/74ZWg.

France 24 (2021) 'Cameroun: Des fausses images des récents affrontements entre Arabes choas et Mousgoum'. 10 December. https://bit.ly/3tvU9q4.

Freedom House (2022) *Country Report Cameroon*. https://freedomhouse.org/country/cameroon/freedom-world/2022.

Gillis, A. (2020) 'How the Dictator of Cameroon Gives Millions to American Companies to Polish his Reputation with "Fake News"'. *Mondiaal Nieuws*.

Howard, P. N. (2020) *Lie Machines: How to Save Democracy From Troll Armies, Deceitful Robots, Junk News Operations, and Political Operatives*. New Haven, CT: Yale University Press, 15.

International Crisis Group (2017) *Cameroon's Anglophone Crisis at the Crossroads*. Brussels, Africa Report No.250, 2 August. https://bit.ly/3tpD954.

Jeune Afrique (2018) *Présidentielle au Cameroun: Maurice Kamto revendique sa victoire avant la proclamation des résultats*, October. https://shorturl.at/hnvM1.

Jeune Afrique (2019) *Cameroun: plusieurs militants du MRC blessés au cours d'une marche à Douala*, January. https://shorturl.at/rN015.

Kouam, J. (2022) 'Cameroonian President Paul Biya Marks 40 Years in Power'. *ABC News*, https://abcn.ws/3hGM0fX (accessed 14 November 2022).

Koumnde Mbaga, G. O. (2021) *Mishandling Strategic Communication: The Anglophone Crisis in Cameroon*. Quantico: United States Marine Corps University.

Laws on Expression Online: Tracker and Analysis (2022). https://lexota.org.

Le Bled Parle (2018) 'Cameroun: Le journal l'Anecdote se lâche sur Maurice Kamto'. 18 October. https://bit.ly/3MfEFPK.

Libom Li Likeng, M. (2020) 'Dérives médiatiques, la désinformation, le discrédit de l'action gouvernementale et des hautes personnalités dans les réseaux sociaux'. *Press Conference Adress from Minister of Posts and Telecommunications*, July. https://bit.ly/3TjBYiL.

MINAT (2021) *Partis politiques légalisés 2021*. http://www.minat.gov.cm/index.php/fr/annuaires/partis-politiques?view=partis.

Mississippi State University Library. *Evaluating False News and Misinformation*. https://guides.library.msstate.edu/c.php?g=672253&p=4772779.

NetBlocks (2018) *Facebook and WhatsApp Restricted in Cameroon on eve of Election Results*. October. https://bit.ly/3K55tQs.

Nfi, J. L. (2017) 'The Dismantling of the Cameroon Federation in 1972: The Petroleum Factor'. *International Journal of Innovative Legal & Political Studies*, 5 (3): 1–6.

Ngange, K.L. and Mokondo, M.S. (2019) 'Understanding Social Media's Role in Propagating Falsehood in Conflict Situations: Case of the Cameroon Anglophone Crisis'. *Studies in Media and Communication*, 7 (2): 55–67.

Ngapout, A. M. (2021) 'Nouveaux médias: La menace de la désinformation'. *Cameroon Tribune*, https://shorturl.at/grS27.

Ngono, S. (2021) *Médias audiovisuels et tolérance administrative au Cameroun: Enjeux communicationnels et logiques d'acteurs.* Paris: L'Harmattan.

Nounkeu, C. T. (2020) 'Facebook and Fake News in the "Anglophone Crisis" in Cameroon'. *African Journalism Studies*, 41 (3): 20–35. https://doi.org/10.1080/23743670.2020.1812102.

Présidence de la République (2021) *Présentation du Cameroun, mise à jour le 15 Octobre.* https://bit.ly/3cK7xic.

RFI (2021) *Cameroun: L'État veut accentuer le contrôle des ONG étrangères*, August. https://shorturl.at/mrXY1.

Roberts, T. and Mohamed Ali, A. (2021) 'Opening and Closing Online Civic Space in Africa: An Introduction to the Ten Digital Rights Landscape Reports'. In T. Roberts (ed.), *Digital Rights in Closing Civic Space: Lessons from Ten African Countries.* Brighton: Institute of Development Studies. https://opendocs.ids.ac.uk/opendocs/handle/20.500.12413/15964.

Sa'ah, R. J. (2022) 'Seul le commerce des cercueils est en plein essor'. *BBC News*, 23 August. https://bbc.in/3E9fpXM (accessed 10 November 2022).

Seignour, A. (2011) 'Méthode d'analyse des discours: L'exemple de l'allocution d'un dirigeant d'entreprise publique'. *Revue française de gestion*, 211: 29–45. https://www.cairn.info/revue--2011-2-page-29.htm.

Smidt, H. (2018) *Shrinking Civic Space in Africa: When Governments Crack Down on Civil Society.* (GIGA Focus Afrika, 4). Hamburg: GIGA German Institute of Global and Area Studies - Leibniz-Institut für Globale und Regionale Studien, Institut für Afrika-Studien. https://nbn-resolving.org/urn:nbn:de:0168-ssoar-60572-3.

Sombaye Eyango, J. R. (2018) 'Inside the Virtual Ambazonia: Separatism, Hate Speech , Disinformation and Diaspora in the Cameroonian Anglophone Crisis'. Master's Theses. 1158, https://repository.usfca.edu/thes/1158.

Takougang, J. (1993) 'The Post-Ahidjo era in Cameroon: Continuity and Change'. *Journal of Third World Studies*, 10 (2), Third World Problems and Issues: 268–302.

Tande, D. (2011) *Presidential Election: How Candidates Are Navigating the Social Media Landscape.* https://bit.ly/3EnjSrG.

The World Bank (2020) *Individuals Using the Internet (% of Population) – Cameroon.* https://data.worldbank.org/indicator/IT.NET.USER.ZS?end=2020&locations=CM&start=1990&view=chart

Toussi, S. (2019) 'Overview of Cameroon's Digital Landscape'. *CIPESA*, September. https://cipesa.org/2019/09/overview-of-cameroons-digital-landscape/.

TV5 Monde (2018) *Cameroun: Faux observateurs électoraux et vraie polémique*, October. https://shorturl.at/gmpL9.

United Nations (General Assembly) (1966) 'International Covenant on Civil and Political Rights.' Treaty Series 999 (December): 171.

Wardle, C. and Derakhshan, H. (2017) *Information Disorder: Toward an Interdisciplinary Framework for Research and Policy Making.* https://bit.ly/3e6s7Od.

Chapter 9

Disinformation in Uganda's 2021 elections

Juliet N. Nanfuka

The 2021 presidential election in Uganda was marked by an explosion of disinformation which undermined the opportunity for free and fair elections. The dissemination of intentionally false and misleading information – disinformation – in the Ugandan digital landscape represents a threat to the very tenets of a free, fair and open elections. For elections to be free and fair, any electorate needs to have unimpeded access to a diversity of trustworthy information sources and to independent analysis. Social media was hailed as a means by which citizens could access such information from spaces not policed in state-controlled media, however a proliferation of disinformation has put those advantages in jeopardy. As the elections approached in Uganda, the deployment of disinformation was among the primary tactics by political groups: evidenced in the form of doctored images, falsified videos and untrue text, polluting open debate and deliberation. This chapter looks at the way that disinformation manifested during the election period and examines the power relations between the state, opposition parties and online citizen groups that were reflected in and affected by the disinformation campaigns identified. The term disinformation here refers to the intentional dissemination of false information for political purposes.

In the belief that election disinformation can only ever be adequately understood in the wider context of political economy, and because of Uganda's particular history of state-controlled media, the chapter begins by providing the reader with some historical context. A review of definitions of disinformation and the wider literature is then used to argue that that the specific practice of election disinformation is best understood as one element within a wider toolkit of digital authoritarian practices. This chapter then presents a range of empirical examples of disinformation that were deployed by both pro-government and opposition groups during the 2021 presidential elections. These examples are then analysed through the lens of power and authoritarian practices to answer the question of whose interests were served by the production and dissemination of this political disinformation. The chapter seeks to understand how power relations between the state and opposition actors shaped and are were shaped by the use of disinformation.

These questions were explored using desk research to review existing literature, by conducting social media analysis of the content of specific #hashtag campaigns during the election and through qualitative analysis of the most influential social media accounts and examples of disinformation. This is the first study to analyse the evolution of disinformation in Ugandan elections through the lens of digital authoritarianism. As online channels become the primary platform for social and political communication in Uganda much more research is necessary in this space. The chapter concludes with some tentative recommendations that arise from this analysis for policy, practice and further study.

Background

Disinformation in Ugandan politics predates the digital era. Broadcasting was introduced to the country in 1954 with the establishment of the Uganda Broadcasting Service. The service was established to communicate Britain's colonial agenda including disinformation to counteract growing anti-colonial sentiment and pro-independence voices (Lugalambi and Mwesige 2010). After independence, post-colonial administrations in Uganda maintained a tight hold on media outlets and suppressed press freedom (Chataba and Fourie 2007). Despite being an early adopter of several technology-related legal frameworks, Uganda has a history of blocking the free flow of information and the use of disinformation, particularly during elections. These disruptions to accessing trustworthy information came at the expense of civic engagement, access to information and freedom of expression.

Political environment

Uganda is located in East Africa. It is bordered by the Democratic Republic of the Congo, South Sudan, Kenya, Tanzania and Rwanda. The southern part of the country includes a substantial portion of Lake Victoria, which is shared with Kenya and Tanzania (Figure 9.1).

The country gets its name from the Kingdom of Buganda whose region in the country was declared a British protectorate in 1894. The country gained independence on 9 October 1962 and Milton Obote who led the Uganda People's Congress (UPC) party, was elected as Prime Minister. Between 1967 and 1969, the Obote regime clamped down upon independent media including '*Transition*' which was then Africa's leading literary magazine due to its criticism of government policy(Tabaire 2007). In 1971 Obote was overthrown by General Idi Amin who was the Army Chief of Staff at the time. In relation to political narrative in Uganda, it is during Amin's rule that the use of 'cutting-edge media technology, populism and radical ideologies' to maintain a grip on power came into use (Burke 2019).

In 1977, General Amin was accused of disseminating disinformation about the deaths of the Archbishop of the Church of Uganda Janani Luwum and two

Figure 9.1 Uganda map (CIA Factbook public domain image).

Uganda Cabinet Ministers – Erinayo Wilson Oryema and Charles Oboth Ofumbi. The official government account of their deaths was that they had died in a car accident. Investigative journalists argued that the trio had been had not died in an auto crash as officially reported but had instead been murdered (NY Times 1977). Amin dismissed the claims labeling the newspaper reports 'anti-Uganda propaganda' It eventually emerged that the deaths were possibly related to Amin's insecurity due to Anglican Church guests who were slated to visit the country in 1977 for the Church's centenary celebrations, many of them from the United Kingdom and the United States (New Vision 2015).

In 1980, President Obote returned to power when President Amin was overthrown but following a guerilla war the National Resistance Army (NRA) came to power in 1986 and General Yoweri Museveni's became president. The National Resistance Movement (NRM) which emerged from the NRA under Museveni created a 'no-party democracy' which banned political parties. The first multiparty election was held in 1996 but widespread claims of of voter intimidation and election rigging. Museveni has won every election since, and has held on to power for almost four decades. Opposition candidates face intimidation, frequent arrest and difficulty getting a fair hearing on state-controlled media.

Currently, Uganda is characterized as a 'hybrid regime' (The Economist 2022), one that combines democratic characteristics with autocratic ones. This description of regime-type is mirrored by the country's categorization as 'partly free' in the 2021 Freedom on the Net ranking (Freedom House 2021) with digital authoritarian- practices repeatedly in evidence, particularly at election times including through the use of restrictive laws, unwarranted arrests and disruptions to communications (Shahbaz 2018).

Digital landscape

This section briefly reviews the rapid uptake in mobile internet and social media use . According to the Uganda Bureau of Statistics, Uganda's population as of 2022 stood at 44 million with just over 50 per cent of the population being female. Meanwhile, the country has a median age of 16.7 against a global value of 30.3 years (World Economics 2022). At the time of the election there were 28 million mobile phone connections, 12 million internet users and 3.4 million social media users in Uganda (DataReportal 2021). Twitter was only used by 1 per cent of the population although that 1 per cent were disproportionately journalists, politicians and other political influencers. Mobile devices are the primary means through which the internet is accessed in Uganda (Data Reportal 2022).

The cost of mobile data in Uganda ranks among the highest in the region, with 1 GB of data costing up to 16.2 per cent of an average Ugandan's monthly income compared to the Sub-Saharan average of 9.3 per cent (CIPESA 2022). Despite the country embarking upon the utilization of online channels as avenues to engage with citizens, Uganda's e-Participation Index ranked at 95 out of 193 in 2020, marking a decline from eighty-seven in 2018 (UN 2022). The index measures the access and use of information technologies of United Nations member states.

Analysing the 2021 election

In the leadup to the elections of January 2021, online narratives were rife with political debate. This period is notable as it was in the midst of the Covid-19 pandemic during which political campaigning was forced to move online, necessitating increased reliance by candidates on digital tools to communicate with voters as physical gatherings had been banned (MoICT 2020).

However, this election, was not immune from the recurring characteristic of elections in Uganda: state control of public narratives (CIPESA 2014). This has included the introduction of regressive laws and the blocking of online communication channels (Shahbaz 2018). These authoritarian tactics go against the grain of freedom of access to information, freedom of expression and of assembly, resulting in the shrinking of civic spaces and the avenues for free and robust journalism, public accountability and civic engagement on political discourse at such a critical time as elections.

Defining disinformation

As discussed in the introduction, in this book the term disinformation refers to the intentional dissemination of false information for political gain. Wardle and Derakhshan (2017) argue that disinformation is one of three mechanisms of 'information disorder: misinformation – where false information is shared, but no harm is meant; mal-information – where true information is shared to cause harm and disinformation where false information is knowingly sharing to cause harm'.

Kuo and Marwick (2021) argue that the language of disinformaton often acts to depolitize the practice. They write that 'in public discourse disinformation is tied inextricably to social media and technology platforms, and often curiously depoliticized, framed as "polluting" or "infecting" an otherwise healthy information ecosystem'. They argue that some framings 'disconnect disinformation from the broader politics of knowledge production and systems of power that undergird it; in other words, who benefits and why?'

The Africa Center for Strategic Studies, a US Department of Defence entity, merges the afore definition which recognizes the relationship between politics and power in their definition of disinformation as the intentional dissemination of false information with the intent of advancing a political objective (2022).

These tendencies can be understood through the framework of digital authoritarianism, the use of digital technologies to reduce citizen freedoms and rights (Freedom House 2018). Speaking about the same process, Feldstein (2021) writes that such 'digital repression' comprises six techniques which include surveillance, censorship, social manipulation and harassment, cyberattacks, internet shutdowns and targeted persecution against online users. He notes that these techniques are not mutually exclusive, but each offer a specific set of objectives from a unique set of tools in order to fulfill its function, per Table 9.1. Indeed, in the case of Uganda, all these techniques have been employed in recent years, some of which will be discussed in this chapter.

Lemaire, Selvik and Garbe (2021) write that several African governments have resorted to two primary strategies to tackle what they termed as fake news, which are technological and legal content regulation. In Uganda, both strategies have been employed in the lead up to elections including through the reliance on existing laws such as the 2011 Computer Misuse Act being used to selectively arrest and prosecute critics for spreading 'inciteful, annoying, or false information' (The Conversation 2019) or the repeated disruption of citizen's access to social media and sometimes the internet in its entirety (BBC 2021).

Ahead of the January 2021 general elections, violations of human rights and the deployment of forms of digital authoritarianism were in evidence. This was not only due to the Covid-19 management measures introduced in 2020, which in their nature also introduced various human rights concerns (HRW 2020). opposition candidate Robert Kyagulanyi was making extensive use of social media and would face several different kinds of digital authoritarian repression of his campaign. As had occurred in previous elections the regression of digital rights including freedom of expression, access to information and even online assembly and again,

Table 9.1 Techniques of Digital Repression

		Techniques of Digital Repression			
Surveillance	Censorship	Disinformation	Cyber attacks and hacking	Internet shutdowns	Targeted arrests and violence
AI surveillance (facial recognition systems, intelligent video surveillance, smart policing, smart cities/ safe cities)	*Political and social content blocked/ filtered; use of friction & flooding* **Social media/ICT apps blocked** *Content removal*	Government/ pro-government outlets peddle disinformation, false content	State-sponsored technical attacks which manipulate software, data, computer systems, or networks to degrade operational capabilities or collect Information	*Internet or electronic communications disrupted* Total internet shutdowns Partial shutdowns (restricted website/ social media access, blackouts, slowdowns, throttling)	ICT user prolonged detention for political/social content ICT user physically attacked or killed
Communications surveillance (internet/social media monitoring, mobile phone tapping/SIM registration, location monitoring, intrusion spyware. packet inspection, network interception, cable tapping, telecom surveillance)	*Censorship laws/ directives:* Religion/blasphemy Cyber crime False news Political/hate speech Lèse-majesty Security/terrorism Sedition Copyright Infringement	Cyber trolling, social media manipulation/ harassment by pro-government actors (astroturfing, bots, sockpuppets. impersonation	*Categories:* Attacks harming operational capacity Intrusion and surveillance attacks *Illustrative Tools:* Vandalism Distributed denial of service Man-In-lhe-middle Phishing Advanced	*Infrastructure restrictions* (internet firewall; closed ICT Infrastructure)	
Surveillance laws (Intelligence/ national security laws, data disclosure, data retention, data localization)	Defamation/libel Indecency/antI-IGBT **Financial targeting of groups**	Election manipulation (for example, data exploitation)	persistent threat Spoofing Border Gateway Protocol		

Source: The Global Expansion of AI Surveillance (Feldstein 2021).

excessive police used upon journalists and citizens would take place (CIVICUS 2021). Kyaguanyi, a pop star turned opposition leader of the National Unity Party (NUP) is better known by his stage name of Bobi Wine and his campaign employed a range of social media #hashtags to mobilize popular support.

Digital disinformation in Ugandan elections 2006–19

To understand the role of disinformation and wider digital authoritarian practices in the Ugandan election of 2021, one has to retrace their steps to just under two decades ago. Internet access and use was still nascent in the country, and the state had already recognized the potential of online spaces as an avenue for public dialogue and for movement building – with the latter posing a potential threat to the interests of the ruling party due to the platform online spaces provide for state critics and opposition parties.

As such, in the lead up to the first multiparty election in 2006, the state blocked a critical website Radio Katwe. The ruling party – the National Resistance Movement (NRM) – reportedly complained to the Brinkster Communications Corporation – which hosted the server for Radio Katwe – that the website was publishing 'malicious and false information against the party and its presidential candidate'. This claim by the state that disinformation was being deployed against the president would be repeated in multiple elections in order to justify repression of opposition parties and independent media channels in the coming years. However, Brinkster denied receipt of any official communication or request from the Ugandan government to shut down the site (IFEX 2006). Incumbent, Yoweri Museveni, in power since 1986, would go on to win the elections.

Blockage of websites would go on to become a key tool used by the state against critics alongside unwarranted arrests, intimidation in addition to laws that infringed upon various rights including privacy of communications, freedom of expression and freedom of assembly (CIPESA 2014). Radio stations and print media were not spared as they would also face disruptions to their content production and consumption. Similar but evolving tactics would be used in all elections that have taken place since 2006.

During the February 2011 elections, websites and SMS were blocked to suppress election-related content. In the wake of the 2010 Arab Spring where long-serving authoritarian presidents were removed from power by social media using youth movements, the power of the internet and, in particular, social media become a cause of great concern to incumbent politicians. In Uganda, the state instructed telecommunications service providers to block all Short Messaging Services (SMS) that included words related to the Arab Spring including 'Ben Ali', 'Tunisia', 'UPDF' (Uganda Police Defense Force), 'army' 'dictator', 'gun', 'police' and 'teargas'. Following the disputed elections in Uganda, which saw Museveni remain in power, social media platforms Facebook and Twitter were blocked as opposition leaders took to these spaces to garner support through the 'Walk to Work' (#WalkToWork) campaign which highlighted the escalating price of food and fuel in the country and was met with significant police violence (Balancing Act 2011).

An analysis of the #WalkToWork campaign (on Twitter) (Okurut 2011) explains how the government used its power over telecoms companies to effect an internet shutdown to disrupt the use of social media to coordinate the protests. The state used the tools most readily available which included arrests, censorship and internet disruption.

The government justified its action citing maintenance of 'public order' or 'national security' as the basis for blocking the flow of information. In an examples of government disinformation, the state denied any involvement in the disruptions to the platforms. However, a letter leaked to the public later confirmed that the Uganda Communications Commission (UCC) which is the state telecommunications regulator, issued a directive to telecommunications companies to block the sites (Echwalu 2011). In all instances a common thread emerging is the use of state apparatus to block communication channels especially during times where public narrative was critical of the state. During the 2016 elections and the election that followed, online disinformation became more apparent.

In the 2016 elections, a different approach would be used with president Museveni allegedly paying about UGX 400 million (USD 107,000) to popular local musicians to compose songs supporting him. Although not contesting in the elections, Bobi Wine reported that the communications regulator allegedly banned his song 'Dembe' which had commentary on the elections and was deemed as warmongering, a claim the regulator would deny with some commentators arguing that the musician was simply 'seeking listenership or interest' in the song (Daily Monitor 2016).

The most dramatic evidence of disinformation came when an automated 'bot army' was found to be campaigning online for the president. In 2016, an estimated 5,000 bots were identified promoting pro-Museveni narratives on Twitter (CIPESA 2016). A 'bot' is piece of software that generates automated messages online and which can be mistaken for an authentic human user. The automated bot accounts amplified posts that supported the incumbent or boosted comments that criticized or derided the opposition leader Besigye. Suspicions were aroused when multiple accounts were tweeting identically worded messages. It was never established whether the US political marketing firms employed by the ruling party to support its election campaign were implicated in the deployment of the 5,000 strong bot army. The use of online campaigns of 'coordinated inauthentic behaviour' by pro-ruling party actors would remerge as a tactic in the 2021 election campaign.

The shift in narrative, blatant disinformation

For the 2016 election, presidential aspirants proactively embraced social media as part of their campaign strategies. However, within three months and on two occasions related to the elections, social media platforms as well as mobile money services were shut down. The state argued that the action was taken to protect the peace and stability of the country (Ojok 2016).

Just two years later, in July 2018, following a presidential directive the Ugandan state would impose a controversial 'social media tax' to reduce 'gossip' and disinformation on including on messaging on Whatsapp, Facebook, Skype and Viber. Among the arguments for the tax was that the government needed resources 'to cope with the consequences' of social media users' 'opinions, prejudices [and] insults'. After the election, the social media tax was dropped and replaced by a 12 per cent direct tax on internet data (CIPESA 2022).

Between the 2006 and 2011 elections, the Ugandan government was active in blocking websites, SMS messaging and in arresting political actors or journalists. To justify its action the government made false claims (never substantiated in a court of law) that citizens were inciting violence and destablizing the country. These false claims meet the definition of disinformation: falsehoods deployed intentionally to serve political aims. In 2016, one analyst commented, 'I think the government intends to keep the people uninformed. You see, uninformed people are easy to manipulate . . .' in reference to the ways in which speech critical of the government was routinely obstructed.

In 2019, the communications regulator UCC issued orders to thirteen radio and TV stations to 'suspend' thirty-nine news executives and producers in an attempt to stop them from covering opposition activity (RSF 2019). These actions have served to only push more opposition and critical content to more easily accessible social media platforms online.

Digital disinformation in 2021 Ugandan elections

The 2021 Uganda elections took place against the backdrop of the Covid-19 pandemic which had forced both national and global audiences to increase their reliance on online channels of communication. The Electoral Commission issued Covid-19 management guidelines which banned physical rallies and encouraged aspirants to explore alternative options of engaging potential voters including through the use of online channels. Later, gatherings of up to 200 supporters at a single rally were allowed (Samuel-Stone 2021). The pandemic forced election campaigning to go online where the footprint of disinformation had steadily grown. Juxtaposed against this were arrests, media disruptions, public protests, amendments to laws and regulations and eventually, a state-imposed complete shutdown to internet access. As witnessed in previous elections, information has often been distorted, faced censorship or outright blocked.

Social media was rife with allegations and reports of abuse and fraud by state related factions, while this narrative was countered with narrative pointing to opportunistic violence, flouting of Covid-19 regulations and the promotion of sectarianism (WION 2021).

Examples of election disinformation

Having provided sufficient historical context on the political and technological landscape this section presents a range of examples of disinformation deployed in the 2021 election both by the ruling and opposition parties in Uganda. Kakande (2020) studied the political use of Twitter in the election and found that the two primary presidential candidates dominated tweet volumes related to the elections. This dominance was replicated in studies of Facebook as well.

Online, various hashtags emerged in support of the two primary candidates – these were primarily their surnames – #Museveni and #Kyagulanyi (Bobi Wine). Many other hashtags also emerged to reinforce narratives and affiliation such as #Vote4Kyagulanyi or #MuseveniMustLead. The hashtag #WeAreRemovingaDictator were driven by the opposition, while #SecureYourFuture or #StopHooliganism supported pro-ruling party narratives (CIPESA 2021). Additional hashtags emerged which were used by both camps to suit promote their interests such as #Tweberemu ('let's be in for our own sake').

One influencer whose services were used during the 2021 election noted, 'We were given pre-designed messages and videos from rival camps, which we shared on various platforms through mostly Twitter and Facebook.' Another stated, 'It is a game of trending and no one cares what kind of information they push out there. Each tweet put out is paid for at the end of the day, . . .' (Buule 2021).

Online narratives: A case of dominance and disinformation delinquency

To identify the most important online influencers social media analysis was conducted to identify trending hashtags in the election period. Samples of the top trending hashtags were studied over a two-week period to identify the Twitter accounts with the greatest impact. Twitter was chosen as the primary platform for investigation both because of its use by politicians and journalists and because its contents were at the time of research freely available to researchers. The social media analysis software NodeXL was used to harvest all Tweets using the hashtags #StopHooliganism and #StopPoliceBrutalityInUganda over the fourteen-day period from Monday, 16 November 2020 to Monday, 30 November 2020. The selected time frame coincided with known incidence of political unrest and related arrests that occurred during the same period in the election campaign. These Twitter data sources are complemented by supporting examples from Facebook and YouTube.

Within the sampled data a range of disinformation cases were evidence. These examples often deployed false information in the form of misidentified still or video images. One example of this are tweets which used the text, 'Below is a pic where hooligans are destroying a road worth billions of tax payers' money. why does bobi wine and his NUP like trading in violence? #StopHooliganism #StopHooliganism.' Analysis of the image by the Digital Forensic Research Lab showed that the image was actually from a 2011 riot and was shared by pro-ruling party accounts which supported the #StopHooliganism hashtag. It noted that 'one user, @AsantejnrRuhima, who was tagged in @k_siima's image, posted the photograph 11 times'. (DFR Lab 2020). Deploying untrue information knowingly to further a political objective meets the definition of disinformation.

Another instance of disinformation using false images related to claims of police brutality. An example is an image of women falling while uniformed individuals appear to be chasing and stepping on them. This is a tweet from the Twitter account of @heisalana on 6 November 2020 which stated, 'The victims also have sons daughters and people they take care of 😔😔 just like u officer in office 👮👮 #StopPoliceBrutalityinuganda' accompanying upon investigation it transpired that the image is from a 2017 protest in the Democratic Republic of Congo (DRC). Although the inauthenticity of the imagery was established, the disinformation had already spread.

Pro-ruling party disinformation often relied upon a false narrative that opposition candidates relied on foreign funding and were responsible for the 'popularisation of homosexuality'. No evidence was provided to evidence the foreign-funding claim and a person's sexuality is not determined by 'popularisation'. Twitter user @HotLeaksUg was among those deploying this disinformation in posts such as '*Stella Nyanzi, Bobi Wine Turn to Homosexual Community for Campaign Funds . . .*' and this post by a news site's account '*I'm Going To Destroy #BobiWine's Kingdom: Veteran Journalist #BassajjaMivule Officially Joins NRM, Accuses Bobi Wine's #NUP Of Being Homosexuals,Lumpens*'. Anti-homosexuality commentary has previously won Museveni praise within government and among his supporters.

There was a surge in the use of both the #StopHooliganism and #StopPoliceBrutalityInUganda hashtags following the arrest of Bobi Wine on 18 November 2020. Police used tear gas and live bullets to disperse the presidential candidate's supporters who were protesting his arrest (*Al Jazeera* 2020). Many instances of what occurred on the day of Bobi Wine's arrest were shared on social media providing crucial data for a *BBC Africa Eye* report. The *BBC* programme would document in an investigative feature the zealous use of live ammunition against mostly unarmed citizens and bystanders (*BBC Africa Eye* 2021). To justify this use of police violence the state claimed that the peaceful demonstrations were violent. This disinformation was deployed using the #StopHooliganism hashtag. While legitimate cases of 'hooliganism' were documented such as video and pictures of a female police officer being beaten by citizens, the investigation revealed that contrary to the pro-ruling party disinformation, there was no evidence that any of the seven people shot on Kampala Road were rioting on that day. Following the screening of the investigation, the Criminal Investigations Department summoned the media group's managing editor on allegations of 'criminal libel, incitement to violence, and false news publication' (*BBC* 2021; CPJ 2021). It is ironic that having been caught deploying disinformation the state arrested the editor on charges of 'false news publication'.

The account of Bobi Wine (@hebobiwine) was a dominant presence in both hashtags. However, among the top ten accounts associated with the

#StopPoliceBrutalityInUganda hashtag were the official account of the Uganda Police Force (@policeug) and the official Yoweri Museveni account (@kagutamuseveni). These accounts were often referred to in tweets, as Twitter users pointed out various legitimate or suspicious cases of police brutality, or sometimes shared outright disinformation. Accounts associated with the #StopHooliganism hashtag also included the Uganda Police Force account and accounts sympathetic to the ruling party, including that of the Chief Executive Editor of the state-owned national newspaper, New Vision, Don Wanyama (@nyamadon). Other accounts included those of human rights activists, media personalities and avid tweeps sharing content using their preferred hashtags to contribute to skewed on line narrative.

In one instance, an account accused Bobi Wine of posting disinformation (@nuwamanyaisaac 2020). It stated, '*@NUP_Ug and Bobi Wine the chief strategists of fake news. See how Bobi posted that this is Northern Uganda. He has used photos of Hon Julius Malema's campaign that happened years ago in South Africa. #StopHooliganism.*' However, the account referred to was itself a fake account. The unverified account was not operated by Bobi Wine. The image in the post depicted multitudes of people at a rally but investigation showed that the image was originally taken in South Africa at a Julius Malema rally. The same account (@nuwamanyaisaac 2020) would also tweet altered images of the Daily Monitor newspaper with an falsified headline containing massively inflated numbers of deaths following a riot. The account would allege that these are efforts made by opposition supporters to spread disinformation. These examples meet the definition of disinformation as the represent deliberate efforts to disseminate untruths to further political objectives by manipulating the public perception of opposition actors.

Meanwhile, it appears that people engaging with the hashtags were located beyond the Ugandan borders, including in neighbouring East African countries, some Southern African countries, parts of Europe and Asia, as well as some states in North America. However, divergence was registered in West Africa, where more engagement appeared in support of the #StopPoliceBrutalityInUganda.

Another example of using images from other countries to fuel disinformation relates to the #EndSARs protests in Nigeria and the resulting Lekki Toll Gate massacre (DW 2021; Oladapo and Ojebode 2021) which saw the spread of disinformation, including tweets accompanied with old images and false information. Using the #StopPoliceBrutalityIn Uganda hashtag the Nigeria based account @ifemosumichael 2020 posted an image depicting naked bodies on the ground, accompanied by the text, 'When you see this please retweet widely. #StopPoliceBrutalityinuganda #EndSARS'. However, the image was not of Ugandan origin but fed into the political interest and narrative of opposition interest groups.

Opposition: Seeking avenues to inform

While documentation has been focused around the disinformation perpetuated by pro-ruling party accounts, in the lead up to the 2021 elections, disinformation was also evidenced being spread by opposition supporters. Accounts which fueled opposition disinformation appeared to have relied on the limited digital literacy levels of users to promote the content. The fact checking platform, PesaCheck, documented numerous social media entries which were either hoaxes, doctored images or plainly false information that was shared by both opposition and ruling party supporters (PesaCheck n.d.).

An example of this is a Facebook video post originally published on 24 February 2020 (Masinde 2020) that showed uniformed individuals violently bundling up individuals into a police truck. The post was accompanied with the text. 'This is how they maintain law and order in Uganda' and received mixed responses including some that challenged its authenticity pointing out that the uniforms did not match those of the Ugandan Police Force. A fact checker later conducted image analysis and was able to establish that the image was actually from a riot which took place in Zimbabwe (Enywaru 2020). This example clearly meets the definition of disinformation as false information intentionally shared to serve political interests.

BBC Reality Check also conducted investigations on videos which were widely shared on social media during the election including one featuring US President-elect Joe Biden at an event calling for the release of Bobi Wine. The video turned out to be a two-year old recording of Nick Carter, a Democratic politician who was contesting a local election in Boston. In another example, a screenshot was shared which appears to show the Barack Obama Twitter handle supporting Bobi Wine with the hashtag #FreeBobiWine. The tweet was retweeted almost 1 million times (Mwai 2020). However, a *BBC Reality Check* search of Barack Obama's tweets revealed that he had not posted on the subject on that date, proving that this was another example of disinformation: intentionally false information designed to serve political ends.

With online spaces including YouTube providing additional channels to disseminate information, opposition supporters, government critics, journalists and political activists made extensive use of social media especially in light being barred from state-contolled television and radio platforms (RSF 2019). It is online that the voice of opposition rang loudest and were deemed a 'national security risk' which had to be addressed (Dispatch 2020). However, the state maintained an upper hand due to its inclination to arrest or intimidate opposition actors and the media, a practice that was established in prior elections (IFEX 2006).

The Uganda Communications Commission (UCC) submitted a letter on 9 December, 2020 to Google requesting the company to take down seventeen YouTube accounts[1] that focused on publishing pro-Bobi Wine content. Among the accounts was one belonging to Bobi Wine himself. By mid-December 2020, the channels had amassed over 59 million views and 300,000 subscribers (URN 2020). The UCC argued that the channels did not meet the minimum broadcasting standards and were sensationalizing news reports resulting in riots that led to the loss of several lives (Dispatch 2020). They further argued that the channels were

---

1. Ghetto TV, KKTV, Bobi Wine 2021, JB Muwonge 2, Namungo Media, Ekyooto TV, Map Mediya TV, Uganda Empya, Busesa Media Updates, Uganda News Updates, Uganda Yaffe, Trending Channel UG, Lumbuye Fred and TMO online.

broadcasting without broadcasting licenses and were thus in violation of the law. However, in response, the Google Head of Communication and Public Affairs for Africa, Dorothy Ooko, stated that 'it is very hard to just have a channel removed due to a government request'.

Government: A takedown of accounts

As in the 2016 election, pro-government actors orchestrated a sophisticated online campaign of meeting the definition of 'coordinated inauthentic behaviour'. On 11 January 2021 Facebook suspended the accounts of a number of government officials and NRM party officials for what it described as coordinated inauthentic behaviour aimed at manipulating public debate ahead of the presidential elections. Twitter also suspended similar accounts. Facebook removed 220 accounts, thirty-two pages, fifty-nine groups and 139 Instagram accounts. These accounts had links with the media arm of the government – the Government Citizens Interaction Center. About USD 5,000 worth of ad spend was associated with these accounts. (Facebook 2021).

The coordinated inauthentic behaviour was first identified by the Digital Forensic Research (DFR Lab) whose investigation picked up that various accounts posted exactly the same message on Facebook and Twitter. The messages were supporting a police crackdown on opposition supporters. The investigation revealed two Uganda- based private companies – *Kampala Times*, a news website, and Robusto Communications, a public relations firm – as being part of the machinery behind the online campaign which fueled anti-opposition disinformation. Both companies were incorporated less than two years year before the elections and appear to be linked to each other (DFRLab 2021).

Despite the takedowns, many cases of disinformation remained available online such as the following tweet which was further amplified by the account of President Museveni's son Muhoozi Kainerugaba, who holds the title of senior presidential advisor on Special Operations in Uganda. The tweet claims that Bobi Wine supporters were burning property and praises the army and police force for restoring order. However, the images used were from unrelated events from 2009 and 2011. The image on the left was from a 2009 demonstration in the capital related to restrictions placed a Buganda Kingdom representatives from participating in a political rally. The image on the right was from a 2011 protest following the arrest of Besigye (*Africa Uncensored* 2021).

The action taken by the platforms to remove the state-linked accounts that violated their terms of use sparked a debate on who has the authority to curate online content especially where government content is involved. President Museveni's press secretary, Don Wanyama, (whose Facebook and Instagram accounts were also suspended) took to Twitter and accused Facebook of trying to influence the elections. He stated, 'Shame on the foreign powers who think they can impose a puppet government on Uganda by disabling the online accounts of NRM supporters' (Wanyama 2021). Wanyama's account was among those that shared anti-opposition narrative.

Online disinformation channels blocked: A total internet shutdown

On 12 January, forty-eight hours before polling opened, reports of social media being blocked in Uganda started emerging. Eventually a nationwide internet shutdown was implemented (OONI 2021). The election slated for 14 January would be conducted in a complete internet blackout. Using its position, the state's communication regulatory authority, the Uganda Communications Commission instructed ISPs to block internet access (Nanfuka 2021).

Disinformation and power relations

The preceding sections have documented the rise of digital disinformation in Ugandan electoral politics. Although social media use is limited in the country, its rising importance as a site of contesting narratives and political authority is clear. Increasing investments are being made by a range of domestic actors, with foreign consultancy and on global platforms have complicated the media landscape for future elections.

The relationship between opposition actors, the state and platforms has been put to the test over the years in Uganda – especially with the growth in social media access and the increasing use of online communications. Parallel to this has been the emergence of pronounced digital authoritarianism; as online civic space has expanded it has been perceived as a threat by the ruling party which has responded with a range of authoritarian practices to control that online civic space. While this chapter has focused primarily on the use authoritarian use of disinformation, it is clear that to fully understand digital disinformation it must be considered within the context of a wider digital authoritarianism including, digital surveillance and internet shutdowns. This increase in digital authoritarianism has limited the avenues of critical expression, freedom of expression and public discourse during elections and at times of public protest (Roberts et al. 2021).

The examples of coordinated campaigns of inauthentic online behaviour on the part of the Ugandan state are clear evidence that the government is increasing its investments in disinformation capabilities across social media including Twitter, Facebook and YouTube. These disinformation capabilities help it to manage the flow of online information and to structured narratives that meet state interests.

However, it is not only the state that is making use of disinformation. Examples provided show that during the last two elections opposition groups have also deployed disinformation in pursuit of their political objectives. This is not a false claim of equivalence. It does not appear that opposition use has been as well-structured, as clearly orchestrated, or as well financed as that conducted by NRM-related accounts, nor was any opposition disinformation activity labeled as 'coordinated inauthentic activity' as defined by social media platforms. However, this does not negate the fact that it was present. While fact checking entities have stepped up their efforts to monitor and assess electoral disinformation even when this is achieved, by the time it is flagged, the intended political purpose of the disinformation has often already been served.

One possible implication of platforms blocking state disinformation and not opposition disinformation is that the state is likely to take even more oppressive measures to manage online content. One such measure is additional repressive legislation, including the the Computer Misuse (Amendment) Act passed in 8 September, 2022. Among the regressive provisions is the prohibition of the 'misuse of social media', which is defined as the publishing, distributing or sharing of information prohibited under Uganda's laws. Perpetrators of this offence face imprisonment of up to five years of a fine of up to UGX 10 million (USD 2,619), or both. Other prohibitions in the act include the sending or sharing of unsolicited information through a computer and prohibition of sending, sharing or transmitting of malicious information about or relating to any personWanyama 2022).

Barely two weeks after its enactment, a blogger known as Kasagga Bashir (also known as Kasagga Matovu) was charged under the Act. A police statement indicated that Kasagga, 'with requisite intent and knowledge, used his social engineering techniques to create, obtain and modify tweets and screenshots of twitter handles of the Defence Spokesperson @UPDFspokesperson, Uganda Police Force @PoliceUg, Annita Annet Among @AnitaAmong and Balaam Barugahare Ateenyi @Balaam 1980' (UPF 2022). Among is the speaker of Parliament and Balaam is a leading events promoter with a strong leaning to the ruling party.

The law could be used in a more targeted manner against critical voices online in the long run – especially where it appears that the state cannot rely on platforms to take down content even in cases where legitimate disinformation is present. Commentators following the developments during the 2021 Uganda elections which included the takedown of CIB accounts argued that by blocking pro-ruling party accounts, platforms had given government 'the perfect excuse to do what it had already planned' that is block digital communications (*BBC* 2021).

Researcher Odanga Madung, noted that 'Any casual observer of Ugandan politics expected the government to impose internet restrictions ahead of the elections, so Facebook's decision – especially the absence of tact when punishing infringements of its terms of service – offered Museveni a timely ruse to clothe the inevitable shutdown as a retaliation' (*BBC* 2021). However, the undercurrent of opposition inspired disinformation appears to have been lost in the power-play between the government and platforms. While both platforms and the state have argued the need to prevent the spread of falsehoods, the UCC stated that it needed to control content that does not meet the minimum broadcasting standards (Kyeyune 2020).

Although platforms potentially have a position of power, their lack of understanding of the contexts in which they are working worked against them. In an article by the *BBC*, political analyst Nanjala Nyabola noted that social media companies need to have a greater presence on the continent with local staff and a commitment to understand the social and political context to prevent the enforcement of their policies playing Into the hands of authoritarian governments (2021).

While platforms may want to apply their rules equally, the broad spectrum of users, regions and contexts and even political regimes means that they may play into the interests of authoritarian governments – such as platforms recognition of the presence of disinformation but only the takedown of pro-ruling party accounts. The possible hyper-focus on oppressive regime actors and their content by platforms may allow for just as problematic content from opposition actors to go without penalty and thus add fuel authoritarian governments moves to limit or block online communications at the cost of free speech, access to information and broader civic engagement.

Conclusion

Disinformation is as old as politics itself. This chapter began by providing examples of colonial and post-colonial disinformation from before the age of social media. Understanding how each successive political settlement used its monopoly of broadcast media to shape political narratives to serve its interests helps avoid the fallacy that social media has caused disinformation. The rapid expansion of mobile internet access and social media provides a powerul new tool for those wishing to disseminate political disinformation. Unlike state-owned broadcast media it can be used by a wider group of actors. The examples from the 2021 election in Uganda show that while the state still dominates election (dis)information there has been some democratization of who can produce and disseminate electoral messaging.

The ruling party in Uganda has retained power for forty years and has done so using not one single tactic but rather a wide range of methods. While this chapter focused primarily on the practice of digital disinformation, it also included examples of internet shutdowns and repressive laws that are also elements of a wider toolkit of digital authoritarianism.

The use of intentionally misleading information to further political interests and objectives has been evident since the beginning of recorded political history in Uganda. The use of disinformation by state actors is the most well-documented and this has been the case with the most recent elections considered in this chapter. This chapter has shown that social media has somewhat democratized the ability to produce and broadcast election (dis)information in Uganda. One emerging effect has been the ability to document disinformation deployment by non-state actors – in the case of this study by pro-opposition actors. Despite this, a power imbalance remains between the incumbent government and the ruling NDM party and the opposition. The ruling party maintain an upper hand through their access to the large state budget and institutions denied to opposition groups. Among those resources is the ability to use other tactics and mechanisms of digital authoritarianism to suppress opposition and retain power. This power imbalance was exhibited when Twitter and Facebook took down pro-ruling party disinformation accounts – the state was able to mobilize its power to effect a nationwide shutdown of the entire internet just before and during the elections.

Disinformation in Ugandan has emerged as a tool of power – either by the incumbent to reinforce and retain power, or by the opposition to wrestle for power. Platforms have become intermediaries in this power contestation such that their regulations and practices impact on the electoral processes in every nation.

For free and fair elections, the electorate in any country need to have access to a diversity of trustworthy information and independent analysis. Social media was supposed to help expand these democratic freedoms in online space even in settings where offline freedoms were shrinking. The expansion of state disinformation and creeping digital authoritarianism puts these freedoms at risk.

Arising from this analysis of disinformation in Uganda the following tentative suggestions arise for how online freedoms might best be defended and expanded. Further research and documentation are needed into the drivers, mechanisms and effects of the deployment of digital disinformation tactics by both state and non-state actors. It was not possible to ascertain who developed the strategy and orchestrating the online campaigns of coordinated inauthentic behaviour. There is a compelling need to effect national legislation and platform regulation that protects citizens' digital rights and their ability to participate in unfettered political association and expression. For social media platforms to be able to adequately moderate political debate they must employ local staff that understand the languages and political culture being contested. For citizens to be able to filter online content for disinformation there is an urgent need to raise awareness of disinformation as part of a wider critical digital literacy. Governments need to see social media not as a threat to their retention of power but rather as a means to engage citizens in democratic deliberation and participatory democracy.

Bibliography

Africa Center for Strategic Studies (2022) *Mapping Disinformation in Africa*. 26 April. https://africacenter.org/spotlight/mapping-disinformation-in-africa/ (accessed 23 May 2022).

Al Jazeera (2020) *Deadly protests in Uganda after Bobi Wine arrested again*. 18 November. https://www.aljazeera.com/news/2020/11/18/bobi-wine-uganda-opposition-presidential-candidate-arrested.

Balancing Act (2011) *Uganda: Govt Blocks Facebook, Twitter as 'Walk to Work' Protest Gathers Momentum*. 21 April. https://www.balancingact-africa.com/news/telecoms-en/21762/uganda-govt-blocks-facebook-twitter-as-walk-to-work-protest-gathers-momentum (accessed 10 June 2022).

BBC (2018) 'Cameroon Drops Fake News Charges against Mimi Mefo'. November. https://www.bbc.com/news/world-africa-46194532.

BBC (2021) *Uganda social media ban raises questions over regulation in Africa*. 15 January. https://www.bbc.com/news/world-africa-55618994.

Buule, Gabriel (2021) *Daily Monitor, How social media influencers have become tools for blackmail*. 16 August. https://www.monitor.co.ug/uganda/special-reports/how-social-media-influencers-have-become-tools-for-blackmail-3512422.

Chibita, M. and Fourie, P. (2007) 'A Socio-History of the Media and Participation in Uganda'. *Communicatio: South African Journal for Communication Theory and Research*, 33 (1): 1–25, https://www.tandfonline.com/doi/abs/10.1080/02500160701398938.

CIPESA (2014) *State of Internet Freedom in Uganda*. 28 September. https://cipesa.org/?wpfb_dl=181 (accessed 29 July 2022).

CIPESA (2016) *Analysis of Twitter Activity During the 2016 Presidential Debates in Uganda*. February. https://www.cipesa.org/?wpfb_dl=210.

CIPESA (2021) *How Online Narratives Played Out on Twitter Before, During and After the 2021 Uganda Elections*. May. https://cipesa.org/wp-content/uploads/2022/03/

How-Online-Narratives-Played-Out-on-Twitter-Before-During-and-After-the-2021-Uganda-Elections-copy.pdf (accessed 27 August 2022).

CIPESA (2022) *Disinformation Pathways and Effects: Case Studies from Five African Countries.* May. https://cipesa.org/?wpfb_dl=497 (accessed 29 June 2022).

DataReportal (2021) *Uganda.* https://datareportal.com/reports/digital-2021-uganda.

DataReportal (2022) *Uganda.* https://datareportal.com/reports/digital-2022-uganda (accessed 30 July 2022).

Dispatch (2020) *Pro-Bobi Wine YouTube Channels are a National Security Risk, UCC Writes to Google.* 15 December. https://www.dispatch.ug/2020/12/15/pro-bobi-wine-youtube-channels-are-a-national-security-risk-ucc-writes-to-google/.

Echwalu, Edward (2011) *Ugandan Media Censored Over Walk to Work Protests.* 19 April. https://cpj.org/2011/04/ugandan-media-censored-over-walk-to-work-protests/ (accessed 5 June 2022).

Freedom House (2021) *Freedom on the Net 2021; The Global Drive to Control Big Tech.* September. https://freedomhouse.org/sites/default/files/2021-09/FOTN_2021_Complete_Booklet_09162021_FINAL_UPDATED.pdf.

Freedom House (2021) *Freedom on the Net.* Uganda. https://freedomhouse.org/country/uganda/freedom-net/2021.

Howard, Philip N. (2020) *Lie Machines: How to Save Democracy from Troll Armies, Deceitful Robots, Junk News Operations, and Political Operatives.* New Haven, CT: Yale University Press.

HRW (2020) *Uganda: Respect Rights in COVID-19 Response.* 2 April. https://www.hrw.org/news/2020/04/02/uganda-respect-rights-covid-19-response.

IFEX (2006) *Critical Website Radio Katwe Blocked on Eve of Presidential Election.* 23 February. https://ifex.org/critical-website-radio-katwe-blocked-on-eve-of-presidential-election/.

Jeune Afrique (2019) Cameroun : plusieurs militants du MRC blessés au cours d'une marche à Douala, January. https://shorturl.at/rN015.

Kakande, Arthur (2020) *Analysis of Uganda's Social Media Data Regarding the 2021 General Presidential Elections.* 22 November. https://towardsdatascience.com/analysis-of-ugandas-social-media-data-regarding-the-2021-general-presidential-elections-3dd52a23cedb.

Kuo, Rachel, and Rachel Marwick (2021) *Misinformation Review: Critical disinformation studies: History, power, and politics.* 12 August. https://misinforeview.hks.harvard.edu/article/critical-disinformation-studies-history-power-and-politics/.

Kyeyune, Hamza (2020) *Google rejects Uganda move to close YouTube channels.* 29 December. Google rejects Uganda move to close YouTube channels.

Lemaire, Pauline, Selvik, Lisa-Marie and Garbe, Lisa (2021) *Democracy in Africa.* December. http://democracyinafrica.org/how-african-countries-respond-to-fake-news-and-hate-speech/ (accessed 14 August 2022).

Lugalambi, G. and Mwesige, P. (2010) *On Air Uganda.* Nairobi: Open Society Foundation. https://www.opensocietyfoundations.org/uploads/98954150-a6df-49ee-a680-d9d4a8cd07fe/uganda-public-broadcasting-20100701.pdf.

MoICT (2020) *Call to embrace the scientific campaign roadmap.* 21 June. https://ict.go.ug/wp-content/uploads/2020/06/Press-Statement-on-Scientific-Electoctions-Road-Map.pdf.

Mwai, Peter (2020) *Uganda election: False claims about Joe Biden and others.* 20 December. Peter Mwai.

Nanfuka, Juliet (2021) *Uganda's 2021 Election: A Textbook Case of Disruption to Democracy and Digital Networks in Authoritarian Countries.* 13 January. https://cipesa.org/2021/01/ugandas-2021-election-a-textbook-case-of-disruption-to-democracy-and-digital-networks-in-authoritarian-countries/.

New York Times (1977) *Uganda Issues Warning to Americans and British Who 'Tell Lies' About It*. https://www.nytimes.com/1977/03/14/archives/uganda-issues-warning-to-americans-and-british-who-tell-lies-about.html.

Ojok, Donna (2016) *Social Media Lockdown and Elections in Uganda*. 2 March. https://blogs.lse.ac.uk/africaatlse/2016/03/02/social-media-lockdown-and-elections-in-uganda/ (accessed 5 June 2022).

OONI (2021) *Uganda: Data on Internet Blocks and Nationwide Internet Outage Amid 2021 General Election*. https://ooni.org/post/2021-uganda-general-election-blocks-and-outage/.

Roberts, T. and Mohamed Ali, A. (2021) 'Opening and Closing Online Civic Space in Africa: An Introduction to the Ten Digital Rights Landscape Reports'. In T. Roberts (ed.), *Digital Rights in Closing Civic Space: Lessons from Ten African Countries*. Brighton: Institute of Development Studies. https://opendocs.ids.ac.uk/opendocs/handle/20.500.12413/15964.

RSF (2019) *Uganda 'Suspends' 39 Journalists for Covering Politician's Arrest*. 2 May. https://rsf.org/en/uganda-suspends-39-journalists-covering-politician-s-arrest (accessed 13 July 2022).

Samuel-Stone, Songa (2021) *Digital Voter Manipulation: A Situational Analysis of How Online Spaces Were Used as a Manipulative Tool During Uganda's 2021 General Election*. https://www.kas.de/documents/280229/0/Digital+Voter+Manipulation+Report.pdf/910ccef1-3d4e-1f58-0d4c-70f0509a1e89?version=1.1&t=1624704090405.

Shahbaz, Adrian (2018) *The Rise of Digital Authoritarianism*. https://freedomhouse.org/report/freedom-net/2018/rise-digital-authoritarianism.

Tabaire, B. (2007) 'The Press and Political Repression in Uganda: Back to the Future?' *Journal of Eastern African Studies*, 1 (2): 193–211. https://www.tandfonline.com/doi/pdf/10.1080/17531050701452408.

The Conversation (2019) *How Uganda is Using Old and New Laws to Block Activists on Social Media*. 8 September. https://theconversation.com/how-uganda-is-using-old-and-new-laws-to-block-activists-on-social-media-121823 (accessed 13 July 2022).

The Economist (2022) *A New Low for Global Democracy*. 10 February. https://www.economist.com/graphic-detail/2022/02/09/a-new-low-for-global-democracy.

Uganda Bureau of Statistics (2022) 'Statistical Abstract'. https://www.ubos.org/wp-content/uploads/publications/05_20232022_Statistical_Abstract.pdf.

UN (2022) *e-Government Knowledge Base*. https://publicadministration.un.org/egovkb/en-us/Data/Country-Information/id/179-Uganda.

United Nations (General Assembly) (1966) 'International Covenant on Civil and Political Rights'. *Treaty Series* 999 (December): 171.

URN (2020) *Lawyers Amazed at UCC 'ignorance' as Google Tells Regulator to Go to Court*. 17 December. https://observer.ug/news/headlines/67794-lawyers-amazed-at-ucc-ignorance-as-google-tells-regulator-to-go-to-court (accessed 13 July 2022).

Wanyama, Don (2021) *Don Wanyama Twitter Account*. 9 January. https://twitter.com/nyamadon/status/1347816013514088448.

Wardle, Claire and Derakhshan, Hossein (2017) *Information Disorder: Toward an Interdisciplinary Framework for Research and Policy Making*. Strasbourg: Council of Europe.

WION (2021) *Bobi Wine vs Yoweri Museveni: Who will become Uganda's next president?* 13 January. https://www.wionews.com/world/bobi-wine-vs-yoweri-museveni-who-will-become-ugandas-next-president-356521.

World Economics (2022) *Uganda's Median Age*. https://www.worldeconomics.com/Demographics/Median-Age/Uganda.aspx.nya (accessed August 29, 2021).

Chapter 10

Online disinformation and 'meme-fication' in Angola's 2022 election

Edmilson Angelo

Introduction

After a protracted anti-colonial war, Angola has been under one-party rule since 1975 with power held continuously by the People's Movement of the Liberation of Angola (MPLA). The country held its fourth multi-party general election in August 2022, which proved to be the most closely contested in the nation's history with the ruling MPLA losing the capital city Luanda to opposition rivals National Union for the Total Independence of Angola (UNITA). For decades the ruling party has maintained firm control of the political narrative through state-controlled TV and radio. However, the arrival of social media has broken the state's monopoly on political information and platforms such as WhatsApp, Facebook, Instagram and Twitter have emerged as significant sites of political contestation. This chapter focuses primarily on the deployment of digital disinformation by the state and on counter-disinformation in the forms of online memes deployed by young citizens in the run up to the 2022 general elections.

The term disinformation, discussed in greater detail in the introduction to this book, is used in this chapter to refer to false information shared intentionally for political objectives. An internet meme is 'a piece of culture, typically a joke, which gains influence through online transmission' (Davison 2012). Disinformation has been exercised in Angola by colonial powerholders and political parties long before the arrival of digital technologies. In the colonial and post-colonial administration those in power have often used their control over state media channels to deploy racist pseudo-science and other disinformation to legitimize incumbent power (Kuo and Marwick 2021).

In context where state control of media limits open debate about democratic alternatives, the arrival of social media provided a new form of civic space where issues and voices underrepresented by establishment media and political parties could be heard (Roberts et al. 2021).

Young Angolans have made creative use of online civic space, using memes to disrupt state disinformation, claims rights and demand change. Although there has been an enormous amount of research attention to online politics in the last decade, there has been comparatively little research on digital politics in Africa and even less in Lusophony Africa. Research on disinformation in Angola is almost entirely absent in the existing literature as this is the first ever study analysing the role of disinformation in Angolan electoral politics in the digital era.

This chapter addresses the gap in the literature by examining the mechanisms of disinformation by those in power and its influence on e-citizens' political behaviour in Angola. In other words, the chapter explains how disinformation is fabricated and distributed by those in power, and how young people in online spaces in Angola have responded by disrupting state control of the political narrative.

The chapter conducts a digital ethnography of state disinformation during Angola's 2022 election as well as an analysis of meme-based counter-disinformation by citizens. Gaventa's concepts of power and space are used to provide a framework to analyse how in an authoritarian country deprived of offline civic spaces, the youth in Angola are creating new online democratic spaces where they feel unrestricted to express their rights to freedom of expression and demand change.

The rest of the chapter is organized as follows: the first section provides some historical and political context for the reader unfamiliar with the political and technological conditions that shape disinformation in Angola. The methodology is then briefly discussed before reviewing the existing conceptual literature defining disinformation and presenting the conceptual framing of power in digital spaces. Then the chapter continues with examples of state disinformation and citizens countering the disinformation often in the form of memes before these examples are analysed to answer the main question of this chapter.

Background

The borders of present-day Angola were defined by Portuguese colonialization, with the Democratic Republic of the Congo to its north, Zambia to the east, Namibia to its south and the Pacific Ocean along its west coast (Figure 10.1).

The government's position was boosted by a post-independence oil-fuelled economic miracle that repositioned Angola, a war-torn 'failed state', as one of the world's fastest growing economies with a GDP of US$121billion, the third-highest in Africa (OPEC, 2007). The country's oil production hit a peak of almost 2 million barrels per day by 2010 and has ranged around 1.85 million since 2012 (De Oliveira 2014). Despite the impressive oil-driven growth in the early 2000s, pervasive poverty, inequality, infrastructure crisis, corruption and other social issues remain noteworthy problems. Rather than being used for the benefit of the people, oil revenues have been used to promote an authoritarian hegemonic dispensation concentrated around former MPLA President Dos Santos and his inner circle (De Oliveira 2014).

Hidden behind Angola's economic boom are alarming figures on indices such as the United Nations Development Programme (UNDP). Although subjective, Angola ranks 148th among 186 countries on human development index (UNDP 2022). This suggests large income inequalities, which explains Angola 119th position on the Global Corruption Index (Transparency International 2023).

Figure 10.1 Angola. *Source*: Open Street Map @cc-license.

As the economy grew so did Angola's population and particularly youth as a proportion of the total population. Results from the 2014 census projected the youth population of the country to significantly rise in the following years (INE 2014). Today, it is estimated that 34.48 million is the total population, with youths under thirty-five making up more than 50 per cent of the population (Simon Kemp 2022). These young Angolans, for whom the memory of the civil war is becoming a distant recollection, have been increasingly vocal politically.

The youth in Angola are increasingly taking to the streets and using social media to express their concerns, discontent and on occasion fury at the level of police brutality, corruption, unemployment and rising living costs among other issues faced by a majority of the population in Angola (Amnesty International 2020). As reported by Amnesty International (2020) the series of peaceful demonstrations that took place in several Angolan provinces brought together thousands of people across the country who demanded the end of police abuses in Angola.

Much of this youth-led anti-government protest is being organized on social media, which is becoming an increasingly important dimension of Angola's political sphere. Platforms such as Facebook and Instagram have become powerful tools for young people to mobilize against the state. Social media has not only allowed the youth to actively express their political discontentment but also to create a political identity in a way that is convenient and potentially safer in a country with restricted civic space offline. As the government continues to struggle to deal with this 'new' reality of digital political activism, attempts to limit and control these virtual spaces have prompted wider protests and even online *meme-fication* of the executive power.

New laws to control online political speech are evidence that Angola's ruling party sees the new political dynamics happening online as a threat to its power. To fight this new digital threat to political power, the government proposed a new article (333º) in the Penal Code of Angola that condemns mimicry, jokes or critical commentary of the president of the Republic and organs of sovereignty, particularly online (Luamba 2020). This is a proposal that has been seen by local analysts as a threat to freedom of expression and creation, which has prompted a new wave of online protests led by the youth reflecting the importance and power of social media in Angola's political sphere (Luamba 2020).

Media landscape

A report by the Media Institute of Southern Africa (MISA 2003) examined the level of freedom of press in Angola since the end of the civil war. It reported that state media such as Angola Public Television (TPA), National Radio of Angola (RNA) and Journal of Angola were by far the biggest channels of information in the country with a visible potential to play an active role in the reconstruction and democratization of Angola. However, these organizations faced state control of public media institutions and the individuals in it (directors, journalists, commentors) who work in them (MISA 2003). Moreover, local journalists received extra benefits for belonging to the ruling party in the form of a house allowance, cars or the like, particularly for those on national television (MISA 2003). This illustrates the historical hegemonic power of the political system in Angola and the clientelist relations within the channels of (dis)information.

In recent years, the country has witnessed a growing number of violations of freedom of press against journalists and the state takeover of private media companies such as TV ZIMBO which is currently the most watched channel in the country (Lusa 2020). This has presented further obstacles to democratic debate, shrinking civic space for opposition parties during elections, as I discuss further in this chapter.

Digital uptake in Angola

The growing digital presence and actions of political actors in the warmup to the 2022 general election echoes the rise of digital spaces within Angola's political realm and how post-colonial hegemonic parties are reinventing themselves online to maintain power and control.

Table 10.1 is derived from a data report Kepios (2022) and shows that almost 12.41 million people use the internet in Angola. Access to the internet remains inaccessible in many rural areas, but it is used intensively by youths in urban areas like Luanda. In a context where spaces for political contestation remains limited, new digital spaces such as Facebook and Instagram and other social media platforms have provided a relatively safe space, not mediated by mainstream media or political parties, where young people are able to rehearse resistance, protest and mobilize against the ruling party.

What is more, the digital space in Angola is also being used as a tool for opposition parties and leaders to project their political agendas. The importance of the current digital space in Angola was strengthened in 2017 when President Lourenco launched an official Facebook page after assuming office via a post that read, 'comrades and friends, this is my official page on social media, please follow me and let us discuss on daily basis the main issue that affect the youth' (Lourenço 2017).

This act can be interpreted as a normal practice of digital communication which African leaders and governments are following for a better online presence and communication. However, in his introductory post quoted earlier, the communication was directed at a specific segment of the population, which is the youth. By mentioning the youth in his post, he highlights the significance of youth in Angola today, but also draws a clear picture of the relationship between the digital spaces and the youth in Angola today, especially during elections as he is the first presidential candidate from Angola's ruling party MPLA to create a social media account to campaign.

Strategies for political campaign online by political parties during Angola's 2022 elections reveal how social media has become a leading tool for political communication and mobilization in Angola. These new online spaces are not only facilitating greater access to both false and true information but are providing a simple path to active interaction between political parties and electorates, especially the younger generation.

Table 10.1 Digital Angola 2022 Statistics

Population of Angola	34.48 million
Internet users	12.41 million
Youth	55 per cent under twenty-five, 78 per cent under thirty-five
Internet users	36 per cent of the overall population
Social media users in adult population	13.5 per cent
Facebook	81 per cent of internet users
Pinterest	12.4 per cent
YouTube	3.7 per cent
Twitter	1.32 per cent
Instagram	0.6 per cent

Source: (Kepios, 2022).

On 24 August 2022, civil society in Angola casted their vote to elect the next president. The election contest between MPLA and opposition UNITA was the closest in the country's electoral history since the end of the civil war in 2002 (Burke 2022). Even though MPLA was re-elected with 51 per cent of the overall votes, it faced a devastating and historical defeat to opposition UNITA by 63 per cent to 31 per cent in the capital city (Neusa and Silva 2022). This marked the first time in the history of the country that the ruling MPLA lost in Luanda, which is the main political, economic and social gate of Angola.

Under a new context where digital discourse has become significantly important for partisan communication and electorate mobilization, particularly among the youth, who, like in other parts of the world, are influenced and inspired by new practices of communication and interaction that shape governance at the local and global level with social media at the center of this new paradigm.

Methodology

This chapter examines the mechanisms of disinformation used by those in power and their influence on e-citizens' political behaviour in Angola. To answer this question, I employed a qualitative mixed-method approach composed of digital ethnography within two 'public' online spaces (Facebook and Instagram) where political discourse and campaigns were taking place heavily. In doing that, I examined the techniques and actors behind the main episodes of digital disinformation in the lead-up to the 2022 election.

Digital ethnography also known as online ethnography is an online research method that adapts ethnography to the study of the communities and cultures created through online-mediated social interaction (Hine 2011). While traditional ethnography study observes the interactions between individuals who are co-located, digital ethnography extends ethnographic study to settings where interactions are technologically mediated and not face-to-face (Hine 2011). Unlike in other countries in Africa and beyond (South Africa, Nigeria, Zimbabwe, United States, United Kingdom . . .), where Twitter is the main tool for politics online, in Angola Facebook and Instagram rather than Twitter are at the center of the online political discourse both in terms of number and impact, and are the two online spaces used for this chapter. To complement the ethnographic research method, twelve semi-structure interviews were conducted with well-identified social media account holders, predominantly youths who accounted for the largest electoral group.

The research described in this chapter is part of a larger doctoral research project which includes digital ethnography on additional platforms and other election issues. As the focus for this chapter was election disinformation, I began monitoring online posts in the six months before the August 2022 election and for one month after. I narrowed my focus to just two digital platforms (Facebook and Instagram), as Facebook has the largest number of social media users in Angola and Instagram is the platform on which most Angolan counter-disinformation memes originate.

Initially, I followed the main election hashtags (#2022VaisGostar, #JáEstá) to discern which individual accounts were most influential – that is, most mentioned and most reposted. After two months monitoring in this way it was possible to focus in on those hashtags and accounts that generated the most disinformation and counter disinformation to maintain a record of those posts that met my definition of disinformation (and counter disinformation memes) for further analysis.

Disinformation and digital space

Bennett and Livingston (2018: 124) define disinformation as the deliberate spreading of falsehoods to advance political goals. Bradshaw, Bailey and Howard (2020) use the term to refer to purposefully crafted and strategically placed information that deceives someone, tricks them into believing a lie or taking action that serves someone else's political interest. This chapter adopts the definition of disinformation provided by Benkler et al. (2018), who define the concept as an act designed to manipulate and mislead people intentionally to achieve a political end, as most appropriate for this study of political disinformation.

According to Davison (2012), an internet meme is a piece of culture, typically a joke, which gains influence through online transmission. Memes are most often shared as visual images, passed from person to person, often modified along the way, with some memes gaining sufficient traction to go viral and become a shared social phenomenon. Chris Tenove (2019) defines political memes as a purposefully designed visual framing of a position, represented in the form of jokes about a politician, public figure or political issue.

Memes today represent a new genre of political communication that work when widely shared and help cultivate a sense of belonging to an 'in-group' presenting a compelling and complementary normative illustration about a figure. They are easily created, consumed, changed and disseminated and can quickly communicate the creator's position on the subject. The stronger the emotional response provoked by a political meme, the greater the potential effect (Tenove 2019).

The rapid expansion of access to mobile internet and to social media such as Facebook and Instagram in Angola has meant that the latter have become popular and effective ways for young people to express themselves politically. Many young people in the country who feel alienated and unrepresented by the established political parties and state media have found alternative civic spaces on social media for a new kind of unruly politics. Those with access to mobile internet are expressing themselves politically in this new online civic space by posting, sharing, commenting and interacting with those who rule, those who aspire to rule and the wider civil society on political matters.

These new digital communication platforms are not only used by the youth but also by establishment political parties to communicate, mobilize and propagate their political messaging. In hegemonic political regimes like Angola, with state-controlled media, these new online platforms represent a new virtual space in which they can exercise their power. Yet, it also represents a space where counter-power and counter-narratives can be projected not only by opposition parties but also by the electorate, especially in times of election.

Conceptualizing digital spaces of power

There is an extensive literature documenting studies on the spaces in which citizens challenge dominate power and claim rights (Schmelzkopf 1995; Cornwall and Coelho 2004; Gaventa 2006; Gaventa 2010). There has been far less attention dedicated to studying the emerging digital spaces for citizen engagement and political contestation using the lens of space and power. This chapter borrows from theories of how power operates in offline spaces to analyse what new forms of power arise in emerging online spaces and asks how they reflect offline power relations and affect them.

Gaventa views power not as a finite zero-sum resource to be fought over, but as a resource that can be produced, shared and used by actors and their networks in many multiple ways (Gaventa J. 2006). Gaventa sees power as something produced actively and collectively in spaces, which helps us better examine where and how power is exercised by those who rule vis-à-vis those who are ruled. In the paper 'Finding the Spaces for Change: A Power Analysis', John Gaventa (2006) explores the effectiveness of potential new democratic spaces for citizen engagement by studying the power dynamics inside and outside of these spaces (2006: 3).

Through the lenses of a 'power cube', Gaventa (2006) examines the concepts of places, spaces and forms of power and their inter-relationship. He argues that such three-dimensional analysis helps us understand how 'spaces' represent opportunities, moments and channels where citizens can come together to contest political power and create relationships that affect their lives and interests (2006: 26). Gaventa sub-divides spaces of power into three categories: the first *closed spaces* are created by elites and are spaces where decisions are made behind closed doors without public consultation or involvement (2006: 26). In other words, they are spaces of exclusion found often in non-democratic states with very centralized decision-making like Angola.

In the paper 'Seeing like a Citizen', Gaventa (2010) explains why it is important to frame citizens as rights-bearing actors, arguing that civil society is one of the few arenas in which citizens can express their political identities and claim their rights. From this perspective, citizenship is viewed as a process in which rights-bearing actors engage constantly with the states, and civil society itself (Gaventa 2010: 59). Through his *citizen-centred approach*, Gaventa (2010) argues that the starting point to our understanding of citizenship should not be institutional design but rather citizens' perceptions of themselves – an understanding attained by questioning how they interact and view state institutions to claim entitlements and benefits.

From this perspective citizenship is not a status given to citizens by the state, but it instead is an active process of citizen engagement in civic and political life to claim their rights and to assert their voice (Gaventa 2010: 59). Through this active process citizens exercise power over decisions which affect their lives, and democracy is extended from one of voters to a democracy of citizens (Gaventa 2010). It is this view of active citizens exercising rights in spaces of power that informs the analysis of online civic space in this chapter.

Disinformation, election and the MPLA

This section provides four examples of lies intentionally deployed by the ruling party for political gain during the 2022 election. These include two manufactured lies about opposition presidential candidate Adalberto Costa Junior: first, the false claim that he had lied about his academic qualifications and second the lie that he was not Angolan.

Case I: #IsACJreallyAnEngineer?

The first example of disinformation deployed by the ruling party MPLA in the run up to the 2022 election was an accusation that the opposition candidate was academically unqualified – a claim that was later shown to be false. Two months before the election, a disinformation campaign was launched via a well-known journal in Portugal questioning the veracity of his academic degree from Porto Institute of Engineering. This was rapidly shared online by well-known figures of the ruling party MPLA with large social media following and the youth wing of the party. The social media posts urged the leader of the opposition to respond to the news and publicly show his degree to prove his academic qualifications. What is more, the news became a national debate as it headlined on national television and was a topic of televised debate for a few days (Novo Jornal 2022). This tripartite strategy is a well-documented propaganda strategy: first, seed a story in a foreign publication, second, using domestic influencers to circulate the story on social media, third, use establishment media to present it as 'news' (Howard 2020; Jones 2022).

Questioning the legitimacy of his academic degree was part of a series of defamation attempts to denigrate the image of the opposition party and undermine its leader in the run-up to the election (NJ 2022). To end the immediate noise generated around the disinformation on his academic background, the School of Engineering at the Polytechnic of Porto (Portugal) released a statement rejecting the news and confirming the legitimacy of Adalberto's degree (Lusa 2022).

The dissemination of the disinformation was done by four key actors: the Portuguese media, old figures of the ruling party, the youth of the party and Angola's national television. Even though the source of the disinformation was a Portuguese tabloid, the news automatically carried weight in Angola as it came from Portugal, where the media is deemed to be independent and continues to influence public opinion in Angola given the history of the two countries. This sheds light on the role of foreign actors in purveying disinformation campaigns in Africa (Africa Centre for Strategic Studies 2022).

Veteran members of the central committee of the MPLA, together with leaders of the youth wing of the party, turned this false information into a classic political propaganda in the form of audio and texts posted on social media, to demoralize the opposition and promote the agenda of the ruling party (Jones 2022). This attempt to mislead the public was specifically directed at the youth who represented the larger electorate group in Angola. While giving his opinion during a televised debate on the topic, a political analyst associated with the MPLA repeatedly questioned whether the youth in Angola would trust a leader who lies about his academic qualifications to lead their future (Bali O Chionga 2022). However, rather than creating a feeling of unrest towards the opposition party, the disinformation made the youth become more supportive of Adalberto Costa Junior by creating the hashtag #ACJ2022 and #MyPresident which was shared and used as captions by a significant number of accounts by and for the youth in Angola. This was a common denominator, as I found in my examination of the disinformation attempts against the opposition party in Angola in the run-up to the 2022 elections.

In other words, unsuccessful disinformation from the state had an opposite effect to the one intended, which has led to a political opening. To that end, if a piece of political (dis)information can be shown to be a cynical lie to serve political interest then it can increase the size and strength of the opposition.

Case II: Is he Angolan or Portuguese?

Soon after stating his desire to lead the opposition party UNITA and subsequently become a presidential candidate under his party's umbrella, speculation around Adalberto Costa Junior's nationality started emerging from within his party during UNITA's XII Ordinary Congress to elect its leader.

Adalberto Junior was born in Benguela (Angola) and for many years served as the head of UNITA in Portugal. His long spell in Portugal granted him Portuguese citizenship at a specific time of his life. However, neither the Angola Constitution nor the regulations of his party permit dual nationality for presidency (Constitution of the Republic of Angola 2010). To that end, his rise to the leadership seat of the opposition party was challenged by internal groups within UNITA who questioned the legitimacy of him becoming the leader of the party given his dual citizenship (Sul 2019).

Soon after speculation on whether Adalberto revoked his Portuguese citizenship before becoming the leader of UNITA started coming out, as with the previous case, the subject became of topic of discussion on national television, as it represented an opportunity to stop Adalberto from running from the number one seat in the country and perhaps have another leader in the opposition party who is less popular among civil society.

In the run up to the general elections, the supreme court decided to intervene and invalidated the UNITA's congress where Adalberto Costa Junior had been elected as president of UNITA, based on the finding that there had been 'clear irregularities within the electoral process that took place in UNITA's XIII Congress' (Lusa 2021). The decision to cancel UNITA's congress increased the propagation of the narrative on Adalberto's nationality on television and social media by structures of the ruling party, with his patriotic commitment being questioned based on his dual citizenship status, which is prohibited for anyone running for election in Angola.

In 2019, Arlete Chimbinda, Member of Parliament for UNITA and spokesperson for Adalberto Costa Junior's candidacy for UNITA's leadership, had already stated that the candidate had formally revoked his Portuguese nationally before his election as the president of UNITA (Jornal de Angola 2019). She referred to article 37/81 of the Portuguese constitution, which states that 'those who, being nationals of another state, declare that they do not want to be Portuguese, lose their nationality' (Constitution of Portuguese Republic 2005). According to UNITA's spokesperson, their leader had formally declared his wish to revoke his Portuguese citizenship to the respective institution in that country before submitting his candidacy to lead UNITA.

In addition, Adalberto Costa Junior commented on the speculation of his future after the decision by the supreme court, claiming to be an act based on disinformation about the status of his nationality fabricated by the ruling party and instrumentalized by an institution (the supreme court) that serves as partisan instrument rather than an independent body that serves the country (Lusa 2021).

As the decision from the supreme court came just months from the general elections, UNITA was forced to organize a new Ordinary Congress in a space of a month to elect its leader (VOA 2021). This saw the re-election of Adalberto Costa Junior who came out of this congress with higher political support from his party and civil society.

Again, the outcome of the disinformation played in favour of UNITA and its leader, rather the ruling party MPLA. This case illudes to how in authoritarian regimes like Angola all states' institutions and powers such as the judiciary, can easier become instruments within the machine of disinformation to maintain the status quo.

Case III: Anti-MPLA vandalism a seed of violence by UNITA

Given the historical background of the country's prolonged conflict, one of the mostly used electoral propaganda campaigns to defame the opposition was the war narrative framed on the opposition in Angola for many decades. In other words, UNITA was a synonym of war, an image built by the ruling power to deflate the opposition and maintain power without any contestation or political threat particularly during elections.

On 10 January, an office of the ruling party was set ablaze in the capital city of Luanda (Mendes and Almeida 2022). Videos and images of unidentified individuals who claimed to be members of UNITA were quickly shared and linked with anti-MPLA/government protest to reinforce the narrative against the opposition. What is more, national television channels such as TPA and Zimbo started a series of interviews with religious leaders, civil society and opened a general debate with political leaders on the importance of maintaining the peace and avoiding the influence of political parties with a history of war making.

Angolan national television (TPA) ran a series of broadcasts that indirectly portrayed the opposition party to be directly involved in the act of vandalism that took place in one of the offices of the ruling party (Televisão Publica de Angola 2022). Like the previous cases presented earlier, once broadcasted on national television, the accusations were immediately spread on social media through pages associated with the ruling party attempting to portray the opposition as promoter of violence who will take the country back to the times of conflict though much of the protest was a result of public discontentment against the government over the ongoing issues of inequality and unemployment (Nebe 2020). Perhaps this suggests a degree of professionalism and central coordination in the disinformation campaigns by the ruling party in Angola.

After investigations, testimonies and the arrestment of seventeen people, it was later found that the act of vandalism which led to the burning of a local office of the MPLA had nothing to do with the opposition party but happened as part of a radical protest by taxi drivers to force the government to scrap restrictions limiting passenger capacity to 50 per cent (Mendes and Almeida 2022).

As stated by the head of the New Alliance of Luanda's Taxi Driver Association, Francisco Paciente, '*the strike and protest was over the daily discrimination by police and the earlier decree limiting passenger numbers inside vehicles*' (African Insider 2022). This debunked the disinformation made by the MPLA secretary in Luanda on national television who claim that the protest was political motivated by 'well-identified players who are behind these attacks' (African Insider 2022). A claim that was followed by an old video, with no connection to the incident, of an activist threatening the MPLA while expressing his support to UNITA. Disinformation in this case operates to manipulate and hinder public's image of opposition party through a narrative of war that remain sensitive for a country like Angola that has experience more than two decades of civil conflict.

Case IV: UNITA using money from Dos Santos' family (Corruption)

Former president Jose Eduardo dos Santos ruled the country for over thirty-eight years and was accused of ruling the country as his own family business with a small number of shareholders during his marathon rule (Lynsey 2018). In 2017, Joao Lourenco, then minister of defence, succeeded Dos Santos as president and picked the fight against corruption as his main flag for his mandate (AFP 2018).

Since taking power, President Lourenco has cracked down on corruption, going after members of his own party. His anti-corruption campaign was not only applauded by the international community, but it increased, though temporary, sympathy, optimism and enthusiasm towards his leadership by the public in Angola. The various episodes of corruption scandals that were exposed and continue to be dealt with by the supreme court since Lourenco came into power are mainly involving the family or close allies of former president Dos Santos. Among them is Isabel dos Santos, daughter of the former president and one of Africa's richest women who headed Sonangol[1] (2016–17), and her brother Filomeno dos Santos who led Angola's Wealth Fund (2013–18) and was granted a five year sentence by the supreme court for corruption and money laundering (BBC 2020).

The combat against corruption led by President Lourenco created a narrative of corruption being the main cause of Angola's problems, making those involved in corruption scandals enemies of the state. To that end, anyone who associated themselves with money derived from Dos Santos family could be seen to be promoting corruption that has affected the country deeply. In the warmup to the 2022 election, (dis)information emerged from a tabloid claiming that opposition leader, Adalberto Costa Junior, was receiving funds from the Dos Santos family to restructure his party (Folha 9 2022).

Political analysis linked to MPLA were calling for an investigation on UNITA's donors list and questioned the integrity of the opposition leader and his party for receiving money from an individual with legal cases of corruption. This was done via televised interventions during news hours and for few days. It is important to mention these analysts had different slots of intervention during the televised programmes, but the message was always the same, which reinforces the professionalism and central coordination in the disinformation campaigns by the ruling party.

This forced the leader of the opposition party to demystify such claims during a political rally in the province of Lunda Norte, where he called the accusations 'lies and hypocrisy' coming from people who were practicing acts of corruption with the former president of Angola, and are now going against him and his family as if they are not part of the same party (Novo Jornal 2022).

Additionally, both daughters of former president Dos Santos called the news fake and a politically motivated 'witch-hunt' led by President Lourenco (Browning and Zhdannikov 2020).

By analysing the dynamics of the Angolan state disinformation, a pattern emerges of how it is coordinated. In important ways this echoes the mechanics of the 'Lie Machine' described by Philip Howard (2020) in his work on computational propaganda, with different operatives responsible for distinct stages in the disinformation campaign. The machinery of disinformation led by the Institute for Propaganda and Psychological Action created by the ruling party, and the (dis)information that serves the MPLA on a daily basis, managed to provide misleading information in the hope of resuscitating the image of UNITA in the eyes of the youth who represent the largest electorate group in the country.

---

1. Sonangol is the economic heart of Angola that formerly oversees petroleum and natural gas production in the country.

The counter-disinformation mechanism

Once state actors deployed disinformation, youth activists were quick to question the truthiness of the information and started mocking the clear attempt at deception using memes. On social media, the disinformation was quickly debunked by youth commentators on social media who stood by the side of the opposition party and its leader who constantly had to publicly deny the disinformation coming from the structures of the ruling party.

Among the various accounts, one of the most liked and shared by young people in Angola is Mankiko. The account belongs to a well-known cartoonist, Sergio Piçarra, who turns political (dis)information into creative images with funny messages to illustrate how civil society interprets and reacts to the actions of the government during the electoral process.

In the meme reproduced in Figure 10.2, the president is dressed in judiciary attire sitting on the chair of the judge while holding two clowns representing the supreme court and the constitutional court standing on two podiums that read 'fight against corruption' and 'fight against opposition'. This was in response to the decision of the supreme court to call off the opposition party's congress that elected Adalberto Costa Junior as president.

The message here is clear as it questions the independence of the judiciary system in Angola, suggesting that there is no separation of power with the rule of law under the hand of the executive power led by the president. This post with over 2,000 likes and shares on social media worked as a counter disinformation that created a popular response to state control news channels and reinforce the hashtags created to by the youth to challenge the state. This is only one of the various new forms of counter disinformation taking place in the digital space in Angola.

Figure 10.2 *Source*: @mankikoofficial (Instagram).

Another highly shared post created online on an anonymous page was one which was posted around the time where the nationality of the leader of the opposition party was being discussed. This post was part of a sequence of posts that supported the hashtag #2022VaisGostar (#In2022YouWillSee).

It was an illustration of how based on the sentiment of the overall population the voting queues will look like for the five political parties running for election. While the ruling party is represented with only one vote coming from its own president, the main opposition party is demonstrated as the options for majority of the population despite all the negative (dis)information against the opposition party and its leader.

Recent online trends created by the youth in Angola showcase the solidification of social media in the political sphere and the start of *meme-ification* of the ruling powers' attempt to disinform the youth for political purposes. The hashtag #In2022YouWillSee was created as a response to the continuous government failure to deliver services and promises from previous elections to warn the government that the youth will not vote for the MPLA in 2022.

One of the creators who asked for his identity to be hidden explains how the goal behind the creation and spread of such a hashtag is to 'communicate the discontentment of the youth in a way that is funny, easy to understand for other youth' and to effectively demand a reaction from those governing the country (CC-P7).

This was in line with other content creators such as CC-P2, who is one of the youths behind the most followed and shared social media page on Instagram, who said, 'we create visual communication in a form of memes to respond to any government decision that violates our rights or take us for a joke, this is us showing them that they are the real jokers if they think we are not aware of what is going on' (P2). A preference for Instagram rather than other social media such as Twitter is based on the idea of anonymity and the power of visual communication going as far as comparing it with the traditional analogues of (dis)information such as television and its influence.

> Most digital influencers in Angola have Facebook accounts as it the most used social media in country, however, its mainly used for written communication that often starts and ends on Facebook only. Also, Facebook pages are well identified and easy for the government to find, for these reason Instagram is allowing us to communicate our voices in a creative way using short funny videos that summarises the sentiment of the youth towards the current government in a way that is funny and safer for us. (CC-P7)

The comparison of social media with traditional forms of communication such as television was further discussed on the issue of disinformation in Angola. As one of the interviewees stated,

> the government here (in Angola) controls the media and everything that comes out of it. There are no credibility and people no longer believe in state owned media they are believing us, our memes, our videos, the post and even

our news . . . today we are not just creators of memes, we are also source of information for and against the government. (CC-P10)

Once state actors deployed some of the disinformation presented earlier, young people started questioning, via social media, the legitimacy of the (dis)information showed on national television. Through memes and hashtags, they demonstrated support to the leader of the opposition party who was seen to be a victim of defamation by the ruling party in the run up to the 2022 election. In the following I highlight another example of counter-disinformation led by the youth related to Case III on Anti-MPLA Vandalism, a seed of violence by UNITA.

When an office of the ruling party MPLA was set ablaze in the capital city of Luanda during a protest by the taxi driver association, social media was quick to question the information displayed on national television indirectly accusing the opposition party to be behind such acts. The post from Picaro summarized in a creative and funny manner how many people interpreted the event that took place during the protest from the taxi driver. It is important to mention that the post reproduced in Figure 10.3 goes in line with many descriptive posts and comments from various people on the pages that shared the news regarding the act of vandalism in one of the offices of the MPLA in Luanda.

The post gives a summary of the position of the ruling MPLA, the Taxi Drivers Association, the opposition party UNITA and the ordinary citizen in Angola. On the top left side is a drawing of the former general secretary of the ruling party

Figure 10.3 *Source*: @mankikoofficial (Instagram).

in Luanda, Bento Bento, claiming that the act of vandalism against the office of the MPLA has nothing to do with the taxi drivers' protest, on the top right corner is the spokesperson of Angola's taxi drivers association questioning why the government lied about them cancelling the protest, while on the bottom left corner is the general secretary of the opposition, UNITA, wondering why the local media ignored the press release statement from UNITA denying any involvement in the protest by the taxi drivers. Lastly, on the bottom right corner are two ordinary citizens talking to each other about how they already understand what is going on as they wait for the next episode of election propaganda, which they know will have no positive impact on the lives of the everyday citizen.

In the process of mapping the architects of political disinformation in Angola I observed the existence of closed spaces within the ruling party for the creation of digital content for disinformation which plays a significant role in its outcome. Old-fashioned hierarchical structures within authoritarian political parties like the MPLA in Angola are incredible slow at adapting and handling new digital communication techniques and this hinders the intended outcome of most of the political disinformation. What is more, such limited and inexcusable understanding and adaption of social media by high-ranking members of the ruling party in Angola has resulted in the practice of online counter-disinformation being regarded as disrespectful youth behaviour against the power structures of the state.

These new digital trends led by young people in Angola are demonstrating an evolution of new spaces of resistance in a country where youth represent the main social voice (Gaventa 2006). The use of memes to fight government not only demonstrate the power of the digital space in Angola but also illustrate how the country is undergoing a new phase of social dynamics and state-citizen relation especially in times of elections. Here, the benchmark of prosperity for the youth is no longer the end of the civil war but rather the political promises made by the ruling party versus the socio-economic reality of most of the Angolans which contradicts the political promises.

What is more, despite the visible element of resistance for the youth within these digital spaces there is also a space of online counter-disinformation and disinformation led by young people in Angola aimed at the ruling party which has directly benefitted the opposition party rather than vacuum it in times of elections. This leans on Gaventa's (2010) concept of power and space as this is a space for building power, counter-power and counter-narrative.

Traditional sources of disinformation such as state television in Angola act as the seed of online disinformation created to diminish opposition. *Evening News Hour* is the starting point of all disinformation created by the Institute for Propaganda and Psychological Action which is then posted online by high-ranking offices of the party and quickly shared by members of youth structures of the MPLA. If the outcome of the disinformation is the one intended on the online space, the disinformation is immediately returned to national television as headline news to be solidified as important information for all Angolans. All of this is usually done through 15–30 minutes of coverage on evening news hour and through a televised political debate led by civil and political opinion makers supported of the regime. However, if the planned outcome is not achieved, the disinformation is brought to an immediate end through accusation, intimidation and impressment of social media account holders on national television.

The Angolan case alludes to digital spaces and its power on everyday citizenship particularly among the youth. Spaces such as Facebook and Instagram have become key instruments of effective citizenship, resistance and (dis)information among the youth in a way that is influencing power political behaviour in Angola. Moreover, it helps understand how old analogues and new digital dynamics of communication are competing to influence public opinion and state-citizen relations during election time in Angola. Social media has become a tool of day-to-day citizenship for young Angolans as it is safer, easily maximized and widely referenced within the politics of the country. This goes in line with the concept of new democratic spaces which continue to widen in Africa (Cornwall and Coelho 2004).

Social media in Angola has provided a space in which opposition voices and alternative views are heard now more than ever. This is a space with very different power dynamics than the offline public sphere dominated by establishment media channels and political parties. Although politicians have set up social media profiles and have propaganda departments to strategize how to dominate these new online spaces, it remains a space in which different power relations operate. Unlike in mainstream media, it is possible for alternative views to be heard on Facebook and Instagram in Angola. People who did not see themselves represented in establishment media/parties are creating new online spaces on Facebook, Instagram and other social media platforms where a new form of unruly power emerged in the shape of irreverent memes that speak truth to power in ways not permitted in offline spaces.

When the MPLA deployed disinformation in digital spaces, it was often young people who held them accountable, who called them liars and posted counter-disinformation – not a form of power that is possible on the state-controlled TV, radio or press. The hidden power that allows establishment media editors to determine the terms of the debate (what gets on the news agenda) is contested in online spaces. Everyone has the opportunity to speak and the extent that opposition voices form networks and alliances amplifies and makes their voices more powerful. Hashtags and memes are emerging digital communications for building networks and produce counter-power and counter-narratives. The example from Angola shows that there is power in digital spaces.

Conclusion

This chapter set out to examine how disinformation is fabricated and distributed by those in power and its influence on e-citizens' political behaviour during election in Angola using a theoretical framework of power and space. In summary, all disinformation attempts created by the ruling power in Angola in the run up to the 2022 general elections failed to deliver its intended political outcome. Young people in Angola are exposing state lies challenging the status quo while playing an active role in creating their own identities though active online participation in a country where they account for the majority of the population.

Social media such as Facebook and Instagram have afforded the youth in Angola new communication instruments, such as memes, to respond to state disinformation and find new spaces to challenge power while raising their voices in a constrained political, economic and social environment. The Angolan case alludes to how young people in Africa are not waning in political engagement but are rather using non-conventional forms of political participation to resist, inform, counter-disinform and influence politics in Africa, especially during elections. The most important channel for their political expression is now social media, which has become the facto instrument of defence against the state, and the recent wave of political memes directed at the ruling party in the warmup to the 2022 elections reflects this phenomenon.

Bibliography

AFP (2018) *Lourenco vs Dos Santos: Angola's President Steps Up Fight Against Corruption.* 23 November. Retrieved from Africa News: https://www.africanews .com/2018/11/23/lourenco-vs-dos-santos-angola-s-president-steps-up-fight-against -corruption/.

Africa Center for Strategic Studies (2022) *Mapping Disinformation in Africa.* 26 April. Retrieved from Africa Center for Strategic Studies: https://africacenter.org/spotlight/ mapping-disinformation-in-africa/.

African Insider (2022) *Angola's Ruling Party Office Torched During Taxi Strike.* 11 January. Retrieved from African Insider: https://www.africaninsider.com/politics/angolas -ruling-party-office-torched-taxi-strike/.

Amnesty International (2020) *The Police Are Not on the Ground to Distribute Sweets.* 12 September. https://www.amnesty.org/en/latest/campaigns/2020/10/security-forces -brutality-in-angola/#:~:text=The%20protests%20brought%20together%20thousands %20of%20people%20across,of%20teenagers%20and%20young%20men%20by%20the %20police.

Bali O Chionga (2022) 22 April. https://www.tvzimbo.ao/ao/zimbo-online/.

BBC (2020) *José Filomeno dos Santos: Son of Angola's ex-leader Jailed for Five Years.* 14 August. Retrieved from BBC News: https://www.bbc.co.uk/news/world-africa -53774288.

Benkler, Y., Faris, R. and Roberts, H. (2018) *Network Propaganda: Manipulation, Disinformation, and Radicalization in American Politics.* Oxford: Oxford University Press.

Bennett, W. L. and Livingston, S. (2018) 'The Disinformation Order: Disruptive Communication and the Decline of Democratic Institutions'. *European Journal of Communication,* 33: 122–39.

Bradshaw, S., Bailey, H. and Howard, P. N. (2020) *Industrialized Disinformation: 2020 Global Inventory of Organized Social Media Manipulation.* Oxford: Oxford Internet Institute.

Browning, N. and Zhdannikov, D. (2020) *I'm a Scapegoat: Angola's Isabel dos Santos Decries Corruption 'Witch Hunt'*. 10 January. Retrieved from Reuters: https://www .reuters.com/article/us-angola-corruption-idUSKBN1Z91E4.

Burke, J. (2022) *Angolans go to Polls in Most Competitive Election in Decades*. 24 August. Retrieved from The Guardian: https://www.theguardian.com/world/2022/aug/24/ angolans-go-to-polls-most-competitive-election-decades.

Constitution of Portuguese Republic (2005) 3 October. https://www.parlamento.pt/sites/ EN/Parliament/Documents/Constitution7th.pdf.

Constitution of the Republic of Angola (2010) *Constitution of the Republic of Angola*. 21 January. Retrieved from Comissao Constitucional: file:///Users/edmilsonangelo/D ownloads/Angola%20Constitution%202010.pdf.

Cornwall, A. and Coehlo, V. (2004) 'New Democratic Spaces?'. *IDS Bulletin*, 35: 1–9.

Davison, P. (2012) 'The Language of Internet Memes'. In M. Mandiberg (ed.), *The Social Media Reader* (p. JSTOR), 120–21. New York: New York University Press.

De Oliveira, R. (2014) *Magnificent and Beggar Land: Angola Since the Civil War*. Oxford: Oxford University Press.

Folha 9 (2022) *Família 'dos Santos' quer voltar ao poder... através da UNITA!*. 11 March. Retrieved from Folha9 Noticias em primeira mao: https://folha9.com/2022/03/11 /familia-dos-santos-quer-voltar-ao-poder-atraves-da-unita-2/#:~:text=A%20alian %C3%A7a%20criada%20entre%20Isabel%20dos%20Santos%20e,Governo%20no %20%C3%A2mbito%20do%20combate%20contra%20a%20corrup%C3%A7%C3 %A3o.

Gaventa, J. (2006) 'Finding the Spaces for Change: A Power Analysis'. *IDS Bulletin*, 37: 23–33.

Gaventa, J. (2010) 'Seeing Like a Citizen: Re-claiming in a Neoliberal World'. In A. Fowler and C. Mulunga (eds), *NGO Management: The Earthscan Companion*, 55–67. London: Routledge.

Hine, C. (2011) *The Virtual Objects of Ethnograpgy*. Retrieved 29 March 2020, from http:// methods.sagepub.com.ezproxy.sussex.ac.uk/base/download/BookChapter/virtual -ethnography/n3.xml.

Howard, P. (2020) *Political Lies*. London: Yale University Press.

INE (2014) *Recenseamento Geral da População e Habitação –2014*. 23 September. https:// andine.ine.gov.ao/nada/index.php/catalog/3.

INE (2014) *Resultados preliminares do recenseamento geral da população da habitação de Angola 2014*. Retrieved 15 September 2016, from Censo: https://unstats.un.org/unsd/ demographic/sources/census/wphc/Angola/Angola%202014%20Census.pdf.

Jones, M. (2022) *Digital Authoritarianism in the Middle East: Deception, Disinformation and Social Media*. London: Hurst Publishers.

Jornal de Angola (2019) *Adalberto Costa abdica cidadania lusa adquirida*. 10 October. Retrieved from Jornal de Angola: https://www.jornaldeangola.ao/ao/noticias/detalhes .php?id=437483#:~:text=Adalberto%20Costa%20abdica%20cidadania%20lusa %20adquirida%20A%20deputada,perda%20da%20nacionalidade%20portuguesa. %2010%2F10%2F2019%20%C3%9Altima%20atualiza%C3%A7%C3%A3o%2009H41.

Kepios (2022) *Digital 2022: Angola*. 15 February. Retrieved from Data Reportal: https:// datareportal.com/reports/digital-2022-angola.

Kuo, R. and Marwick, A. (2021) *Critical Disinformation Studies: History, Power and Politics*. 25 March. Retrieved from Havard Misinformation Review: https:// misinforeview.hks.harvard.edu/article/critical-disinformation-studies-history-power -and-politics/.

Lourenço, J. (2017) *Joao Lourenco Status*. 28 September. Retrieved from Facebook: https://www.facebook.com/cdajoaolourenco/.

Luamba, M. (2020) *Artigo 333: Estará a liberdade de expressão em causa ?*. 12 November. Retrieved from DW Made for Minds: https://www.dw.com/pt-002/artigo-333%C2%BA-estar%C3%A1-a-liberdade-de-express%C3%A3o-em-causa-em-angola/a-55625968.

Lusa (2020) *Grupo da TV Zimbo passa paara as mãos do governo angolano*. 31 July. Retrieved from DW Made for Minds: https://www.dw.com/pt-002/grupo-da-tv-zimbo-passa-para-as-m%C3%A3os-do-governo-angolano/a-54395509.

Lusa (2021) *Tribunal Constitucional de Angola anula congresso da UNITA*. 5 October. Retrieved from PUBLICO: https://www.publico.pt/2021/10/05/mundo/noticia/tribunal-constitucional-angola-anula-congresso-unita-1979978.

Lusa (2021) *Tribunal Constitucional de Angola anula congresso da UNITA*. 5 October. Retrieved from DW Made for Minds: https://www.dw.com/pt-002/tribunal-constitucional-de-angola-anula-congresso-da-unita/a-59412324.

Lusa (2022) *ISEP confirma que Adalberto Costa Júnior concluiu formação*. 13 June. Retrieved from DW Made for Minds: https://www.dw.com/pt-002/isep-confirma-que-l%C3%ADder-da-unita-concluiu-forma%C3%A7%C3%A3o-de-engenharia-eletrot%C3%A9cnica/a-62119052.

Lynsey, C. (2018) *The Downfall of an Angolan Dynasty*. May 2. Retrieved from Foreign Policy: https://foreignpolicy.com/2021/05/05/angola-isabel-dos-santos-corruption/.

Mendes, C. and Almeida, H. (2022) *Angola Taxi Drivers' Strike Sparks Protests Against Ruling Party*. 10 January. Retrieved from Bloomberg: https://www.bloomberg.com/news/articles/2022-01-10/angola-taxi-drivers-strike-sparks-protests-against-ruling-party?leadSource=uverify%20wall.

MISA (2003) *Mission Report: The Media Situation in Angola - Obstacles and Possibilities*. https://allafrica.com/download/resource/main/main/idatcs/00010262:976cc44800926cbc58f806dcc6a22ff7.pdf.

Nebe, C. (2020) *Angola Braces for Anti-Government Protests*. 11 October. Retrieved from DW Made for Minds: https://www.dw.com/en/angola-braces-for-anti-government-protests/a-55543686.

Neusa, & Silva (2022) *Angola: Vitória do MPLA com sabor a derrota?* 29 August. Retrieved from DW Made for Minds: https://www.dw.com/pt-002/angola-vit%C3%B3ria-do-mpla-com-sabor-a-derrota/a-62964898.

NJ (2022) *O grau de engenheiro, o riso de ACJ, e, por fim, a resposta 'Eu estudei lá'*. 8 July. Retrieved from Novo Jornal: https://www.novojornal.co.ao/politica/interior/o-grau-de-engenheiro-o-riso-de-acj-e-por-fim-a-resposta-eu-estudei-la-108494.html.

Novo Jornal (2022) *Presidente da UNITA nega aliança com marimbondos*. 11 August. Retrieved from Novo Jornal: https://novojornal.co.ao/politica/interior/eleicoes-presidente-da-unita-nega-alianca-com-marimbondos-e-diz-que-corrutos-sao-os-que-gastaram-30-mil-milhoes-em-dez-anos-com-a-construcao-de-estradas-intransitaveis-109414.html.

OPEC. (2007) *New Member Angola to Underpin OPEC Efforts to Stabilize Market*. 15 June. Retrieved from OPEC: https://www.opec.org/opec_web/en/.

Roberts, T., Ali, A., Karekwaivanane, G., Msonza, N., Phiri, S., Zorro, . . . Ojebode, A. (2021) *Digital Rights in Closing Civic Space: Lessons from Ten African Countries*. Brighton: Institute of Development Studies.

Schmelzkopf, K. (1995) 'Urban Community Gardens as Contested Space'. *Geographical Review*, 85: 364–81.

Simon Kemp (2022) *Digital 2022: Angola*. 15 January. Retrieved from Data Reportal: https://datareportal.com/reports/digital-2022-angola.

Sul, N. F. (2019) *Novo Lider da Unita Sinaliza rutura com o passado*. 20 November. Retrieved from DW Made for Mindes: https://www.dw.com/pt-002/novo-l%C3 %ADder-da-unita-sinaliza-rutura-com-o-passado/a-51331749#:~:text=Novo%20l %C3%ADder%20da%20UNITA%20sinaliza%20rutura%20com%20o,partido%20da %20oposi%C3%A7%C3%A3o%20em%20Angola%20enfrenta%20v%C3%A1rios %20desafios.

Televisão Publica de Angola (2022) *Militantes da UNITA Vandalizam Comité do MPLA*. 20 March. Retrieved from Televisão Publica de Angola: https://www.youtube.com/ watch?v=YHY25y6LL-E.

Tenove, C. (2019) *The Meme-ification of Politics: Politicians & Their 'Lit' Memes*. 4 February. Retrieved from The Conversation: https://theconversation.com/the-meme -ification-of-politics-politicians-and-their-lit-memes-110017.

Transparency International (2023) *2022 Corruption Perceptions Index Reveals Scant Progress Against Corruption as World Becomes More Violent*. 31 January. Retrieved from Transparency International: The Global Coalition against Corruption: https:// www.transparency.org/en/countries/angola.

UNDP (2022) *Human Development Report 2021–22*. 8 September. Retrieved from Human Development Reports: https://hdr.undp.org/content/human-development-report -2021–22.

VOA (2021) *Congresso da UNITA confirmado para 2 a 4 de Dezembro*. 29 October. Retrieved from VOA Porugues: https://www.voaportugues.com/a/congresso-da -unita-confirmado-para-2-a-4-de-dezembro/6331762.html#:~:text=LUANDA%20 %E2%80%94%20A%20Comiss%C3%A3o%20Pol%C3%ADtica%20%28CP%29 %20da%20UNITA,a%20favor%2C%2015%20votos%20contra%20e%20tr%C3%AAs %20absten%C3%A7%C3%B5.

Chapter 11

'Anyone can be a mercenary'

Disinformation and Kenyan news media in the 2022 general election

Wambui Wamunyu

The news media has long been considered an important actor in democratic processes, a provider of credible information that citizens can use to choose leaders or hold them accountable. Kenya's news media has portrayed itself as a trustworthy actor in the democratic process. However, it became both victim and purveyor of digital disinformation in the country's recent elections held in August 2022. This alarming turn contributes to a weakening of the integrity of an institution perceived to be vital for healthy democratic processes.

The tactic of disinformation deployment had been used in the previous two polls in 2013 and 2017, with the British consulting firm Cambridge Analytica playing a prominent role as it handled one Kenyan political party's political campaigns (Nyabola 2018). The consulting firm had also been retained for other electoral races in other parts of the world, revealing both global and local aspects or a 'glocalized' approach to politics enabled by digital technologies such as social media companies. By some accounts, the firm's tactics included using social media to distribute sponsored posts, attack advertisements aimed at competitors and disinformation. The firm would eventually be suspended from Facebook for the illegal mining of user data (Dahir 2018a; Ekdale and Tully 2020).

In the period leading up to Kenya's 9 August 2022 general election, the phenomenon of digital disinformation was on full display as politicians sought the votes of a citizenry divided along the lines of class, ethnicity, gender and age. Disinformation campaigns were targeted not only at politicians but also at other players including government entities (such as the Independent Electoral and Boundaries Commission (IEBC) which oversaw the poll) and the news media. The IEBC was the subject of multiple falsehoods about election schedules and officials shared on social media before, during and after the election.

In one instance, a fake listing of IEBC vacancies for election officers and clerks was shared on Facebook in March 2022. It was debunked by the fact-checking organization Africa Check (Gichuhi 2022). After the election, the Nation Media Group reported that individuals associated with presidential candidate Raila Odinga had spread false information about two commissioners breaking rank against the commission chair on claims that the chair had conspired to rig the election with Odinga's opponent William Ruto (Mbuthia 2022). Odinga's loss to Ruto was eventually upheld by the Supreme Court (Magak 2022).

It is the news media – which worked to provide accurate information while fighting (not always successfully) a daily deluge of false information – that is the focus of this chapter.

Disinformation can be termed as the deliberate sharing of falsehoods or misleading information (Guess and Lyons 2020) and, in a political context, is a potent form of election manipulation. It is dangerous because of the ways in which it can undermine healthy political processes and institutions, while engendering distrust and political participation apathy in the citizenry.

In the leadup to Kenya's 2022 general election, the expression of disinformation emerged early with social media primarily serving as the arena of battle. While much had been made of foreign actors in political disinformation during the 2013 and 2017 polls, the 2022 election had a difference. It was characterized by a more home-grown approach with local politicians engaging social media teams whose tasks included the promotion of the politicians and responding to attacks from opponents, with the messages spreading on various platforms including the mainstream media.

Pithy political narratives and slogans were spread and amplified through relentless messaging on social media. For instance the 'Kieleweke' camp referred to the incumbent president and his allies, while the 'Tanga Tanga' camp was linked to the deputy president (whose rift with the president in the period leading up to the election had grown) and his allies. The terms *Kieleweke* and *Tanga Tanga* are from the Kiswahili language and mean 'it is understood' and 'loiterers' respectively. In the messaging, disinformation would be woven in as in a 2020 Facebook post, where Martha Karua, who would end up as the deputy running mate for Raila Odinga, called out the *Tanga Tanga* side for spreading fake news about her (Kenyans.co.ke 2020).

This chapter addresses how political disinformation manifested itself in the news media during the August 2022 general election. Using a qualitative approach, the chapter interrogates data drawn from document review, interviews with journalists and a media researcher and a focus group discussion held with media analysts who regularly monitor news media content.

The rest of the chapter is organized as follows: the next section provides political and technological context for the occurrence of disinformation in the 2022 general election. I then describe the methodological approach taken before presenting examples of digital disinformation in and about the news media drawn from Kenya's 2022 election. In the final section I discuss findings and draw some conclusions.

Background

Historical context: Disinformation and the Kenyan news media

The history of Kenya's news media dates back to the establishment of the print press in the late 1800s with the subsequent introduction of radio and television in

1928 and 1962 respectively. While the broadcast sector was under the ownership and governance of colonial authorities, newspapers were established by multiple players, including members of different races, political activists and supporters of government (Karikari 2007; Mbeke et al. 2010). There were differing agendas for these publications – such as pro-colonial government or pro-Independence – and with varying success rates (Frederiksen 2006).

The Second World War and period leading up to Independence in 1963 were significant for the types of disinformation created and distributed by colonial authorities and indigenous Africans (Gadsden 1986; Osborne 2015). Pamphlets, films and songs carrying coded messages were among the media used to pass on information, whether accurate, misleading or outrightly false. The news coverage of the Mau Mau, a movement of Africans fighting for a return of their lands and freedom from colonial rule, also generated substantial responses from government propaganda and coverage in the British press. Those responses were presented in the press, with the Mau Mau falsely portrayed as terrorists who were being effectively contained by the British colonial authorities (Tully 2010). This meets this chapter's definition of disinformation as lies deployed intentionally for political gain.

The 1970s and 1980s saw significant changes across the political, and socio-economic environments of many African countries, Kenya among them. These changes included increasingly repressive regimes, changes of leadership, continued economic dependence on former colonial authorities, and significant societal challenges. These would then be followed by citizen demands for greater political freedoms and multi-party politics (Berger 2012; Karikari 2007).

Claims of political disinformation continued, such as those relating to the African leadership that had taken over power post-Independence. The example that follows indicates the type of false or misleading information that was shared through the press. In one instance, Oliver and Galby (2022) described a smear campaign run by the British government's Foreign Office in the 1960s against Jaramogi Oginga Odinga. He was Kenya's first post-Independence vice president and constitutionally the first in line to take over leadership from the president. Oliver and Galby (2022) indicated he was not the preferred choice for the British, and through written pamphlets that would receive widespread news media coverage, he was falsely described as a communist. Odinga protested against the portrayal and against the use of the press to vilify him. This example meets the definition of disinformation as untruths disseminated intentionally for political objectives.

As citizens clamoured against the political authoritarianism increased in Kenya, it led in the 1990s to the liberalization of the state-controlled news media sector and the entry of new players such as privately owned television and FM radio stations. It is also during this liberalization period that Kenyan news media also begun to adopt the use of the internet (Mureithi 2017; Ogola 2015). The news media would invest in digital technologies, adopting their use in journalism, including news reporting and dissemination on mobile and online platforms (Wamunyu and Wahutu 2019; Wamunyu 2021).

The tactic of disinformation deployment had been used in the previous two polls in 2013 and 2017 with the British consulting firm Cambridge Analytica playing a prominent role as it handled one Kenyan political party's political campaigns (Nyabola 2018).

A consistent characteristic of the Kenyan news media through the generations has been to view itself as an essential pillar of democratic society, playing the functional roles of information provision, political engagement and entertainment (Fourie 2007). However, the news media operate in an environment where the state or powerful individuals in the political sphere have sought to control the news media in various ways such as by owning the media, incurring debt by delaying paying of advertising in the news media, and interfering with editorial decision-making. The families of Daniel Arap Moi and Uhuru Kenyatta (the second and fourth presidents of the country) have large shareholdings or own in the news media companies Standard Group and MediaMax respectively (Ogola 2011).

Additionally, while mainstream media remain an important source of information for the citizenry, their audience numbers and advertising revenues have declined over the last decade, and in the period of and before the Covid-19 pandemic, the journalism sector experienced widespread retrenchments and steep pay cuts (Business Today 2020; Kimani 2022; Mare et al. 2019; Tully 2021).

These challenges have contributed towards the sharing of falsehoods or misleading information by and through the Kenyan press. A journalist interviewed for this study worked for a media house that owned print, broadcast and online media outlets. On its multiple digital platforms alone, the media house reached an estimated 10 million users monthly. In one instance of disinformation, one of the media house's social media accounts was blacklisted for posting false information. Blacklisting is a term where a social media platform requires the amendment of content that violates its guidelines.

By the journalist's admission, the false information occurred because of personnel constraints where inexperienced journalists were left to run the websites particularly on slower weekend shifts. Their lack of experience meant that they could make poor decisions with little oversight, and it came with a heavy price.

> If [social media platforms] flag you as a website that communicates fake news, they can sanction you. That is what happened to us. Once you are blacklisted, they no longer promote your stories. So for anyone searching stories, no one will get the stories. They also don't allow adverts. They will block the ads, so it hurts you financially. (Key Interviewee 2)

The mainstream media's reliance on social media to reach audiences creates a vulnerability to disinformation and can lead to reduced trust from audiences (Marwick and Lewis 2017).

Disinformation in Kenya predates the digital era, so cannot reasonably be seen as caused by social media. This section provides a brief historical context for the reader who is not familiar with Kenya's political, media and digital developments.

Technical context: Digital technologies and disinformation

While disinformation had occurred prior to the availability of the internet, its quantity and range of creators have increased significantly with the adoption of digital technologies. Social media is distinct from mainstream media primarily because the former is unfiltered and much of the information that is spread on the platform is unverified and veracity of facts rarely checked. However, even where information is subjected to fact-checking, the process does little to correct disinformation as the sources being used to check for facts may be in dispute (Rich et al. 2020).

The rise of disinformation is primarily attributable to the unfiltered nature of information shared on social media where cyber propaganda and disinformation are used to shape public opinion (Maweu 2020). Internet access and other digital technologies enable contemporary disinformation, which spreads far and wide quickly. Across the African continent, disinformation has gradually increased over the past few years (Africa Center for Strategic Studies 2021). In Kenya, the two factors contributing to this growth have been the proliferation of digital technologies and the lucrative nature of disinformation.

Kenyans of different generations would also increasingly turn to various social media applications as sources of information. Varying levels of trust in the news media as an institution contributed to this turn to alternative sources of information with citizens expressing a concern with fake news. One report indicated that 79 per cent of Kenyans had been victims of fake news (Media Council of Kenya 2023; Mudavadi and Shanahan, 2022; Mwita 2021).

Internet access was first made available in Kenya in 1995. It was costly and exclusive because it was availed on a limited number of leased telephone lines only offered by one government entity through internet service providers (ISPs). News media companies were among the early clients of the ISPs, using their services to set up websites that served local news to Kenyans in the diaspora (Mureithi 2017; Ogola 2015).

Statistics from government bodies and independent researchers show the country has since experienced a great expansion in internet access and mobile telephony, with a subsequent growth of social media use in the country. For instance, between 2007 to 2012, the percentage of Kenyans over the age of fifteen with access to the internet had increased from 15 per cent to 26.3 per cent. Government policy had identified internet access as a priority for economic growth and providing services (Communications Commission of Kenya 2010; Research ICT Africa 2012). By the October–December 2022 quarter, there were a recorded 47.7 million data/internet subscribers in the country, with smartphone penetration at 60 per cent countrywide. The mobile phone served as the primary mode of access to the internet (Communications Authority of Kenya 2021, 2023).

A 2019 study indicated that among Kenyans there was pervasive use of a variety of social media applications. The majority of Kenyans used WhatsApp, (88.6 per cent), Facebook (88.5 per cent) and Youtube (51.2 per cent). Other platforms used were Instagram (39 per cent) and Twitter (27.9 per cent). The social media sites were used not only as fora to connect with others, but as source of news, entertainment and political information (SIMElab Africa 2019). The extensive adoption of new digital technologies in the Kenyan context partly explains why TikTok would become not just an video-sharing application but a widely used disinformation platform in the Election 2022 season (Madung 2022).

In the 2010s, the investments in digital infrastructures had allowed for the citizenry to have increased access to social media applications. Social media became a new frontier for hacks-for-hire who would malign reputations and spread unsubstantiated or false information (Laibuta 2013; Otieno, 2015). The use of digital technologies in the spread of disinformation escalated in the elections of 2013 and 2017 with the accompanying recognition that foreign actors could use social media and user data to manipulate political messages and influence electoral contests around the world (Ekdale and Tully 2020).

Cambridge Analytica, a British political consulting firm, was retained to run the Jubilee Party's political campaign during those polls, such as by conducting research and creating targeted messaging. Their tactics reportedly included the use of sponsored posts, attack advertisements aimed at competitors as well as disinformation. The company also primarily shared much of the messaging on Facebook and WhatsApp (Dahir 2018a). Cambridge Analytica would eventually be suspended from Facebook for illegally mining data from millions of its user profiles. In 2017, Facebook took measures to limit the spread of fake news stories by placing advertisements in Kenyan mainstream print and broadcast media outlets aimed at providing the public with guidelines on how to recognize false stories (Dahir 2018a).

In that period, the news media had also become targets of disinformation such as with the doctoring of their headlines or front pages. The manipulation of visual messages – such as screenshots and videos – from news media content would be escalated in the 2022 election.

Various political events have seen synchronized efforts at disinformation, including the registration of websites that disseminated fake news, and information shared by opinion influencers (Freedom House 2018). Global Disinformation Index noted that even established mainstream media online publications were at risk of spreading false information based on weak operational structures, and a reduction in personnel following retrenchments and pay cuts (Wamunyu 2021).

In the 2022 election, the Kenya Kwanza Alliance and the Azimio la Umoja – One Kenya Coalition emerged as the two leading opposing sides and they each sought to portray themselves positively while denigrating their opponents. Examples are shared later in the chapter.

Methodology

Qualitative data were collected between December 2021 and February 2022 from document review, interviews and a focus group discussion. These three types of data established how disinformation occurred in and through the Kenyan news media during the 2022 elections.

As the emphasis of the study was disinformation experienced in and among the news media during the election of 2022, the document review entailed analysing articles that debunked or verified content from news websites as well as the experiences of journalists. The two fact-checking sites selected were owned by credible organizations which verified or debunked claims made in particular news stories carried in Kenyan local news media. Only the stories related to the general election of 2022 and published on the organizations' websites were analysed.

For the interviews, a senior editor and journalist covering digital news platforms from two different news organizations were purposively sampled based on their organization's public responses to disinformation tactics. A media researcher was also interviewed to provide context around the nature of disinformation in the 2022 election. Five news content analysts who regularly monitor content – on Kenya's print, broadcast and online news media – provided perspective in a focus group discussion on disinformation trends observed in the leadup to the election.

Each of the research interviewees and FGD participants were provided with an overview of the research and informed of their right to choose whether to participate. Voluntary consent to participate was obtained from every participant prior to the start of the interviews or focus group discussion. More specific information on the data collection tools is presented in Table 11.1.

Participant confidentiality was subsequently upheld by anonymizing each participant who is identified in this study by a number and the type of data collection tool they were associated with e.g. 'Key Interviewee 1' and 'FGD Participant 1'. Thematic analysis was deployed where the data were organized as a collective whole and themes identified by an inductive process (Braun and Clarke 2006).

The next section provides six illustrations of disinformation that occurred during the general election of 2022. The targets of disinformation in these illustrations are journalists, media houses, and political leaders in the two leading political coalitions.

Table 11.1 Data Collection Tools

Data collection tool	Number	Comment
Document review – Fact checking sites	163 articles	Africa Check (136 articles) Kenya Editors Guild (twenty-seven articles)
Interviews	4	Two journalists, one media researcher, one social media influencer
Focus Group	1	Five media analysts engaged in news content monitoring during the general election of 2022

Examples of disinformation in Kenyan news media

In previous elections, extensive disinformation campaigns had been associated with foreign or external actors as with Cambridge Analytica's involvement in the 2013 and 2017 elections. While there emerged reports of continued external influence even in the 2022 election (Kirchgaessner et al. 2023), the 2022 incarnation of political disinformation had a more domestic flavour as politicians hired local content creators and social media teams. One report described how in the leadup to the 2022 election, Kenyan politicians or their affiliates would hire Twitter influencers (individuals with large social media followings) or rent social media accounts to promote the politicians' agenda (Mozilla Foundation 2021).

Disinformation was waged by different political parties and politicians, intent on attacking their rivals. In July 2022, a newspaper story indicated that there was a 'fake news smear campaign . . . waged by operatives of the rival coalitions, who are also doctoring polls to give the impression that their preferred candidates are in the lead, and has become more pronounced in this year's election as it is increasingly being fought online' (Chelangat and Shikanda 2022).

The following six examples reveal several patterns that emerged related to the news media disseminating, falling victim to or experiencing the impact of disinformation. These patterns were politicians' use of news media to spread disinformation, the targeting of disinformation campaigns against prominent/ credible news brands or journalists; the timing of disinformation around significant events (such as the announcement of alliances) and the extensive use of visual forms of disinformation (such as manipulated videos and photographs) which were easy to spread via social media platforms.

Example one – Incorrect information disseminated on news outlets

On 24 May 2022 a radio station broadcasting in one of Kenya's local languages interviewed Rigathi Gachagua, running mate to then presidential aspirant William Ruto. The duo would win after the poll was concluded. As deputy presidential aspirant, Gachagua claimed that Kenya owed China KSh. 11.2 trillion (Kenya Editors Guild 2022). The country's debt was a primary issue given the country's economic woes during the campaign period (Africanews 2022; Iraki 2022). The claim was not challenged during the interview.

The claim was ultimately proven wrong through a fact-check provided by a media professional body. The Kenya Editors' Guild (KEG) had set up a fact-checking desk which interviewed an expert in the language confirming the error made during the interview, KEG also presented information from National Treasury report showing that KSh. 783 billion was what was actually owed. KEG also interviewed an economics expert to explain the discrepancy. The information was published in English on the KEG website (Kenya Editors Guild 2022) and the link to the original interview availed on the same site (Inooro FM 2022).

Inooro FM, the station on which the debt amountclaim was made, has more than 470,000 followers on Facebook where the interview was carried (Inooro FM 2022). Additionally, local language stations do not always have the personnel to undertake fact checks in the languages in which they broadcast. There is no guarantee therefore that the listeners of the interview in which the debt claim made by Gachagua received a fact-check in the language in which they had heard the interview.

In 2022, television and radio were the primary sources of news for Kenyans (Media Council of Kenya 2023), reinforcing the news media's role to provide credible, accurate information. Inooro FM and Citizen TV are co-owned by Royal Media Services and are among the leading broadcast outlets in terms of national audience reach. When disinformation is shared and not corrected/retracted on such platforms, it reaches millions and carries with it the credibility associated with the broadcast outlet.

Example two – Political ownership of news outlets

On 4 February 2022, *The Star* newspaper published an infographic based on IEBC figures indicating the votes presidential candidates Raila Odinga and Musalia Mudavadi had garnered in the region from which Mudavadi hails. The figures had interchanged Mudavadi's data with that of Odinga, indicating that Odinga had lost to Mudavadi. The story would be corrected on 10 February 2022 showing that Mudavadi had trailed behind, garnering 31 per cent of the 1.2 million votes garnered between him and Odinga (Star Editor 2022).

The Star shared an apology for the error stating that '[t]he mix up happened at the data preparation stage'. However, the focus group discussion participants indicated their perception of a hidden agenda in the error, based on the ownership of the newspaper. At the time of the February 2022 publication, Mudavadi had allied himself with William Ruto who was vying for presidency against Odinga. Ruto had been identified alongside then President Uhuru Kenyatta as having an interest in owning a stake in *The Star* (Africa Intelligence 2019), which was alluded to in the focus group discussion. *The Star* is among a stable of media outlets owned by the company Radio Africa.

> From our analysis we felt that that was very deliberate because of the ownership aspects. It is in the public domain that Ruto owns some shares in Radio Africa. So [with] Mudavadi being in the Kenya Kwanza Alliance, the numbers were skewed to favour them and that was intentional. (FGD 2)

There are sections of the political class that own various commercial or community news media in Kenya, a strategy that contributes to a decline in the independence of the news media. One report indicated that this ownership trend was 'part of a wider co-option of journalists and civic activists by politicians to blunt their criticism, exploit their networks and even influence other journalists' (Mungai 2022).

The analysts' perception of how political elites control or manipulate news narratives even through 'intentional errors' that could subsequently be corrected reveals the insidious ways in which disinformation can be deployed using news brands, which have traditionally been trusted source of information (Africa Intelligence 2019; Wasserman and Madrid-Morales 2019).

Example three – False newspaper/magazine covers

Apart from being used as conduits of disinformation, news media brands or journalists were also targets. There were three primary approaches taken by disinformation agents, namely the generation of false front pages of news publications, false quotes attributed to individuals, or false information about well-known reputable journalists.

False front pages abounded as they were easily created and shared on digital platforms. The 26 March 2022 edition of *Taifa Leo*, a Kiswahili daily, carried a headline claiming that Jubilee Party favoured more elderly individuals (Africa Check 2022b). Fact-checking organization Africa Check found the newspaper's front page had been altered. The Jubilee Party was associated with President Uhuru Kenyatta who was supporting Raila Odinga's presidential bid.

Such content was easy to read and share, but it was difficult to establish who had created it. The two journalists interviewed for this study each admitted that a challenge they faced was having enough personnel with the know-how to quickly catch or counter disinformation posts. Additionally, they indicated having unconfirmed suspicions of the sources of the disinformation, primarily unnamed local content creators/influencers. But one of the journalists – Key Interviewee 3 – made the further claim that digital infrastructures made it possible for literally anyone to be culpable, creating 'information mercenaries for hire'.

> We like to take pride in the fact that we are a digital economy. The penetration of the Internet is quite high and the diffusion of gadgets is high. But on the downside this means that anyone can be a mercenary. (Key Interviewee 3)

The notion of 'mercenaries for hire' reveals the commercial angle that disinformation had taken in Kenya's digital sphere even prior to the election. A focus group participant expounded on the transactional nature of disinformation.

> In the circles I belong to, it's being said that these elections are going to be won on social media. The reason is, people now are buying influencers to push content on social media. (FGD Participant 2)

There were differing accounts as to the amounts politicians or their agents paid to push a disinformation agenda. A Mozilla Foundation (2021) report indicated that Twitter influencers – broadly defined as individuals with large social media followings – were paid between US$10 and US$15 to engage in three campaigns daily. The payments were made through the mobile money platform M-Pesa. Ramadhan and Murimi indicated that the bigger the race, the more the politician would pay. They quoted an anonymized source who claimed that the cost of running hashtags for aspirants ranged between Sh. 20,000 to Sh. 100,000. Presidential candidates would pay the larger amounts since the content had to trend for longer periods of time such as a full day as well as reach different regions across the country. The source did not express remorse or concern for the amount of disinformation he and others generated.

During the February 2022 focus group discussion for this study, two participants observed that as the political heat intensified, the use of influencers to generate and disseminate disinformation had continued at the rate of Kenya Shillings (KSh) 527 for every post generated. Money sent via mobile phone. The payment for the post amounted to KSh. 500 and the extra KSh. 27 was the charge for encashing the money from a mobile money agent.

The substantial private and public investments in digital infrastructures in Kenya had enabled disinformation to mature beyond political strategy to become a source of livelihood for many content creators. Even as there are efforts to detect it, disinformation also has become a rewarding activity, making it more difficult to deter.

Examples four and five – False information attributed to branded news outlets

False quotes carried on branded news websites were a frequently used tactic, and applied to large and relatively small news outlets. In January 2022, a poster bearing the website name 'Kenyans.co.ke' had an image of politician Martha Karua and the following quote: 'I cannot attend an event that is a coalition of thieves! I wish my brother Musalia Mudavadi well; we hoped to create a movement that has clean hands but greed overrides everything. Kenyans open your eyes.' (Africa Check 2022a) Africa Check found the quote to be false and the digital news media company Kenyans.co.ke also denied that it had generated the poster (Kenyans.co.ke 2022). Karua and Mudavadi were leading politicians being courted by the presidential aspirants William Ruto and Raila Odinga to join their respective alliances. The fake poster circulated soon after Mudavadi had allied himself to Ruto.

Another instance of false information attributed to branded news outlets occurred after election day and before the official announcement of the winner of the presidency. A poster bearing the logos of several media brands claimed that Raila Odinga had won 51.1 per cent of the vote while his rival Ruto had 48.2 per cent. The Kenya Editors Guild declared the poster as fake (Kenya Editors Guild 2022).

But the two journalists interviewed for this study said that their efforts were insignificant compared to the deluge of disinformation that targeted news brands, including their employers. The disinformation was easily spread beyond the mainstream news media on social media platforms such as Whatsapp, Facebook and Twitter.

Disinformation that targeted the news media was easily spread on social media, enabling an organic propagation that was strategically incorporated into political discourse and not always caught by the public.

Example six – Journalists as disinformation targets

In 2021, political journalist Francis Gachuri was the victim of disinformation – a campaign poster bearing his name and image indicated he was running for a member of parliament seat on a United Democratic Alliance (UDA) ticket (Africa Check 2021). Gachuri is an experienced broadcaster who at the time was working with Royal Media Services, a leading news media company.

The poster began circulating on social media a day after the incumbent Paul Koinange died. His death would require that the IEBC run a by-election to fill the seat prior to the general election of August 2022. The poster bore Gachuri's image and carried the slogan *'Jamba ya wira' (translated as 'a man who works')* (Africa Check 2021). This by-election was seen to be a test between two political outfits led by the sitting president Uhuru Kenyatta and his deputy William Ruto who had engaged in a public falling-out (Agutu 2021). The use of well-known names or brands is a commonly used ploy in disinformation circles as it creates a level of credibility and name recognition in the intended recipients (Volz and Barry 2020).

Gachuri's response was to deny the claim during a television news broadcast, a day after the poster first circulated. He called the poster 'classical fake news, crafted by kings and queens of fake news with a motive only they know. It should be dismissed with the contempt it deserves' (Citizen TV Kenya 2021). The 'kings and queens of fake news' alluded to the shadowy teams of content creators on social media who, through financial payment, had been co-opted into the industry of disinformation. A fact check by the organization Africa Check further confirmed that the claim was false (Africa Check 2021). The generation of plausible stories/ quotes using well-known journalists or news brands stood out for the speed with which false narratives related to political processes and events emerged and moved across the social media sphere.

The six examples indicate that by the election of 2022, the deployment of disinformation was a political strategy that had created a local industry where posts or campaigns had price tags depending on the political race at stake. The intention was to strategically create and circulate memorable narratives for a public largely unable to counter or cross-check a constant stream of (dis)information. The news media's fight to counter the deluge of disinformation was affected by multiple constraints, including reduced personnel numbers and declining revenues. Of concern was that news media had become perceived purveyor or target of disinformation, denting its normative role of providing credible accurate information to a trusting citizenry.

Discussion

There were five themes that emerged from the data as follows: commercial enterprise; compromised institutional credibility; disproportionate response; dependable digital infrastructures; and the 'uncritical public'. They are discussed as follows.

Theme one – Commercial enterprise

There were two sub-themes under commercial enterprise namely disinformation for hire and political elites' control of narrative.

Commercial enterprise

Disinformation was a strategic tool which politicians used to identify and articulate issues that would resonate with the intended audience. For the influencers hired alone or in teams, generating, disseminating and amplifying disinformation was a source of livelihood. The pricing based on the nature of the race and the scale of the disinformation campaign revealed a thriving industry that relied on an army of digitally savvy content creators who viewed disinformation as a transactional service rather than an ethical dilemma.

While this study did not establish the actual amount of money that was spent on disinformation efforts during the 2022 election, it was evident that there was extensive financial investment from deep-pocketed political outfits and politicians in hiring content creators, among other agents.

Political elites' control of narrative

Ogola (2011) described the control the state exerted over the news media in the five decades since political independence was secured from the British in 1963. Expressions of that control included direct interference with editorial content, late or non-payment of advertising costs and news media ownership.

As indicated in Example two, the FGD participants questioned the genuineness of the editorial error about Raila Odinga and Musalia Mudavadi to a publication with links to William Ruto. Ruto and Odinga were rivals in the race for the presidency. The publication made the correction a week later.

Ruto, Raila, Kenyatta and an assortment of other political leaders outrightly own or have shares in different news media houses. Royal Media Services (RMS) owns three television stations and fourteen vernacular radio stations, several of which are market leaders in their particular niches. The company, whose owner openly supported Odinga's presidential bid, was perceived to be biased in its coverage of the election. When the ownership and/or funding of the mainstream media is largely in the hands of a few for-profit entities, it raises concerns about who controls the stories the public hears (Ogola 2011).

The ownership and business ties that politicians have with the news media indicate that the political elite retain a firm stronghold with the news media, which they can then use to whatever effect they choose, as was indicated by the FGD participants' perception of the Odinga/Mudavadi error. The implication on disinformation in the public sphere is that the news media can then be used to disseminate disinformation widely without sanction, tainting the information that citizens should have about the leaders who will represent the public's interests and steward publicly owned resources.

Theme two – Compromised institutional credibility

The news media were a useful platform for the dissemination of disinformation such as through the sharing of incorrect data, and in aligning journalists to particular political outfits, as in Examples one and six. In February 2022, an FGD participant had predicted that the news media would need to treat information provided by politicians with care. The participant had presented a hypothetical example of aspirants discussing numbers.

> As we get into elections, misquoting numbers will likely increase. There will be need to focus on what these politicians are saying on radio. For example, someone saying 50 million [shillings] has been misappropriated by a governor. But what does each county get in allocation? That needs to be fact-checked. And numbers can be used to spread disinformation. (Focus Group Participant 1)

Example one indicated that the hypothetical scenario had become reality when a radio station hosted a deputy presidential candidate who provided an inflated figure of Kenya's external debt, later debunked in the English language by the Kenya Editors' Guild. It was not clear that the local language station had issued a correction in the same language in which the station had aired.

The media researcher interviewed for this study explained that the genesis of the use of disinformation in a campaign was in politicians' use of strategists to develop overarching narratives and platforms. Paid social media personnel would then create and amplify carefully crafted messages which could be disseminated on social media platforms of mediated through news media platforms or productions, such as political talk shows. Different politicians and political outfits used variations of this approach.

> You want [the messages] to get to mainstream media for example by influencing producers of news segments or talk shows, or preparation of guests on the shows.

With the talk shows, you bring people from competing sides. One [guest] comes with the [prepared] narrative, so they will say it there however false it may be because it is a political talk show. So the political talk show becomes a good way of disseminating disinformation through mainstream media. Because in our context here, we don't properly [fact] check. (Key Interviewee 1)

Theme three – Disproportionate response

The news media made efforts to counterattack disinformation included investing in fact-checking training and personnel, and deploying of increased and more experienced personnel to monitor and gather news from social media platforms. The use of the 'fake' stamp to counter disinformation on Twitter and Whatsapp became a favoured technique among institutional and individual victims of disinformation including state agencies, political entities and the news media during the electioneering period of 2022.

By their own admission, the journalists interviewed said that they had limited resources to cope with the relentless flow of disinformation in the leadup to the election. Key Interviewee three observed that because the public were not always able to distinguish between accurate and false information, it was the news media's role to combat disinformation.

I know we are not doing enough, but we are trying. We are taking baby steps to show the public what is genuine and what is not. It is a big task because not all [members of the public] are on our platforms. No media house can say they are not facing a resource challenge. (Key Interviewee 3)

However, these efforts were insufficient for under-resourced news departments battered by reductions in pay and personnel, and which did not have enough staff or technical expertise to counter the vast amounts of disinformation encountered daily.

Theme four – Dependable digital infrastructures

Kenya has invested heavily in establishing the physical infrastructure and policy frameworks to support countrywide access to high-speed internet. The Kenya National Digital Master Plan 2022–32 and National ICT Policy (2020) are among policies that provide plans for the installation of fibre optic networks, training of citizens in digital literacy, provision of government services online and strengthening of e-commerce (Ministry of ICT, Innovation and Youth Affairs 2022; Kenya Gazette 2020).

The Communications Authority of Kenya reported that in the July–September 2022 quarter, the country had a 54.3 per cent smartphone penetration rate, which had increased to 60.2 per cent by the following quarter (Communications Authority of Kenya 2023; Communications Authority of Kenya 2023). Kenyans used social media applications Facebook, Whatsapp and Instagram among other applications, where they got information on entertainment, politics, education and so on (Kanyi 2020). As Key Interviewee three observed, the stability and reach of internet access was a boon for disinformation agents.

> You have all the tools you need to create elements of disinformation. We have more people adopting digital today than maybe 5 years ago. Kenyans spend a lot of time on social media. [Sources of disinformation] see that as a target where they can reach us. (Key Interviewee 3)

Theme five – The 'uncritical public'

The target of the disinformation was ultimately the citizen, who would consume information designed to sway his or her votes. The citizenry were presumed to be trusting and innocent by both the disinformation agents and news media. As the media researcher indicated, the former could deploy content and have it shared on social media by the citizenry without the content receiving too much scrutiny. One journalist said the news media served as the public's defender against disinformation.

> The intention is to create a narrative that will enter the information ecosystem and ultimately influence and be further spread by a largely uncritical public. (Key Interviewee 1)

> These guys [sources of disinformation] keep on evolving and they find ways to get to the naïve public. So, it is upon us as the media to try and tell [the public] the tell-tale signs that this is most likely doctored or inaccurate. (Key Interviewee 3)

The two observations suggests that the citizens are perceived to lack agency, even in assessing the veracity of the information they consume and more broadly, in using that information to participate in making decisions related to the leaders who represent them and the stewardship of public resources. Some of the disinformation on social media received pushback, not only from news media but also from social media users. But disinformation may also thrive more when greater numbers of a country's citizenry are accepting of all the information they consume and share.

Conclusion

This chapter sought to explore how political disinformation manifested itself in the news media during the August 2022 general election. The qualitative data drawn from documents, interviews and a focus group discussion revealed that disinformation was a thriving commercial enterprise which had targeted the news media establishment.

Disinformation is not a new phenomenon but in its contemporary expression, the capacity to produce and disseminate disinformation is aided by social media platforms which magnify its speed of movement and reach. During Kenya's 2022 election period, political disinformation thrived in a combative, competitive political landscape characterized by the high-stakes nature of the election and a perceived naïve public.

The news media was both victim and purveyor of disinformation amidst other challenges including declining revenues, paycuts and retrenchments. The insufficient number of personnel who could effectively catch and respond to disinformation also contributed to the news media's inability to fully counter it. This is detrimental to its ability to consistently provide accurate, credible information undermines the public's trust. The news media can then potentially become a channel of spreading message that incite societal tensions.

In rhetoric and aspects of practice, the Kenyan news media associated itself with the roles of 'information provider' and pillar of democracy. But in the mundane, day-to-day routines of news gathering and production, the news media could be and were co-opted by various interests, including those that promoted disinformation as was seen in Election 2022. The ownership of the news media by the political elite indicated that news narratives could potentially be controlled even on digital platforms.

Political disinformation was relentlessly deployed by multiple means, including using the news media as a platform to share inaccurate information and targeting journalists and news media establishments. The commercial nature of the disinformation enabled deep-pocketed politicians or political entities to employ armies of content creators who generated memes, videos, hashtags and posts. This, coupled with the political elite's access to the means of news production by virtue of ownership or shareholding, entrenched powerful interests and enabled the telling of particular narratives.

The relentless nature of disinformation on both mainstream and social media platforms also denied citizens continuous access to credible information that would help them make well-considered decisions about the leaders that would represent their interests at national and county levels.

The citizenry was a weak link in the question as to how to fight disinformation, given how 'uncritical' and 'naïve' it was described to be by interviewees for this study. While there was some citizen pushback against some of the disinformation posts, citizens will need to deploy higher levels of skepticism while consuming and sharing information about political candidates, outfits and promises.

The establishment of robust digital infrastructure has been useful on the whole, but has also contributed to the high levels of disinformation experienced during the election. To reboot before the next election, the news media has the task of rebuilding audience trust, investing in business models that enable greater freedom from social media platforms and political ownership and emphasizing that providing information is not the same as providing credible information.

Bibliography

Africa Check (2021) 'No, Citizen TV's Francis Gachuri not Running for Kenyan PARLIAMENT'. *Africa Check*. https://africacheck.org/fact-checks/meta-programme -fact-checks/no-citizen-tvs-francis-gachuri-not-running-kenyan-parliament (accessed 18 April 2023).

Africa Check (2022a) 'Ignore Fake Quote – Not by Kenyan Politician Martha Karua, Not Published by Kenyans.co.ke News Site'. *Africa Check*. https://africacheck.org/ fact-checks/meta-programme-fact-checks/ignore-fake-quote-not-kenyan-politician -martha-karua-not (accessed 18 April 2023).

Africa Check (2022b) 'Jubilee, a Party for the Old? No, Headline Mocking Kenya's Ruling Party on Fake Taifa Leo Front Page'. *Africa Check*. https://africacheck.org/fact-checks/ meta-programme-fact-checks/jubilee-party-old-no-headline-mocking-kenyas-ruling -party (accessed 18 April 2023).

Africa Intelligence (2019) 'Ruto Vies with Kenyatta Clan for Ownership of Star'. *Africa Intelligence*. https://www.africaintelligence.com/eastern-africa-and-the-horn/2019/12 /13/ruto-vies-with-kenyatta-clan-for-ownership-of-star (accessed 18 April 2023).

African Centre for Strategic Studies (2021) 'Domestic Disinformation on the Rise in Africa – Africa Center'. *Africa Center for Strategic Studies*. https://africacenter.org/ spotlight/domestic-disinformation-on-the-rise-in-africa (accessed 18 April 2023).

Africa News (2022) 'Kenya's Presidential Hopeful Promises to Tackle Unemployment and Debt'. 25 July. https://www.africanews.com/2022/07/25/kenyas-presidential-hopeful -promises-to-tackle-unemployment-and-debt/ (accessed 18 April 2023).

Agutu, N. (2021) 'UDA's Njuguna Wins Kiambaa by-election'. *The Star*. 16 July. https:// www.the-star.co.ke/news/2021–07–16-udas-njuguna-wins-kiambaa-by-election/ (accessed 12 March 2023).

Berger, G. (2012) 'Theorising African Communications: The Bad News Signaled by Broadcast Digital Migration Policy'. *Communicatio*, 38 (2): 135–46.

Braun, V. and Clarke, V. (2006) 'Using Thematic Analysis in Psychology'. *Qualitative Research in Psychology*, 3(2): 77–101.

Business Today Reporter (2020) 'Nation Media Group Announces Staff Pay Cuts'. *Business Today*, 29 April. https://businesstoday.co.ke/nmg-pay-cuts-spares-low-income-earners/ (accessed 23 August 2022).

Chelangat, M. and Shikanda, H. (2022) 'Exposed: Names Behind Kenya's August Poll Lies'. *Daily Nation*. 7 July. https://nation.africa/kenya/news/politics/exposed-names-behind -poll-lies-3871518 (accessed 18 April 2023).

Citizen TV Kenya (2021) 'Gachuri's Punchline: Standing Order #84, Personal Statement'. 1 April. https://www.youtube.com/watch?v=mbfjILYKcVA&t=111s (accessed 31 March 2023).

Communications Authority of Kenya (2021) 'Fourth Quarter Sector Statistics Report for the Financial Year 2020/2021(April–June 2021)'. https://www.ca.go.ke/wp-content/ uploads/2021/09/Sector-Statistics-Report-Q4-2020–2021.pdf.

Communications Authority of Kenya (2023) 'Second Quarter Sector Statistics Report for the Financial Year 2022/2023 (1st October –31st December 2022)'. https://www.ca.go .ke/wp-content/uploads/2023/03/Sector-Statistics-Report-Q2-2022–2023.pdf.

Communications Commission of Kenya (2010) *Analysis of 2010 ICT Survey*. Nairobi: Communications Commission of Kenya. https://www.ca.go.ke/wp-content/uploads /2018/02/Analysis-of-2010-ICT-Survey.pdf.

Dahir, A. L. (2018a) '"We'd Stage the Whole Thing": Cambridge Analytica was Filmed Boasting of its Roles in Kenya's Polls'. *Quartz Africa*, 20 March. https://qz.com/africa /1233084/channel-4-news-films-cambridge-analytica-execs-saying-they-staged-kenya -uhuru-kenyatta-elections/ (accessed 12 October 2022).

Ekdale, B. and Tully, M. (2020) 'How the Nigerian and Kenyan Media Handled Cambridge Analytica'. *The Conversation*. https://theconversation.com/how-the-nigerian-and -kenyan-media-handled-cambridge-analytica-128473 (accessed 10 October 2022).

Fourie, P. J. (2007) 'The Role and Functions of the Media in Society'. In P. J. Fourie (ed.), *Media Studies: Media History, Media and Society, Vol.1*, 2nd ed., 185–209. Cape Town: Juta & Co.

Frederiksen, B. F. (2006) 'The Present Battle is the Brain Battle: Writing and Publishing a Kikuyu Newspaper in the pre-Mau Mau Period in Africa'. In K. Barber (ed.), *Africa's Hidden Histories: Everyday Literacy and Making the Self*, 278–313. Bloomington, IN: Indiana University Press.

Freedom House (2018) 'Freedom in the World 2018'. https://freedomhouse.org/sites/ default/files/2020-02/FH_FIW_Report_2018_Final.pdf.

Gadsden, F. (1986) 'Wartime Propaganda in Kenya: The Kenya Information Office, 1939–1945'. *The International Journal of Historical Studies*, 19 (3): 401–20. Available from International African Bibliography Online (accessed 13 March 2023).

Gichuhi, G. (2022) 'Kenya's Electoral Commission Not Hiring Poll Officials Yet – Ignore Fake Job Advert'. *Africa Check*, 31 March. https://africacheck.org/fact-checks/meta -programme-fact-checks/kenyas-electoral-commission-not-hiring-poll-officials-yet (accessed 29 March 2023).

Guess, A. and Lyons, B. (2020) 'Misinformation, Disinformation, and Online Propaganda'. In N. Persily and J. Tucker (eds), *Social Media and Democracy: The State of the Field, Prospects for Reform* (SSRC Anxieties of Democracy), 10–33. Cambridge: Cambridge University Press.

Inooro FM Kenya (2022) 'Rigathi Gachagua'. *Facebook*, 24 May. https://www.facebook.com /InooroFMKenya/videos/546151790353293/ (accessed 2 April 2023).

Iraki, X. N. (2022) 'Kenya's Election Promises: An Economist's Perspective'. 15 July. *The Conversation*. https://theconversation.com/kenyas-election-promises-an-economists -perspective-186480.

Kanyi, P. (2020) 'Social Media Consumption Among Kenyans: Trends and Practices'. In P. Kanyi (ed.), *Analyzing Global Social Media Consumption*, 1st ed., 88–120. Hershey, PA: IGI Global.

Karikari, K. (2007) 'African Media Since Ghana's Independence'. In E. Barratt and G. Berger (eds), *50 Years of Journalism: African Media Since Ghana's Independence*, 10–20. Johannesburg: African Editors Forum, Highway Africa & Media Foundation for West Africa.

Kenya Editors Guild (2022) 'Kenya Doesn't Owe China KSh. 11.2 Trillion as Gachagua Claims'. https://www.kenyaeditorsguild.org/2022/06/16/kenya-doesnt-owe-china-ksh -11-2-trillion-as-gachagua-claims-in-inooro-interview/ (accessed 14 January 2023).

Kenya Editors Guild (2022) 'Kenya Doesn't Owe China KSH. 11.2 Trillion, as Gachagua Claims in Inooro Interview'. *Kenya Editors' Guild*, 16 June. https://www .kenyaeditorsguild.org/2022/06/16/kenya-doesnt-owe-china-ksh-11-2-trillion-as- gachagua-claims-in-inooro-interview/ (accessed 13 March 2023).

Kenya Gazette (2020) 'Gazette Notice 5472: The Kenya Information and Communications Act (No. 2 of 1998)'. https://www.ca.go.ke/wp-content/uploads/2020/10/National-ICT -Policy-Guidelines-2020.pdf.

Kenyans.co.ke (2020) 'Martha Karua Warns Ruto Allies Over Fake News'. 17 April. https://www.facebook.com/Kenyans.co.ke/posts/martha-karua-warns-ruto-allies-over-fake-news/3495703363779310/ (accessed 31 March 2023).

Kenyans.co.ke (2022) 'This Post Did Not Emanate from Our Media House. It Does Not Conform to the In-house Branding Rules and Did Not Go Through the Multiple Approval Checks Set in Place to Prevent Misreporting'. We, Therefore, Flag it as FAKE. 24 January. https://twitter.com/Kenyans/status/1485485902071803905?s=20 (accessed 31 March 2023).

Kimani, B. (2022) 'Reprieve to Citizen TV Journalists in new Salary Directive'. *Kenyans .co.ke*, 22 March. https://www.kenyans.co.ke/news/74131-citizen-tv-journalists-smile-bank-after-new-salary-directive (accessed 12 October 2022).

Kirchgaessner, S., Ganguly, M., Pegg, D., Cadwalladr, C. and Burke, J. (2023) 'Revealed: The Hacking and Disinformation Team Meddling in Elections'. *The Guardian*, 15 February. https://www.theguardian.com/world/2023/feb/15/revealed-disinformation-team-jorge-claim-meddling-elections-tal-hanan.

Laibuta, M. (2013) 'It's Time to Tame Social Media Mercenaries and Bandits'. *Mugambi Laibuta Blog*, 24 May. https://www.laibuta.com/social-commentary/its-time-to-tame-social-media-mercenaries-and-bandits/.

Madung, O. (2022) 'From Dance App to Political Mercenary: How Disinformation on TikTok Gaslights Political Tensions in Kenya'. *Mozilla Foundation*. https://foundation.mozilla.org/en/campaigns/kenya-tiktok/.

Magak, C. (2022) 'Supreme Court Throws Out Raila's Petition, Upholds Ruto's Win'. *People Daily*, 5 September. https://www.pd.co.ke/august-9/supreme-court-upholds-rutos-win-148031/.

Mare, A., Mabweazara, H. M. and Moyo, D. (2019) '"Fake News" and Cyber-Propaganda in Sub-Saharan Africa: Recentering the Research Agenda'. *African Journalism Studies*, 40 (4): 1–12.

Marwick, A. and Lewis, R. (2017) 'Media Manipulation and Disinformation Online. Data & Society Research Institute'. https://datasociety.net/pubs/oh/DataAndSociety_MediaManipulationAndDisinformationOnline.pdf.

Maweu, J. M. (2020) '"Fake Elections"? Cyber Propaganda, Disinformation and the 2017 General Elections in Kenya'. *Africa Journalism Studies*, 40 (4): 62–76. https://doi.org/10.1080/23743670.2020.1719858.

Mbeke, P. O., Ugangu, W. and Okello-Orlale, R. (2010) *The Media We Want: The Kenya Media Vulnerabilities Study*. Nairobi, Kenya: Friedrich Ebert Stiftung.

Mbuthia, W. (2022) 'How Raila Loyalists Spread Fake News About IEBC Commissioners'. *Daily Nation*, 22 August. https://nation.africa/kenya/news/how-raila-loyalists-spread-fake-news-about-iebc-commissioners-3921918.

Media Council of Kenya (2023) *State of Kenya's Media 2022*. https://mediacouncil.or.ke/sites/default/files/downloads/State%20of%20Kenya%27s%20Media%202022%20Report.pdf (accessed 30 March 2023).

Ministry of ICT, Innovation and Youth Affairs (2022) *The Kenya National Digital Master Plan 2022–2032*. https://cms.icta.go.ke/sites/default/files/2022–04/Kenya%20Digital%20Masterplan%202022–2032%20Online%20Version.pdf.

Mozilla Foundation (2021) 'Inside the Shadowy World of Disinformation for Hire in Kenya'. *Mozilla Foundation*. https://assets.mofoprod.net/network/documents/Report_Inside_the_shadowy_world_of_disinformation_for_hire_in_Kenya_5._hcc.pdf.

Mudavadi, K. and Shanahan, J. (2022) 'What Study Tells Us About Media Trust and Public Perception of Journalists in Kenya'. *Daily Nation*, 14 September. https://nation

.africa/kenya/blogs-opinion/blogs/what-study-tells-us-about-media-trust-and-public
-perception-of-journalists-in-kenya-3948432 (accessed 14 September 2022).

Mungai, C. (2022) 'Kenya 2022: Raila and Ruto are Poaching Star Journalists as
the Independent Media Declines'. *The Africa Report*, 30 March. https://www
.theafricareport.com/183317/kenya-2022-raila-and-ruto-are-poaching-star-journalists
-as-the-independent-media-declines/ (accessed 30 March 2023).

Mureithi, M. (2017) 'The Internet Journey for Kenya: The Interplay of Disruptive
Innovation and Entrepreneurship in Fueling Rapid Growth'. In B. Ndemo and T. Weiss
(eds), *Digital Kenya: An Entrepreneurial Revolution in the Making*, 27–44. London:
Palgrave Macmillan.

Mwita, C. (2021) *The Kenya News Media Assessment*. Nairobi: Internews. https://internews
.org/wp-content/uploads/legacy/2021-03/KMAReport_Final_20210325.pdf.

Nyabola, N. (2018) *Digital Democracy, Analogue Politics: How the Internet Era Is
Transforming Politics in Kenya*. London: Zed Books.

Ogola, G. (2011) 'The Political Economy of the Media in Kenya: From Kenyatta's
Nation-Building Press to Kibaki's Local-Language FM Radio'. *Africa Today*, 57 (3):
76–95.

Ogola, G. (2015) 'African Journalism: A Journey of Failures and Triumphs'. *African
Journalism Studies*, 36 (1): 93–102. doi:10.1080/23743670.2015.1008175.

Oliver, J. and Galby, N. (2022) 'Revealed: UK ran Cold War Dirty Tricks Campaign to
Smear Kenya's First Vice-President'. *The Guardian*, 6 August. https://www.theguardian
.com/world/2022/aug/06/revealed-uk-ran-cold-war-dirty-tricks-campaign-to-smear
-kenyas-first-vice-president-oginga-odinga.

Osborne, M. (2015) 'The Rooting out of Mau Mau from the Minds of the Kikuyu is a
Formidable Task: Propaganda and the Mau Mau War'. *The Journal of African History*,
56 (1): 77–97. doi:10.1017/S002185371400067X.

Otieno, O. (2015) 'How Bloggers Have Changed the Game for Power Elite'. *Daily Nation*,
27 June. https://nation.africa/kenya/blogs-opinion/opinion/how-bloggers-have
-changed-the-game-for-power-elite-1106270.

Research ICT Africa (2012) 'Internet Going Mobile: Internet Access and Usage in 11
African Countries'. *Research ICT Africa Policy Brief No. 2*. https://researchictafrica.net
/wp/wp-content/uploads/2020/06/Internet_going_mobile_-_Internet_access_and
_usage_in_11_African_countries1.pdf.

Rich, T. S., Milden, I. and Wagner, M.T. (2020) 'Research Note: Does the Public
Support Fact-Checking Social Media? It Depends Who and How You Ask'. *The
Harvard Kennedy School (HKS) Misinformation Review*, 1 (8). https://dash.harvard.
edu/bitstream/handle/1/37366464/rich_fact_checking_social_media_20201102.
pdf?sequence=1&isAllowed=y.

SIMElab Africa (2019) 'Social Media Consumption in Kenya: Trends and Practices'.
SIMElab Africa. https://www.usiu.ac.ke/assets/file/SIMElab_Social_Media_
Consumption_in_Kenya_report.pdf (accessed 30 August 2022).

Star Editor (2022) *Raila vs Mudavadi Performance in Western Counties – 2013 Poll*. https://
www.the-star.co.ke/news/infographics/2022–02–10-raila-vs-mudavadi-performance-
in-western-counties-2013-poll/ (accessed 30 March 2023).

Tully, M. (2010) 'All's Well in the Colony: Newspaper Coverage of the Mau Mau
Movement, 1952–1956'. In T. Falola and H. Ter Haar (eds), *Narrating War and Peace in
Africa*, 56–75. Martlesham: Boydell & Brewer.

Tully, M. (2021) 'Everyday News Use and Misinformation in Kenya'. *Digital Journalism*, 10
(1): 109–27.

Volz, D., Barry, R. and Strasburg, J. (2020) 'Fake Twitter Accounts Posing as News Organizations Prematurely Declare Election Victories'. *Wall Street Journal*. https://www.wsj.com/articles/fake-twitter-accounts-posing-as-news-organizations-prematurely-declare-election-victories-11604541638.

Wamunyu, W. (2021) 'Exploring Trust/Mistrust in Journalistic Practice: An Actor-network Analysis of a Kenyan Newsroom'. *African Journalism Studies*, 42 (4): 99–120, doi:10.1080/23743670.2022.2026430.

Wamunyu, W. and Wahutu, J. S. (2019) 'Old Habits, New Realities: Digital Newsrooms in Kenya Commercial Media Houses'. *African Journalism Studies*. doi:10.1080/23743670.2019.1583583.

Wasserman, H. and Madrid-Morales, D. (2019) 'An Exploratory Study of "Fake News" and Media Trust in Kenya, Nigeria and South Africa'. *African Journalism Studies*, 40 (1): 107–23.

Index